THE FRENCH ECONOMY

WORLD ECONOMIES

A series of concise modern economic histories of the world's most important national economies. Each book explains how a country's economy works, why it has the shape it has and what distinct challenges it faces. Alongside discussion of familiar indicators of economic growth, the coverage extends to well-being, inequality and corruption, to provide a fresh and more rounded understanding of the wealth of nations.

PUBLISHED

Stephen L. Morgan
THE CHINESE ECONOMY

Matthew Gray
THE ECONOMY OF THE GULF STATES

Frances M. B. Lynch
THE FRENCH ECONOMY

Matthew McCartney
THE INDIAN ECONOMY

Vera Zamagni
THE ITALIAN ECONOMY

Hiroaki Richard Watanabe
THE JAPANESE ECONOMY

The French Economy

Frances M. B. Lynch

agenda
publishing

First edition published in 2021 by Agenda Publishing

Agenda Publishing Limited
The Core
Bath Lane
Newcastle Helix
Newcastle upon Tyne
NE4 5TF

www.agendapub.com

ISBN 978-1-78821-164-2 (hardcover)
ISBN 978-1-78821-165-9 (paperback)

British Library Cataloguing-in-Publication Data
A catalogue record for this book is available from the British Library

Typeset by T&T Productions Ltd, London
Printed and bound in the UK by TJ Books

Contents

Preface

It is regrettable how little the British know about the economy of a neighbouring country in which so many chose to have a second home, retire or simply visit before the United Kingdom left the European Union. A common assumption is that the French economy is based on agriculture and industry, unlike the more modern, service-based British economy. With high taxation and an inflexible labour market, it seemed understandable that many young, educated French people should escape the high unemployment in their country to work in Britain, and in London in particular.

In 2014, when the Socialist government of François Hollande was in power, a leading British economist wrote that what he found to be the most interesting question about France was not why it was doing so badly but rather why it was doing so well in spite of operating "some extremely destructive policies".[1] In fact, before the Covid-19 pandemic struck, the service economy in France made the same contribution to value added as in Britain (about 80 per cent). The two countries also had about the same size of population (around 66 million), and similar levels of GDP and per capita income. Where they differed was that the service sector in France employed about 75 per cent of the active labour force whereas on some counts it employed 85 per cent in the UK. Unemployment in France was for many years much higher than in the UK, but levels of labour productivity were also higher in France. One of the biggest differences between the two countries, however, is that, since the 1980s, the government in France has consistently raised much more in taxation than Britain, in order to redistribute the gains made from closer integration into the European Union to those who did not benefit to the same extent. As a result, France, while not without its problems, has a more equal society than the UK.

When in 2018 I was invited by Agenda Publishing to write a history of the French economy since the Second World War, I happily accepted the challenge. Unlike my previous archive-based work, this book was to be based on published sources. However, I soon discovered that the most recent economic history book, whether written in French or English, dated from 2004. The context for Jean-Pierre Dormois's history of the French economy in the twentieth century was an economy that, having finally abandoned decades of protectionist policies, was successfully meeting the twin challenges of globalization and the introduction of the European single currency, the euro.[2]

Indeed, globalization was officially presented in France, as elsewhere, as the positive outcome of the growing interdependence of advanced economies to which there was no viable alternative. Although French governments had tried since the 1980s to redistribute some of the gains from globalization to those who had not benefited, almost 17 per cent of voters had expressed their dissatisfaction by supporting Jean-Marie Le Pen, the leader of the ultra nationalist party, the Front National, in the first round of the presidential elections in 2002, giving him a place in the runoff second round of voting. The mismatch between the positive assessment of globalization and mounting voter dissatisfaction led a group of economists, critical of neoliberalism, to conclude that many problems in society were being overlooked by governments primarily because they were not being measured. National accounts, they correctly asserted, focused on the growth of GDP as the overarching indicator of the health of the economy. In January 2008, several months before the global financial crisis plunged the advanced economies into recession, they persuaded the incoming French president, Nicolas Sarkozy, to set up a commission within the Organization for Economic Cooperation and Development (OECD) to examine the issue.[3] Chaired by one of the most prominent critics of globalization, Joseph Stiglitz, assisted by Jean-Paul

Fitoussi and Amartya Sen, the commission recommended that national statistics needed to move beyond measuring GDP to capture inequalities in its distribution in terms of not only income and wealth but also other aspects of well-being such as health, education, political voice and access to justice, if trust in public policies was to be restored.[4] However, coinciding with the sovereign debt crisis in the eurozone, which was blamed, by the German government in particular, on public finance excesses, in March 2012, 25 member states of the European Union agreed to embed neoliberal principles even more firmly in a new "fiscal compact" known as the Treaty on Stability, Coordination and Governance.[5] Designed to bring public finances under control, the fiscal compact ushered in years of austerity in many European countries. In 2018 a successor to the Stiglitz, Fitoussi and Sen commission published a second report to draw attention to the impact of these austerity policies on widening inequalities within and between European countries.[6] The rapid spread of the Covid-19 virus was to provide further cruel proof of many of these inequalities.

Paradoxically, while attention had been focused on the damage to the most vulnerable in both developing and developed countries caused by globalization, it was protectionism and not globalization that was on the rise. After 14 years of trying to negotiate tariff reductions in the Doha Round of the World Trade Organization (WTO), the negotiations ended without agreement in 2015, while the bilateral trade negotiations between the EU and the United States (TTIP), launched in 2013, ended without agreement three years later. And within the European single market little progress had been made to open up trade in services, a sector in which most people were employed. The outbreak and rapid spread of the Covid-19 virus led the European Central Bank to temporarily suspend its rules and allow governments to increase public debt. With whole sectors of the economy almost bankrupt, the critical question was how economies could recover from the pandemic without increasing public debt still further or widening inequalities. In France parallels were drawn with the severe challenges facing the country after the Second World War, when it abandoned economic liberalism in favour of government intervention and economic planning. The crisis has thus added a new urgency to the need to understand how the French economy recovered after 1945 and has performed since then.

I begin this history of the French economy since the Second World War by summarizing the perhaps familiar story of its performance in the nineteenth century, and end it in 2018 – the last year for which full annual statistics were available at the time of writing. As Chapter 1 shows, having failed to follow the example of England and stage their own industrial revolution, the majority of French people continued to work in agriculture throughout the nineteenth century. Over the same period the state, despite the Colbertist tradition of economic intervention so frequently cited in textbooks, followed a liberal, laissez-faire approach to policy-making, leaving industry and banks free to develop as they chose, but offering protection to agriculture. Making an exception to economic liberalism during the First World War, it resumed this approach to policy-making during the interwar period. The chapter ends with the catastrophic surrender to Nazi Germany in 1940.

Chapter 2 details the legacy of the war years for economic policy and policy-making. Of all the possible factors that groups on the left and right blamed for the disaster of 1940, it was the economic liberalism of the Third Republic that was singled out. This was replaced after the war by an interventionist state, committed to providing the security the Third Republic had failed to deliver even to the protected agricultural sector. What became known as the French economic model dates from the years 1944–49, when many of the structures of the new interventionist state were put in place. These included nationalizations, economic planning, a welfare state, a modern statistical service and a new training school for civil servants. With many of the postwar reforms lasting for decades while others were replaced, the chapter analyses the evolution of the French economic model over the period 1944–2018.

Having followed its own path to economic development in the nineteenth century and in the interwar period, in what was known as the "30 glorious years" after 1945 the French economy conformed much more closely to developments in other advanced economies.[7] However, as Chapter 3 explains, there was nothing automatic about the way in which the French economy caught up with the more technologically advanced economies after the Second World War. Adopting the same periodization as that identified in Chapter 2, and using traditional metrics, Chapter 3 describes and quantifies the evolution of the French economy since 1945.

If France appeared to have lost its exceptional character in the postwar period, Chapter 4 shows how very distinctive it remained. Nowhere was this more evident than in the continuous attempts by the state to reduce the inequalities between different areas within metropolitan France and between it and its overseas territories. Building on the administrative structures inherited from the revolutionary convention of 1789, the postwar state added a new layer of subnational government, that of the region. But, as we see in this chapter, the questions of how many regions, how much power they should have and for what purpose continued to be debated at length throughout the Fourth and Fifth Republics.

Chapter 5 explores the many ways in which the French state also tried to reduce interpersonal inequalities after the Second World War. It focuses in particular on how taxation was used to reduce differences in income and wealth, while other policies were designed to address inequalities in gender and in the operation of the labour market.

Finally, we come to the question of the French economy and Europe. Although the French were responsible for introducing the first example of supranational governance in postwar Europe, with the formation of the European Coal and Steel Community in 1951, in the subsequent treaties of Rome (1957) and Maastricht (1992) they reacted to initiatives proposed by others, but tried to shape them in ways that would be beneficial to the French economy.

Over the two years or so spent researching and writing this book, I have been very fortunate in the help and support that I have received from a number of people. I would like to thank first of all Steven Gerrard and Andrew Lockett, the editors at Agenda, as well as the anonymous advisers chosen by them to read my initial proposal and first draft, for their useful advice and encouragement. I would also like to thank their chosen type-setter and copyeditor, Sam Clark and Emma Dain at T&T Productions Ltd, for their rigorous work. The University of Westminster generously funded some short trips to the Bibliothèque Nationale and the Bibliothèque de l'INSEE Alain Desrosières in Paris, and allowed me to take some sabbat-ical leave to complete the writing up. Thierry Couderc, Aurélia Jonvaux and Philippe Mustar all gave me valuable guidance in finding research material. I am very grateful to them. Staff at the British Library in Lon-don were equally helpful before they had to close their doors in March 2020 due to the Covid-19 crisis. Others bravely volunteered to read and criticize drafts of chapters. I would like to thank in particular Russell But-ler, Andreas Gestrich, Laura Milward-Lynch and Kate Tranter for their constant and unstinting help and support. My greatest debt remains to Alan Milward. Ten years after his death, his work continues to provide inspiration to me and many others, particularly in these troubled times.

FRANCES M. B. LYNCH
London

Tables and figures

TABLES

FIGURES

Abbreviations

ACP	African, Caribbean and Pacific
CAC	Cotation Assistée en Continu
CAP	Common Agricultural Policy
CEA	Commissariat à l'Énergie Atomique
CEPR	Centre for Economic Policy Research
CFA	Communauté Financière Africaine
CFP	Communauté Financière Pacifique
CFDT	Confédération Française Démocratique du Travail
CGE	Compagnie Générale d'Électricité
CGP	Commissariat Général au Plan
CGT	Confédération générale du travail
CNPF	Confédération nationale du patronat français
CNR	Conseil National de la Résistance
CODER	Commission de Développement Économique Régional
CSG	Contribution Sociale Généralisée
DGEN	Délégation Générale à l'Équipement National
DATAR	Délégation interministérielle à l'aménagement du territoire et à l'attractivité régionale
Dom	Département d'outre-mer
ECU	European Currency Unit
EDC	European Defence Community
EDF	Électricité de France
EEC	European Economic Community
EEZ	exclusive economic zone
EMS	European Monetary System
EMU	Economic and Monetary Union
ENA	École Nationale d'Administration
EPCI	Établissements publiques de coopération intercommunale
EPU	European Payments Union
ERDF	European Regional Development Fund
ERM	exchange rate mechanism
ERP	European Recovery Program

ESA	European Space Agency
ESM	European stability mechanism
EU	European Union
Euratom	European Atomic Energy Community
FDI	foreign direct investment
FJA	Fédération des Jeunes Agriculteurs
FME	Fonds de modernisation et d'équipement
FN	Front National
GDF	Gaz de France
IAR	International Authority for the Ruhr
IMF	International Monetary Fund
INSEE	Institut national de la statistique et des études économiques
ILO	International Labour Organization
LR	Les Républicains
LREM	La République en marche
MATIF	Marché à terme international de France
MRP	Mouvement Républicain Populaire
NATO	North Atlantic Treaty Organization
NTB	non-tariff barrier
OCRPI	Office Central de Répartition des Produits Industriels
OEEC	Organization for European Economic Cooperation
OFCE	Observatoire français des conjonctures économiques
OPEC	Organization of Petroleum Exporting Countries
PS	Parti Socialiste
PWR	pressurized water reactor
RER	Réseau Express Régional
RF	Rassemblement Français
RMI	Revenu mimimum d'insertion
Rom	Région d'outre-mer
RPR	Rassemblement pour la République
RSA	Revenu de solidarité active
SFIO	Section française de l'internationale ouvrière
SGCI	Sécrétariat général du comité interministériel
SMAG	Salaire minimum agricole garanti
SMIC	Salaire minimum interprofessionnel de croissance
SMIG	Salaire minimum interprofessionnel garanti
SNCF	Société nationale des chemins de fer français
SNECMA	Société nationale d'études et de construction de moteurs d'aviation
TTIP	Transatlantic Trade and Investment Partnership
TGV	Train à Grande Vitesse
Tom	Territoire d'outre-mer
UDCA	Union de Défense des Commerçants et Artisans

ABBREVIATIONS

UDF	Union pour la Démocratie Française
UDR	Union pour la Démocratie Républicaine
UMP	Union pour le Mouvement Populaire
UNR	Union pour la Nouvelle République
WEU	West European Union

Map 1 Regions of metropolitan France

Map 2 Departmental boundaries, capitals and former regions of metropolitan France

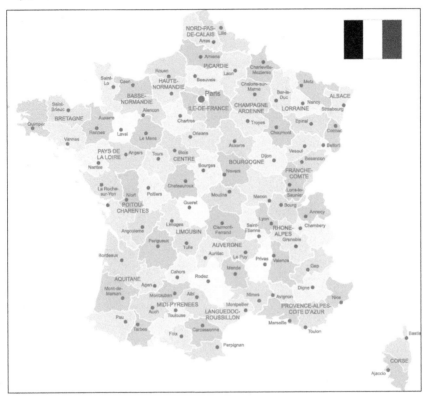

1

Introducing the French Economy

The 30 years after 1945 were the longest and most stable period of growth in measured French history bringing to an end years of economic decline.[1] Immortalized by the French economist Jean Fourastié as the "30 glorious years" (*trente glorieuses*), they were also a time of rapid structural change and economic development.[2] Millions of people moved out of low-productivity jobs in agriculture to work in the industrial and service sectors. The protective walls of tariffs and quantitative restrictions that had long shielded producers from international competition were gradually dismantled as France participated in the European Economic Community (EEC) and in the trade liberalizing rounds of the General Agreement on Tariffs and Trade (GATT) and of its successor the World Trade Organization (WTO). The direction and economic importance of trade also changed, shifting away from the former slowly growing colonial markets and towards the expanding markets of the EEC. What was traded also changed, with France for the first time running a surplus in some agricultural products and foodstuffs as well as in transport equipment and some manufactured goods. Much of this altered after the mid-1970s, when the postwar boom came to an end at the same time as the developed economies moved into recession. In the 40 or so years since the mid-1970s, growth in France, as in other developed economies, has slowed down and employment in industry and agriculture has shrunk, but the service sector has expanded rapidly. With a return of women to the labour market on a scale not seen since before the First World War, the service sector was unable to absorb the millions of men left unemployed as a result of the contraction of industry and agriculture. At the same time, the cost of redistributing income to offset some of the growing inequalities in society led to a tax burden that was higher than anywhere else in the developed world.

Such momentous changes over a lifetime have stimulated considerable debate among historians but little consensus over the causes. What is undisputed is that what happened after 1945 reversed the long period of economic decline that contributed to the shocking surrender of France in 1940. What had to be explained was how France, a country which had been the most powerful in the world at the beginning of the eighteenth century, was to be overtaken in terms of economic growth rates, first by England, then by Germany and Belgium, and finally by the United States, before managing to reverse that decline after 1945.[3]

HISTORIOGRAPHICAL OVERVIEW

For many years economic historians, believing in the universality of the capitalist experience, looked to England, home of the industrial revolution, as the model of economic development for all other countries to follow. What needed to be explained was why France had failed to follow the example of England and stage its own industrial revolution. Attention focused on analysing what was wrong with France, particularly in comparison with England. In this respect it was the very different behaviour of French peasants that was seen to have been the main obstacle to economic development. The abolition of feudal title deeds in the revolution of 1789 had given peasants a new security that was entirely based on land ownership. It was claimed that they had neither the capital nor the ability to innovate, nor the drive to move into the towns, seeing land acquisition as the only way to increase output and improve their lives. Most of their farms were small, and by mid-century, when three quarters of the French population still lived in the countryside, the average surface area of farms was 12 hectares and in half of the departments 50 per cent of farms were less than five hectares.[4]

Without capital to expand, peasants limited their family size to prevent the subdivision of their farms under the equal inheritance code introduced by Napoleon. Whereas at the beginning of the nineteenth century the population of France had been over twice that of Britain, by the end of the century it was lower than in Britain. It was also lower than in Germany. In 1871 the newly unified German Empire had a population of 41.1 million. By 1911 this had risen to 64.9 million, whereas the French population had grown from 36.1 million to 39.6 million over the same period.[5] A slowly growing population was held responsible for a lack of demand for manufactured goods and for the slow growth of industry. Furthermore, there was little demand among peasants for mass produced manufactured goods since most of their needs were met by small-scale rural industry, mainly based in workshops rather than in factories. With consumption restricted largely to the small middle class in towns, who imitated the habits of the wealthier class in Paris, production tended to focus on quality luxury products rather than on cheaper, mass produced goods.

Other factors that were considered to have held back industrial development were: a relative lack of coal and coking coal; the belated development of the railways; an education system based on the grandes écoles in Paris (of which Napoleon's creation of the École Polytechnique in 1800 was the most recent example), which prepared the elite for careers in public service rather than in industry and commerce; banks that preferred to invest abroad rather than in the domestic economy; and industrialists who lacked the spirit of entrepreneurship, preferring the security of the family firm to the large internationally competitive firms in Germany, the United States and Britain.[6]

NOT BACKWARD BUT DIFFERENT

This dominant scholarly narrative of France as a backward economy unable to stage its own industrial revolution began to change in the 1970s. A catalyst for the paradigm shift came in 1973, when Alan Milward and Berrick Saul published the first volume of a two-volume study of the economic development of continental European economies in the nineteenth century.[7] By looking at the experience of almost all European economies in their own right rather than in comparison with Britain, they concluded that there was no universal pattern observable in the economic development of European countries in the nineteenth century. The form that development took depended on specific national factors and circumstances rather than being a global phenomenon. It was driven as much by productivity improvements in the agricultural and service sectors as in the industrial one, and depended as much on demand as supply.

In comparing France with other continental European economies rather than with England, they concluded that by 1870, far from being backward, France was the largest and most dynamic power on the continent. It had simply developed in a different way. This verdict, which chimed with the recognition in the early 1970s that France had become a very successful economy after almost 30 years of rapid and unbroken growth, sparked a huge amount of interest and research into tracing the origins of this success back to the nineteenth century and analysing the performance of the French economy in a more positive light. Instead of emphasizing where France had failed to behave in the same way as England in the nineteenth century, historians asserted that the French model of combining peasant agriculture and rural handicrafts with industrialization was an appropriate and rational response to the situation in which people found themselves in France. Instead of focusing on the periods of crisis such as 1789–1815, 1846–51, 1865–96, the emphasis was on explaining the relatively high growth rates achieved in 1820–45, 1852–65 and 1896–1914.

Each of the factors that were previously considered to have held back the development of the French economy were now analysed differently by historians.

The first question to answer was why, as advances in medicine led to a fall in the death rate across Europe, France should have been the first country to cut its birth rate, when elsewhere it was not until the 1870s that the birth rate began to fall, and in some parts of Spain and Italy this did not happen until after 1930. The traditional answer was that it was the economic constraints facing peasants that caused them to reduce the birth rate in response to the Napoleonic code of 1804, which replaced the right of inheritance of the eldest son by equal inheritance of all children. With research demonstrating that it was the richest groups that reduced their fertility first, the low birth rate has come to be seen as a response to decreased levels of inequality and increased levels of social mobility in nineteenth-century France.[8] In any case, the impact on the economy of a more slowly growing population was now no longer seen as wholly negative, insofar as production was also determined by factors such as the productivity of labour, the length of the working week, the participation rate of women and by the rate of immigration. For its part, consumption was not determined solely by the size of the population but also by its structure, how resources were distributed and by customs. And in fact the period 1895–1913, when the economy was growing rapidly, was also the period when the birth rate was contracting the most.[9] While the lower rate of productivity in agriculture in France in comparison with England was not disputed, it was now attributed to the superior quality and quantity of land available for cultivation in England, rather than to the inability or reluctance of French peasants to innovate.[10]

Similarly, research found little correlation between firm size and productivity, with many small-scale industries, most notably silk production around Lyon, proving to be highly innovative and competitive. It was also demonstrated that, although demand for mass produced goods may have been lower in France, the focus on luxury goods led to an early development of retailing, with the Bon Marché department stores in Paris being the first in the world. The accusation that French banks had starved industry of capital was also challenged by demonstrating that the periods when capital exports were greatest, 1850–70 and 1896–1914, were those of maximum economic growth in France.[11]

However, subsequent research, based on the application of econometric techniques, questioned this positive reassessment of French economic performance in the nineteenth century. Maurice Lévy-Leboyer and François Bourguignon identified the period between the mid-1860s and 1893 as the time when the economy had performed particularly badly. They questioned what had gone wrong after the period from 1830 to 1860 when industrial capacity had doubled, drawing 3.7 million people from the countryside into cities. In the 40 years after 1840 the domestic market had been unified, investment abroad had helped to secure markets for further economic expansion at home and in 1860 the government had signed a free trade agreement with England: the Cobden–Chevalier Treaty, the first such treaty to incorporate a most favoured nation clause. However, instead of stimulating the economy, the intensification of international competition had caused the French to lose their market share, the rate of growth of industrial output dropped by half, while (after some delay) that of agriculture dropped by even more. Export sales, which had formed 18 per cent of national income immediately after the opening of the Suez Canal (1872–75), fell to between 6 and 7 per cent. According to Lévy-Leboyer and Bourguignon, free trade was not to blame, having "paradoxically coincided with a deceleration of growth". The problem, in their view, was that consumption had increased at the expense of investment. As a proportion of gross national product (GNP), investment declined from 10.8 per cent in 1855–69 to 8.4 per cent in 1880–89, and of that investment, excessive government focus on low-productivity sectors such as railways and residential construction had crowded out productive private investment.[12] One famous example of this was the reconstruction of much of Paris in the 1850s and 1860s by Napoleon III's acclaimed Prefect of the Seine department, Baron Haussmann.[13]

Such government investment was seen to have been at the expense of investment in those industries that spearheaded the second wave of industrialization, most notably those of automobiles, aviation and electricity. As a result, the average size of firms in newer industries remained much smaller than in the older industrial sectors. Whereas the average numbers employed between the mid-1860s and mid-1890s ranged between 2,000 and 5,000 in glass or chemicals, 9,000 in heavy industry and between 20,000 and 30,000 in the railway sector, the average employment in automobile firms was 400, with firms preferring to concentrate on design and assembly rather than building large integrated plants and rationalizing methods of working. In general, French firms also tended to be smaller than their foreign counterparts. The two largest, Alstholm and St Gobain, were only between 5 and 7 per cent of the size of ICI or IG Farben.[14] In 1910 output per capita was 40 per cent lower in France than in the United States, 25 per cent lower than in England or Belgium and 10 per cent lower than in Germany.[15]

These conclusions were to focus scholarly attention once again on the reasons for the relatively poor performance of the French economy, particularly in the period after the mid-1860s. Following the tradition of comparing France with England, Jean-Pierre Dormois concluded that it was the enfranchisement of all males aged over 21 in 1848 in France that had given peasants an influence over policy, which increased further under the electoral system of the Third Republic, even as their numbers declined. This meant that the interests of agriculture were prioritized over those of the economy as a whole.[16]

During the great economic depression of 1873–96 agriculture was particularly badly affected, with the purchasing power of peasants falling to 45 per cent of those working in industry. Prices of agricultural produce fell by up to 40 per cent, and the value of the land also declined. Some sectors were worse affected than others. Quality wine production was decimated by the outbreak of phylloxera in 1870–80 but saved from ruin by the judicious export of the root stock to California, where it was grafted and reimported into France as healthy and resistant stock. At the same time, everyday wine faced steep competition from Algeria.[17]

During the depression agricultural interests combined with industrial ones to lobby for tariff protection to prevent further falls in wages and living standards. A coalition of wheat and iron producers succeeded in getting a two-tier system of minimum and maximum tariffs introduced in 1892, with high tariffs of 20 per cent imposed on imported goods that competed with domestic production, and tariffs of 5 per cent or less imposed on those goods that the country lacked. Championed by Jules Méline, the high tariffs were explicitly designed to prevent any structural change in the economy. Méline himself spoke of the virtues of a "static economy", advocating that people should even return to the land. The Radicals who gained control of parliament in 1898 saw it as the duty of politicians to defend the status quo. In France this meant protecting an economy balanced between the three sectors of activity, with agriculture playing an important role in providing for the basic needs of the population. Similarly, small scale uncompetitive firms were to be protected against big business. These views, according to Dormois, were what characterized French economic policy for 50 years after 1892 and held back the development of the economy.[18]

THE EVE OF THE FIRST WORLD WAR

Early proof of the economic damage caused by protection could be found in the years leading up to the First World War, "unaptly named *la belle époque*" according to Dormois, when France was far from being self-sufficient in food. In 1911 40 per cent of the active population was still employed in agriculture, compared with 12 per cent in the United Kingdom, but agriculture contributed only 31 per cent of the value added.[19] Despite prices rising after 1895, agriculture did not regain the level of prosperity that it had before the great depression. The country still needed to import cereals: amounting to as much as 1.5 million tonnes in 1910–11. Indeed, French agriculture had one of the lowest rates of growth and productivity in Europe at the time.[20] According to Dormois, this was not due to natural conditions of the land, as O'Brien and Keydar had argued, but to misguided policy. In an attempt to solve the problem of falling prices and living standards by erecting a system of tariffs, it had only made the problem worse. Indeed, it was in those agricultural products in which France specialized – cereals, wine, fruit and vegetables – that France had the largest trade deficit. In the short term the tariff had reduced imports drastically, almost stopping all imports of the food staples of grain and cattle, but before long the rates of protection had to be increased.

But if Dormois argued that it was the protectionist rather than the liberal policies of the Third Republic which had blocked economic growth and development, Robert Millward, in his comparative study of the relations between business and the state, pointed to the contrast between the French state's refusal to intervene directly, except in isolated instances, in developing the economic fabric of the country, and the behaviour of other states. By the beginning of the twentieth century the French state owned much less economic fabric than elsewhere in Europe. The central or local government in Germany owned over 90 per cent of the railway network, and in Italy almost 80 per cent, compared with under 6 per cent in France. Only 2 per cent of electricity supply in France was owned by the state compared with over 70 per cent in the UK and 80 per cent in Norway. Just over 2 per cent of gas supply was state owned in France compared with 84 per cent in Denmark and 95 per cent in Sweden. Yet like the rest of western Europe, the French state owned all the telegraph lines and the telephone exchanges.[21] It has been suggested that they were seen as a subversive force liable to spread revolutionary ideas. It was not until the 1970s that many parts of rural France were equipped with telephones. Apart from rare exceptions the state was content to regulate rather than to own. Only in certain cases where private firms could not generate profits, even with state subsidies, were they nationalized.[22]

The way that the railways were funded was something of an exception. With the shock of defeat in the Franco-Prussian war, the state now considered "an adequate system of communications [to be] indispensable to the successful pursuit of military operations".[23] Although it did not purchase or nationalize the railways, it passed a law in 1878 under which the development of new state lines was to be covered by the budget of the Ministry of Works and financed directly through government bonds. The government subsidized a number of small companies especially in the south-west and west of France, but beyond an unspecified level of subsidy the government would let the line close – unless it was perceived to be of military value. The network was expanded from 17,440 km in 1870 to 36,800 km by 1900, reaching the most distant and inaccessible towns. Indeed, the widespread extension of the railways was seen as a distinctive feature of France in comparison with other countries.[24]

With the exceptions of the railways and the telegraph, the state was committed to economic liberalism and neutrality in economic affairs. In any case, with strong opposition to the introduction of income taxes before 1914, it lacked the financial means, even had it had the political will, to intervene in the economy. Despite the changes in taxation introduced after the revolution of 1789, which, in sweeping away indirect levies on the basic necessities of life, in particular the reviled tax on salt (*la gabelle*), aimed to replace them with a fairer system of direct taxation, over the course of the nineteenth century the weight of indirect taxes gradually rose. By 1913 they accounted for 55 per cent of all taxes. Of these indirect taxes, customs duties accounted for over 18 per cent. Without additional revenue from income taxes the state was dependent on borrowing to cover its spending. By 1850 public debt was 28 per cent of GNP. On the eve of the war with Prussia it was 42 per cent.[25] However, since expenditure was limited to defence, civil administration and servicing the debt, it was a system that seemed to suit everyone. Taxes were low and the middle class had a guaranteed source of income by subscribing to government bonds and investing in property.

The introduction of income tax on the eve of the First World War failed to generate much extra revenue for the state, however, partly because rates were set at a low level and targeted only the top earners, but it was mainly because the official policy was to borrow from the domestic population

and from the allies in the expectation that Germany would pay reparations, as France had done after the war with Prussia in 1870. With the
heavy loss of life suffered by peasants during the First World War it was
agreed after the war that the agricultural sector would be taxed on the
basis of an estimated income, the forfait, which deliberately underestimated their real income.[26]

THE INTERWAR PERIOD

It was not until 1926 that French finances were stabilized and the currency once again became convertible, at 20 per cent of its pre-war value.
Tariffs were revised upwards in 1928 and the French economy enjoyed a
short period of growth. Industrial output grew and with it the demand
for migrant labour. The government, which had taken over its recruitment during the First World War, continued to organize it during the
1920s. Indeed, so great was the demand in industry that France became
as important an importer of labour as the United States. Industrial production continued to expand for several months after the crash on the
American stock market before a downturn in June 1930. It was to be 20
years before industrial production had regained its 1929 level.

Whereas most developed countries began to recover after 1932, the
French economy continued its decline, with tariff protection no longer
sufficient to maintain living standards, particularly of the peasants. Average incomes in the countryside fell by one third between 1928 and 1935.
Tariffs on wheat imports were raised from 7 francs per quintal in 1914 to
80 francs in 1930. But the policy of suppressing wheat imports was not,
in itself, enough to maintain prices, leading to demands for more direct
financial support. In the first ten months of 1935, the 1,700 million francs
of public money spent supporting wheat dwarfed the 1,170 million francs
spent on national defence at a time of mounting international tension.[27]
After Nazi Germany, in defiance of the League of Nations, remilitarized
the Rhineland and increased its rearmament programme, the left-wing
parties in France overcame some of their ideological differences to form a

united front against fascism. However, they remained divided over many issues, particularly over the role of nationalizations in the transition to socialism, with the Communist party still opposed in principle to any nationalization before the advent of socialism.[28] Speculation against the value of the franc, which was already a concern in 1935, rose even more when a popular front coalition of Socialists and Radicals was elected with the support of the Communists in 1936 under the premiership of the Socialist leader, Léon Blum. In the toxic mix of capital flight and mass strikes the government broke with the liberal policies of its predecessors and focused on a limited number of measures to step up defence production, while trying to meet the needs of workers and peasants. Aircraft production was reorganized into six new state-dominated firms, while firearm and tank production was reorganized into state workshops. The Bank of France was placed under tighter government control. Its executive council, which had been chosen by the governor (himself a government appointee) from among the 200 main shareholders, now became an advisory board, with nine members appointed by the government and two by the entire assembly of shareholders. In 1937 the entire railway system, which had been losing money since before the First World War, was brought into public ownership but with no loss to the shareholders when the charter granting the network to private companies expired.[29] The government also stepped in to intervene more directly in agriculture, setting up marketing boards for sugar, wheat and other cereals, in which the state guaranteed to purchase any surpluses that could not be sold at the official price.

The most controversial policies were the social ones, implemented to bring millions of workers striking for better pay and conditions back to work. Known as the Matignon agreements, they included a reduction of the working week from 49 to 40 hours with no loss of pay, and the introduction for the first time of two weeks paid holidays. Combined with capital flight, the measures put pressure on the value of the currency, and the convertibility of the franc into gold had to be suspended. Having promised not to devalue the franc, the government was forced to do so but the level at which the franc was stabilized was determined following a tripartite agreement with the United Kingdom and the United States. The purpose of the agreement was to avoid subsequent competitive devaluations of sterling and the dollar. However, instead of stimulating production through exports, the economy stagnated, with producers blaming the 40 hour week for reducing capacity. In 1937 the government lost power, bringing its reform programme to an end and, in the case of the 40 hour week, reversing it. In 1938 the franc was devalued, this time unilaterally, and deliberately undervalued. Industrial production picked up, but in the last year of peace it was no more than 80 per cent of the peak level of 1929.

Although Léon Blum was imprisoned by the Vichy state, having been found guilty at his trial in Riom on the spurious charge of contributing to the country's defeat in 1940, there were clearly many factors involved in explaining France's economic decline. No one would have predicted that after a further five years of decline the French economy would enjoy a sustained period of growth, and even fewer would have predicted that, having found the secret of success, it would lose it again. It is to these important questions that we will now turn.

2

The changing French economic model

Of the many changes that transformed the French economy after the Second World War, one of the most marked was the new interventionist role played by the state. In contrast to the laissez-faire economic liberalism of the Third Republic, which had responded to the demands of a narrow but sizeable agricultural lobby group, and to the authoritarian management of Vichy that had served the interests of the German occupation forces and the Nazi war economy, the postwar state was to serve the interests of a much wider range of groups in France demanding economic as well as political security. Under a series of reforms enacted between 1944 and 1948, the structures and instruments that would enable this new-found scale of state intervention in the economy were put in place. Some were inherited from the structures introduced by the Vichy state; others reflected the political aspirations of the resistance groups. Together, the reforms included an extension of the nationalization programme begun under the Popular Front government to include coal, electricity, the main deposit banks, the remaining privately owned firms in the aero engine industry, the Renault car and truck maker and all the air transport companies. These nationalizations were in line, in terms of both the type of industries targeted and the method of implementation, with those introduced in other European states. Where the French were different was in creating a system of indicative planning that, unlike the Soviet system, was designed to operate within a parliamentary democracy. The entire apparatus of state intervention that was put in place was designed to make economic policy-making more democratic than had previously been the case.

It was not just the economic liberalism of the Third Republic that was swept away after 1945, but the entire constitution. Although it had been set up in response to French defeat in the war with Prussia and had survived the First World War, the Third Republic was now associated with decline and defeat. That there would be no return to it in any shape was confirmed by the results of a referendum held five months after the end of the war in Europe. The electorate, which included women for the first time, rejected by an overwhelming majority of 96 per cent the proposal of the Radical party to reinstate the parliamentary regime of the Third Republic. Sixty-six per cent of the electorate in 1945 agreed with Charles de Gaulle, the self-appointed head of the provisional government, that a new constitution, drafted by an assembly elected in October 1945, should be put to a referendum. On 13 November 1945 de Gaulle was unanimously elected as head of a provisional government in which the Communists and Socialists formed the majority. The Communists, as the largest party, with the support of the Socialists, proposed a new constitution based on a single chamber with a weak executive to be put to the country in a referendum. On 20 January 1946, de Gaulle, who instead advocated a strong executive, resigned, seemingly in frustration at his inability to win support for his preferred regime. But, when put to a referendum on 5 May 1946, the constitution proposed by the Communists was rejected by 52.5 per cent of the electorate. In the second constituent assembly a new Christian Democratic party, the Mouvement Républicain Populaire (MRP), won the largest number of seats and, with the support of the Radicals, drafted a constitution based on two chambers and a stronger executive. When voted on by the French people in a referendum on 13 October 1946, it secured a majority (of nine million to eight million votes but with eight million abstentions). On 10 November 1946 elections to the new assembly were held that once again gave the Communist party the largest share of the vote, with 28.8 per cent, closely followed by the MRP with 26.3 per cent, the Socialists with 18.1 per cent, the Radicals with 11.4 per cent and various conservatives and independents with 15.4 per cent. On 14 January 1947, the Socialist Vincent Auriol was elected by the new assembly as president of the new Fourth Republic, with the required absolute majority of 51.19 per cent.

Throughout the short 12-year lifespan of the Fourth Republic there were 21 different governments, dominated by parties collectively known as the "third force" to distinguish them from the Communist party, which was in permanent oppostion from May 1947 until May 1981, and a new party, the Rassemblement du Peuple Français (RPF), formed by de Gaulle in April 1947 and disbanded in 1953. On 23 December 1953 Auriol was replaced as president by René Coty (who in 1940 had voted to give full executive powers to Marshall Pétain). It took 13 votes in the national assembly before he finally secured a majority.

In 1958 the parliamentary system of the Fourth Republic was replaced by the presidential regime of the Fifth Republic as the price demanded by de Gaulle when he was returned to power in the expectation that he alone would be able to bring an end to the Algerian war by retaining Algeria as part of France. The new constitution was ratified in a referendum held in September 1958 by a majority of 82.6 per cent. In a referendum on 28 October 1962 de Gaulle succeeded (62.3 per cent in favour) in amending the constitution of the Fifth Republic to provide for the direct election of the president by universal suffrage rather than by an electoral college. Having survived the election in 1981 of the Socialist president, François Mitterrand (a long-time critic of the constitution), the constitution then survived three periods of cohabitation in which the president and the government were from opposing political parties.[1] In 2000 the presidential mandate was reduced from seven to five years to bring it into line with that of parliament and avoid any further cohabitation. As a result the Fifth Republic has now almost rivalled the Third in terms of longevity (see the appendix for further details).[2]

The reforms enacted in the immediate postwar period, which have come to be known collectively as the French economic model, changed over time in response to developments in the domestic and external political and economic environments. The first main change to the model came in the mid-1960s with the liberalization of the financial system. Other changes over the following three decades were to alter the way in which the state intervened in the economy. From the 1980s onwards, planning gave way to the market and France became more like other countries in the European Community. At the same time the French economy retained many distinctive features. The state intervened less directly in the economy, but its size and its consequent capacity to redistribute income grew. France became a more equal society, but with a significant number of people living precariously. Paris retained its pre-eminent position, but other cities grew in size. French agriculture employed many fewer people but managed to produce a surplus of food. One aspect that remained constant was the ability of the state to collect ever increasing revenue from taxation, which it used for different purposes. In most years, that revenue, expressed as a proportion of GDP, was the largest in the developed world.

In this chapter we examine the French economic model and explain how it changed over time. Then we proceed to analyse the impact of state intervention on the structure and performance of the economy using traditional metrics (Chapter 3), before examining it from other perspectives: on regional inequalities (Chapter 4), on interpersonal inequalities (Chapter 5) and, finally, on relations with France's trading partners in Europe and its former colonies (Chapter 6). This chapter is accordingly divided into five distinct but overlapping sections.

THE LEGACY OF OCCUPATION AND RESISTANCE, 1940–44

In this section we look at the legacies for French policy and policy-making of France's decision to surrender in 1940. Following the armistice signed with Nazi Germany and the occupation of part and then all of France, the Vichy state reorganized the structure of the economy and developed plans for its postwar reconstruction. At the same time, the groups representing the resistance to that occupation developed their own plans for the post-war period.

The French economy that emerged from the Second World War was even weaker than that in the 1930s. In 1944 industrial production was less than half its 1938 level, with output in some sectors, such as metals and construction material, less than one third its 1938 level. The output of jewellery and luxury goods had suffered less during the occupation, having been seen as a safer investment than the national currency. Agricultural production was down by 35 per cent compared with pre-war levels, mainly due to a shortage of labour and fertilizer.[3] Of the 1.5 million agricultural workers mobilized in 1939–40, 500,000 had either died or become prisoners of war. The combination of a collapse in food imports (by 1943 the tonnage of food imports had fallen by 94.4 per cent) and the 15 per cent of agricultural produce requisitioned by the Germans meant that the reduction in food consumption was greater in France than in any other occupied country in western Europe. In 1943–44, bread rations, when they were actually available, were 70 per cent of the pre-war average, while fats were 31 per cent and meat was only 18 per cent.[4] While the official prices for basic foodstuffs doubled between 1938 and 1943, the wages of manual workers rose by less than 50 per cent. For most French people, apart from those working in agriculture, the experience of the war was one of hunger.[5]

Yet out of this reduced output the Vichy government had managed to transfer to Germany not only large quantities of agricultural produce, foodstuffs and alcohol (including 39 per cent of the French production of champagne), but also a sizeable quantity of critical raw materials and manufactured goods. Some industries such as aircraft and automobiles worked entirely for the German war economy. In addition to providing goods, the French government made payments to Germany that amounted to 49 per cent of total public expenditure over the course of the occupation. About one third of these transfers were covered by taxation, some came from printing money (the note circulation increased fivefold) and the rest came from borrowing.

That the Vichy state had managed to control and direct the economy was quite remarkable, particularly since, given the ideological opposition of most governments under the Third Republic to any sort of direct intervention in the economy, France, of all developed countries, was the one least well informed about economic operations. There had been no industrial census since 1931 and no agricultural one since 1929.[6] Nonetheless, with the help of a newly enlarged statistical office, the Vichy state set out to control the entire industrial output in the unoccupied part of France. The verdict of historians is that it represented "the most advanced experience of a managed economy in France".[7] It replaced the Ministry of Armaments with a new Ministry of Industrial Production, comprising separate committees (*comités d'organisation*) created for each branch of production, each charged with setting their own targets. These committees depended in turn on a new central organization (OCRPI) responsible for distributing all raw materials and industrial products, and thus with control over all levels of rationing from initial distribution among producers to final consumption. By the end of the occupation OCRPI employed almost 6,500 people.[8] To enable the transfer payments to be made to Germany, the Vichy state created what was known as the "Treasury circuit". This was a procedure whereby the Treasury issued to the banks national defence bonds, otherwise known as Treasury bills, which by 1945 accounted for two-thirds of retail bank deposits. It also created a new institution, the Délégation Générale à l'Équipement National (DGEN), to draw up a ten-year plan for the postwar period. The main objective of the plan was to overcome what was perceived to be the main economic problem facing France: its technological backwardness. Under the ten-year equipment plan for France and the colonies produced in 1942, this shortcoming was to be addressed by prioritizing investment over consumption through the continued regulation of industry, while recognizing that France's large rural population would have to be conserved. In 1944 DGEN produced a second plan, which was to deal with the immediate tasks of reconstruction once the full extent of the challenges was known.[9]

These challenges, inherited from the depression of the 1930s and the war, were compounded by the fact that other developed economies had not only recovered from the depression after 1932 but expanded rapidly during the war: in the case of the United States the recovery was stimulated by the war. Indeed, in all the main combatant countries, productivity had risen as labour had moved, or been moved, into capital intensive sectors such as the manufacture of aircraft, motor vehicles, armaments and electrical equipment. In France, by contrast, production and productivity in these sectors had declined, partly due to shortages of supply and investment and partly due to the passive resistance of labour to the occupation.

If the Vichy officials were drawing up plans for the postwar nation, so too was the French Resistance. In March 1944, five months before Paris was liberated from German control, the body representing all the resistance groups in France, the Conseil National de la Résistance (CNR), in which the Communists were the only group organized as a political party, circulated its proposals for postwar reform. Reflecting its left-wing majority, the council called for the state to take over the running of the economy by nationalizing the "commanding heights" of energy, transport, banking and credit and involving workers' representatives in drawing up and operating a system of economic planning as well as a comprehensive system of social security.[10] Of all the economic factors that could have been held responsible for the national crisis facing France at the time, the CNR, like the Vichy technocrats, blamed the laissez-faire approach of successive Third Republic governments.

THE POSTWAR REFORMS, 1944–58

For many years the performance of the economy under the Fourth Republic was seen through the lens of its political instability without paying due regard to how the postwar reforms had laid the foundations for politicians and civil servants to manage the challenges associated with the decline of empire, the pressure to modernize the economy, liberalize trade and restore the convertibility of the currency. In this section we examine the series of reforms implemented between 1944 and 1958. These included nationalizations, economic planning, the system of welfare, tax reform and trade liberalization.

Although the entire Vichy state was swept away as France was liberated, there was no immediate agreement, despite the publication of the CNR charter, on what should replace it. In the insurrectionary period before the war ended, the measures taken were piecemeal, responding to immediate economic and political imperatives rather than forming part of a broader coherent strategy. There was little support for the tough austerity measures advocated by the Minister of National Economy, Pierre Mendès France, to control wages and prices until production had increased and a comprehensive plan had been put in place. Quite the contrary. To compensate for the steep decline under the occupation, wages were immediately increased by 50 per cent in the autumn of 1944, and they had increased by 130 per cent by October 1945.[11] There was a consensus that economic recovery depended on expanding domestic demand, on consumption as well as investment. The unions agreed to work a 48 hour week to win what was called the "battle of production", with overtime beyond 40 hours being paid at 25 per cent above the hourly wage. In fact, with wages rising faster than productivity, a guaranteed minimum wage, the *salaire minimum interprofessionnel garanti* (SMIG), was introduced to ensure a rudimentary base level for those workers who lacked the collective force to bargain with their employer. Implemented in February 1950, it initially had eight different rates across the country, reduced to two in 1968. A separate minimum wage was introduced for agricultural workers (SMAG) on 9 October 1950, set at 13.5 per cent below the SMIG before the distinction was ended in 1968. Both were indexed to the cost of living from 1952 onwards, with the calculation mechanism being modified at intervals.[12]

Nationalizations

Similarly, although there was a consensus on the principle of nationalizations, the choice of which firms should be taken into state ownership reflected various motivations. The coal mines in the Nord and Pas-de-Calais, which had been under the direct control of the Germans, were taken over by the state to drive up production at a time when the coal imports on which the economy normally depended were unavailable. Months later, the remaining coal mines were taken under state control to create nine regional state corporations under the central authority of the Charbonnages de France. The purpose of the nationalization of coal was to reduce French dependence on imports through the "battle of production" and to supply cheaper coal to domestic industry.[13]

Other nationalizations were to settle scores dating not only from the occupation but also from the bitter labour disputes of the 1930s. Renault was ostensibly nationalized on the grounds that its owner, Louis Renault, had actively collaborated with the Nazis. However, given that other firms in the motor vehicle sector, such as Berliet, which had worked exclusively for the German war economy, escaped this fate, it is now accepted that the real reason was Renault's harsh treatment of the workforce in the 1930s.[14] Since car production was hardly part of the economic infrastructure of the country, the nationalized firm was to be held up as a model of the highest standards that all manufacturing industries were to follow. Similarly, the aero engine firm Gnôme et Rhône, which had escaped nationalization in 1936, was in no position to resist it in 1945, having been badly bombed by the Allies during the war. Gnôme et Rhône was merged with the previously nationalized aero engine firms to become the Société Nationale d'Études et de Construction de Moteurs d'Aviation (SNECMA).

Gradually, more coherence to the form and purpose of state intervention emerged after months of discussion and debate. In recognition of the central role that civil servants would play in the new interventionist state, a training school, the École Nationale d'Administration (ENA), was set up in October 1945. While it was modelled on the existing *grandes écoles* in terms of selecting students by competitive examinations based on their academic proficiency, it was to be more democratic and transparent in terms of recruitment and training. The perceived problem was not only that civil servants were drawn from an elite and unrepresentative social base but that what they were taught was narrow and specialized. Until the Second World War, each ministry had its own hiring process and selection standards, which meant that few officials were capable of serving in a variety of roles or of having an overview of the needs of society as a whole. Sharing the Vichy state's recognition that civil servants needed to have much greater knowledge about the workings of the economy than was available at the time, the government set up a new national statistical service, the Institut national de la statistique et des études économiques (INSEE), on 27 April 1946.

The rationale for nationalizing the gas and electricity industries in the spring of 1946 was different again. In their case it was to enable them, as the main energy suppliers, to reap the benefits of economies of scale through their monopoly position in the domestic market. At Liberation there were 54 companies running 86 coal-fired power plants, 100 companies running 300 hydroelectric plants, 86 companies transporting that power and 1,150 firms distributing it to customers. Following the creation of Électricité de France (EDF) and Gaz de France (GDF), 34 of the largest insurance companies (almost half the total) were also nationalized in 1946. Two years later, Air France became a mixed company, as did two large firms in maritime transport.[15] Significantly though, the most radical suggestion advocated by the Communist party, to nationalize the iron and steel industry, was not implemented. Its exclusion also meant that a large part of intermediate industry was not directly under state control. However, by nationalizing the Bank of France and the four main deposit banks and by setting up a national credit council (CNC) in December 1945, the state hoped to be in a strong position to control credit for investment in the economy and to do so in an orderly non-inflationary way.

The nationalization of credit was significant, since France subscribed to the values and principles of international cooperation as defined under the Bretton Woods Agreement, which it had signed, together with 43 other countries, in 1944. There was an acceptance that the new international monetary system based on cooperation among member states to achieve stable, convertible currencies was the best foundation for expanding trade. The new system, unlike the gold standard it replaced, recognized that domestic policies to promote economic development should have priority over the need to maintain a fixed exchange rate for the national currency.[16] In December 1945 the French government registered a par value for the franc in terms of gold and the dollar, with a commitment to make it freely convertible at an appropriate time in the future. Monetary policy was to be orthodox rather than Keynesian, but based on interventionist rather than liberal convictions. Initially, both the money supply and inflation were to be managed through selective credit controls. In order to avoid inflation, the Treasury aimed to channel savings and deposits into long-term investment in activities that were perceived to be in the national economic interest rather than for speculative purposes.

It was felt that, in the interwar period, if not earlier, French banks and financial markets had refused to lend to industry, preferring to pursue their own goals, rather than those in the national interest. One difficulty facing policy-makers was that, even had banks been willing to invest in industry, the only type of loans that commercial banks could rediscount at the Bank of France were three-month bills. With Treasury bills now forming two-thirds of bank deposits, the government was in a position to influence the loans made by banks. Unlike Britain and the United States, which had ended the wartime practice of issuing Treasury bills as soon as the war was over in order to allow banks to resume their lending, the system was retained in France until 1964.[17] Banks were now allowed to rediscount bills for up to five years, on the condition that their loans were made for productive rather than speculative purposes. But, in view of the fact that the lack of investment had not been confined to particular firms or sectors but was widespread, one key question was whether the banks, acting on instructions from the CNC, would be able to determine which loans were in the national interest and which sectors should be given priority for investment funds.

Economic planning

It was Jean Monnet who came up with the idea, accepted by de Gaulle in January 1946 shortly before he resigned, of setting up a small planning unit, the Commissariat Général au Plan (CGP), attached to the office of the prime minister rather than to one of the powerful economic or financial ministries, which would draw up a list of investment priorities as part of a four-year development plan. Monnet, a businessman, had spent the war years negotiating supplies for the British war effort from the United States after the fall of France. He now proposed to take such a plan to the Americans as a request for dollar aid. What became known as the Monnet Plan was to modernize and expand the industrial sector in France rather than maintain a balance between industry and agriculture. At a time when the Allies were imposing strict limits on the level of industrial activity permitted in Germany, it was a plan to expand heavy industry in France relative to that permitted in Germany.[18] Initially, it prioritized six basic sectors of the economy for investment: coal, steel, cement, electricity, transport and agricultural machinery. Although only six sectors were selected, almost the whole economy was drawn into the planning process, with 24 modernization commissions bringing together both sides of industry as well as civil servants, set up to agree on production targets for each sector.

Initially, the intention in prioritizing investment in agricultural machinery was to increase the efficiency of the agricultural sector in order to release labour for industry. However, faced with a severe food shortage in 1947, which necessitated the continuation of rations and emergency imports of wheat from the United States under the "Interim Aid" programme, the Monnet Plan was modified in 1948 to include the whole of agriculture as a priority sector. What this meant was that, instead of trying to change the traditional methods of agricultural production in order to create a system of large, highly mechanized farms whose output and productivity would be much higher than those of the existing family farms, the system would be modernized more gradually while retaining the traditional structure. This would be achieved through a variety of methods, ranging from setting up cooperatives for the joint purchase of machinery to providing finance through the specialized agricultural bank, the Crédit Agricole, amalgamating small farms into larger units, subsidizing fuel for tractors and working with agricultural organizations such as the Fédération des Jeunes Agriculteurs (FJA) to educate young farmers in more modern methods. The inclusion of the whole of the agricultural sector also meant that many of the initial production targets of the Monnet Plan were reduced, leading to the accusation by the Communists that the Marshall Plan was favouring the recovery of German industry at the expense of that of France.[19]

A second change introduced in 1948 was the addition of quantitative controls on credit. This was made in recognition of the fact that the existing qualitative controls, exerted by the banks through the CNC, were not sufficient to keep inflation under control. For the first time in their history, banks were required to hold a given proportion of government securities (95 per cent) in their reserves and were subject to a global limit of rediscounting fixed by the Bank of France.

Welfare reforms

A third change made in 1948 was in the organization of social security. Despite the best efforts of Pierre Laroque, the civil servant responsible for setting up the new system, what emerged in 1948 was far removed from the "comprehensive social security programme aimed at ensuring the livelihoods of all citizens, whenever they are not able to do so through work, managed by the representatives of the interested parties and of the state" as set out in the ordinance of 4 October 1945.[20] Opposition had come from a variety of quarters and groups. In the first instance, mutual aid societies, the Catholic trade unions and de Gaulle himself were opposed to the integration of family allowances into a single social security fund. This reflected deep-seated concerns about the slow growth of the French population: concerns that in March 1945 had prompted de Gaulle to call for twelve million beautiful babies to be born over a 10-year period. While these concerns had for a long time been expressed mainly by right-wing groups, the loss of life in the Second World War, and the fact that in some years during the 1930s the population had actually contracted, meant that the birth rate became an issue of wider concern after the war. Indeed, in the first postwar debate about reforming the system of taxation, and the first time, as we have seen, that French women over 21 had the right to vote, the only measure that won a majority in the constituent assembly was to give rebates on income tax to parents. What was agreed was a form of income splitting, known as the family quotient, whereby total household income was divided into a number of parts, with each parent constituting one part and each child 0.5 of a part. For a family of four the total income was therefore divided into three parts, with allowances deducted from each part before the tax on the part was calculated and then multiplied by three to arrive at the total household income tax liability. It was a system that benefited larger, richer families the most, and reduced the revenue from income taxation as a whole.[21]

At the other end of the life cycle, opposition to the proposal to integrate old-age insurance schemes into a single fund came from small and medium-sized business owners, those working in middle management (cadres) as well as self-employed artisans, who all feared that it would impose extra costs on them without delivering proportional benefits. Rather than have a new universal system of social security based on higher taxation and redistribution, what was generally preferred was to retain the principle of differentiated insurance systems with lower contribution rates. Those who belonged to existing insurance-based schemes, such as in coal mining, the railway company (the Société nationale des chemins de fer français (SNCF)) and the civil service, resisted the attempt to force them to merge into one national scheme, and where there was no such professional scheme one was created. Thus, an agricultural scheme was added, as well as ones for independent traders and the liberal professions. In each scheme, to manage risks such as illness, accidents at work, maternity and old age, specialized funds were set up, to which both employers and employees contributed and which were run by representatives of employers and unions, giving the unions a power beyond their numbers.[22] Unemployment was added ten years later, but its financing and management remained independent of social security.[23]

Tax reform

As well as deciding on the form that the new social security regime would take, in 1948 agreement was finally reached on reforming the system of taxation. By 1947 the proportion of households paying any income tax had fallen to its lowest level since 1924. Tax fraud was endemic. Although this had been a problem since the very introduction of income taxation, under the German occupation it had assumed the role of a patriotic duty for many people: a practice that was difficult to reverse after the war. A committee set up in 1946 to investigate how best to increase the revenue from income taxes and reduce fraud failed to produce a majority report. In the absence of any reform, increased claims on the budget arising from the need for additional public investment, as well as to cover the cost of reconstruction, came from the counterpart in French francs of dollar loans and grants from the United States and from advances from the recently nationalized Bank of France. Following a spurious threat made by the United States not to release further counterpart funds of Marshall Aid until the French parliament had reformed the tax system, legislation was finally passed in December 1948. No change was made to the "forfait" mechanism of estimating the tax liability of those working in agriculture. However, in recognition of the fact that tax avoidance was rife among the self-employed, the artisans, small shopkeepers and owners of small and medium-sized firms whereas it was impossible for factory workers to disguise their income, a special complementary tax was introduced in addition to the general income tax, targeted specifically at the self-employed. This was a proportional tax set at 18 per cent. But, instead of reducing fraud, the legislation increased it, since anyone who declared their true income was now seen as an idiot. By 1952 fraud was estimated at between 20 and 25 per cent of tax receipts. In 1954 the system of indirect taxation was changed, with the cumbersome cumulative tax on production replaced by a tax on value added. Not only did VAT not discriminate between production for the domestic market and that for the export market but it could also be used to encourage investment by exempting it from taxation. It was also applied to the service sector. The advantages of the new tax in removing administrative obstacles to trade became so apparent that VAT came to be adopted by the EEC as part of its "*acquis communautaire*".[24]

The Monnet Plan was extended until 1953 to coincide with the end of the Mutual Aid Program, the successor to the European Recovery Program (ERP) – the official name given to the Marshall Plan. But the institutional structures put in place (the CGP, the CNC and the nationalized sector) ensured that planning would continue. Monnet himself had left to become head of the High Authority of the European Coal and Steel Community (ECSC), but economic planning, judged to have been a success, was to continue until the 1990s, even if its influence had faded long before then. From the second plan onwards, the French plans covered the entire economy with the objective of encouraging both public and private investment in order to promote increases in the levels of productivity and competitiveness in France. In view of the rapid turnover of governments – every six months or so in the 1950s – the very survival of the planning organization was an achievement in itself.

Trade liberalization

Controls over credit were effective in maintaining investment and price stability, while the public sector, which became the main base for French trade unions, where jobs were protected for life, was seen as the means of protecting the entire French economy from international competition and market rules.[25] However, it was in the foreign trade sector that the plans were least able to forecast and control growth of demand. Both the first and second plans aimed to substitute domestic production for imports, but the increases in domestic demand were always higher than predicted, as was the growth of foreign demand. Under the second plan imports were not to rise even though GDP was to increase by 25 per cent. At the same time, imports of food were to be reduced by 40 per cent. The problem was that French industry could not produce in sufficient quantity the investment goods needed to modernize the economy, once imports from the United States, funded by Marshall Aid, came to an end. It was imports from West Germany, funded initially by credits from the European Payments Union (EPU) that came to replace them. But what really changed in the 1950s, particularly in comparison with the 1930s, was the changing composition of imports into West Germany. Instead of food and raw materials, West Germany was importing ever greater quantities of metals and engineering products, which French industry was supplying in increasing amounts. Between 1951 and 1958 French exports to West Germany grew at an annual rate of 16.2 per cent, compared with an increase of 2.6 per cent per year to the rest of Western Europe.[26]

The United States had hoped that, in return for dollar aid under the ERP, the 16 European recipients would liberalize their trade and payments to form one large market in Europe, effectively a United States of Europe, with currencies freely convertible into gold and dollars and a partner for the United States in the "free world". However, each time the French government reduced the quantitative barriers to trade, the growth of imports exceeded the capacity to pay for them with exports. Rather than depress consumption and investment, the government reimposed restrictions on imports. It could only be a temporary solution because of the growing pressure, both domestic and external, to liberalize trade. Since imports of equipment goods from West Germany were increasingly important for the modernization of French industry, while imports of consumer goods simply competed with goods already produced in France, forming a small customs union of the six ECSC countries was considered to be more beneficial and less damaging than the large free trade area proposed at the time by the UK. The alternative of seeking refuge in France's protected colonial markets was a counsel of despair. It had not worked in the 1930s, and with countries increasingly demanding independence from France it was even less likely to work in the future. One of the last acts of the French government before it collapsed under the strains of the Algerian war was to sign and ratify the Treaty of Rome, setting up a customs union with the five other members of the ECSC[27] (see Chapter 6).

THE GAULLIST MODEL OF ECONOMIC POLICY-MAKING, 1958–74

In this section we examine how President de Gaulle and his successor, Georges Pompidou, changed the nature of economic planning. On his return to power in 1958 de Gaulle elevated the idea of planning to that of a burning need *"l'ardente obligation"* but abandoned the original objective of democratizing economic policy-making. Just as in his foreign policy, where he sought to make France independent of the United States, challenging American hegemony by taking France out of the military wing of NATO in 1966 and by undermining the privileged position of the dollar in the international monetary system of Bretton Woods, so in his economic policy he portrayed the French model as a third way between American free market capitalism and communism. It was to be based on overcoming French backwardness by promoting the use of modern technology in industry and agriculture, creating large-scale enterprises by encouraging rationalizations and mergers, and advocating strict adherence to the rules of the international monetary system, particularly by the United States. A series of shocks, starting with the general strike of May 1968 and followed by the collapse of the Bretton Woods system and the quadrupling of the price of oil, led to the international recession of 1973–75 and the end of the Gaullist industrial ambitions.

Initially, the transition from the parliamentary multiparty system of the Fourth Republic to the presidential system of the Fifth, which accompanied de Gaulle's return to power in May 1958, resulted in few changes to the structure of economic policy-making. Despite having been a very vocal opponent of any move to dilute national independence within an integrated European organization in the 1950s, sharing responsibility with the Communist party for voting down the proposal to form a European Defence Community (EDC) in 1954, once in power, de Gaulle honoured the Treaty of Rome, setting up the European Economic Community. Indeed, he was responsible for ensuring the creation of a common policy for agricultural protection (CAP), for many years the only common policy agreed in the EEC (see Chapter 6). However, the European Atomic Energy Community (Euratom) was another matter, since de Gaulle was not prepared to relinquish control over any aspect of France's nuclear energy programme. He also accepted the collective commitment of the members of the Organisation for European Economic Cooperation (OEEC) to restore the free convertibility of their currencies into gold and dollars in December 1958 while maintaining national controls over the movement of capital. De Gaulle also supported the system of economic planning that he himself had initiated in 1946, seeing no conflict between national planning and trade liberalization within the EEC. As a measure of his support for planning he appointed Pierre Massé, the very successful head of EDF, to take over as president of the Commissariat au Plan. At that time EDF was considered to be the most efficient and innovative nationalized firm, providing the country with relatively cheap electricity while being sufficiently profitable to rely partially on self-financing and the bond market for investment capital, even if the lion's share of its financing still came from the Treasury.[28] However, over the course of de Gaulle's ten years in power, the system that had been so carefully constructed under the Fourth Republic was gradually weakened to the extent that planning became little more than an ever more sophisticated economic model of government policies, which was largely ignored by private industry (since they were able to raise credit on the money markets) and by the unions. The international monetary system was also weakened by the pressure that the French put on the dollar, ultimately leading to the collapse of the system.

In 1958, given the high rates of inflation fuelled by spending on the war in Algeria, the public spending cuts begun during the last months of

the Fourth Republic were tightened and, under the direction of the orthodox economic adviser, Jacques Rueff, the franc was devalued by 17.5 per
cent (for the second time in two years). To mark the commitment to the
new value, the second devaluation was accompanied by the introduction
of a new franc. Rueff had been a key player in the Tripartite Agreement
with the UK and the United States under which the franc had been devalued in 1936. A firm believer in the gold standard, in which all members
played to the same rules, he felt that France had been living beyond its
means in the 1950s. In 1958, back in a position of influence, he recommended large cuts in social programmes and government subsidies, in
order to balance the budget as part of the measures to stabilize the new
franc. Other measures included a change to the tax system to favour the
self-employed by abolishing the complementary tax, which, as we have
seen, only the self-employed had to pay, while removing parliamentary
control over taxation.[29] The real problem that Rueff saw as undermining
the stability of the international monetary system, though, was not French
profligacy but the way in which the United States took advantage of the
dominant role of the dollar to expand both its domestic consumption and
spending abroad. Through his former assistant, Maurice Couve de Mur-
ville, who served as foreign minister from 1958 to 1968 before becoming
prime minister for one year, Rueff influenced French policy towards the
dollar. The method chosen was to put pressure on the United States to
curb its spending, by instructing the Bank of France to convert the dollars
in its reserves into gold. By December 1964 gold accounted for 73 per cent
of French reserves and it increased still further while the gold component
of the official American reserves fell from just under 25 per cent in 1948
to less than 15 per cent in 1968–71.

At the same time, breaking with the system of controlling bank credit
introduced after the war, the Treasury circuit was ended in 1964, and
semi-public and private organizations took over the financing of the
economy. Between 1961 and 1971 the proportion of total funding provided by the Treasury fell from 22.4 per cent to 9.5 per cent, as the government took measures to encourage the growth of long-term deposits and

greater self-financing of investment by industry. It encouraged mergers in banking and insurance, the creation of mortgage and bond markets, the lifting of restrictions on the number of banking counters and generally encouraged the direct channelling of savings towards companies without state oversight or intervention. Over the course of the 1960s bank participation in the financing of the economy increased in relation to that of the Bank of France and the public and semi-public institutions. Under the Debré–Haberer laws of 1966–67 changes were made to mobilize savings through the use of market mechanisms such as increasing interest rates on deposits and issuing stocks and bonds.[30] According to Haberer, the French economy had suffered from a lack of investment since 1945, so measures needed to be taken to encourage savings and to restore Paris to what he considered its former role as a great international financial centre before the First World War.[31]

Some sectors continued to enjoy state protection and privileged access to medium- and long-term funding from the savings banks. Although the fourth plan (1962–65) was called a plan for economic and social development, in fact planning became more like an industrial policy, in which the state actively promoted mergers and rationalizations to create internationally competitive national champions. This was particularly the case in the fields of aerospace, telecommunications, automobiles, petroleum, computers and the electrification of transport.

In January 1966, when Pierre Massé retired and was replaced by François-Xavier Ortoli, the director of the "cabinet" of Georges Pompidou, the plan became more overtly political.[32] Instead of representing a meeting place for all the economic and social forces in the country, the plan became a way of adjusting between the policies of the various state bodies. Recognizing that not a single French company was among the top 15 firms in the world in sectors such as steel, chemicals, pharmaceuticals, paper making, textiles, electrical engineering or the food industry, the goal of policy now became the creation of international firms that could compete abroad while also defending their market share at home.[33] Building on legislation passed in 1965, under which firms were allowed to take account of inflation when re-evaluating assets and set aside greater amounts for depreciation to reduce corporation tax liability, the government now actively promoted mergers and industrial concentrations. The results were immediate. In metals production, Ugine and Kuhlmann merged, followed by the steel firms Sidelor and de Wendel. In the aeronautics sector Dassault and Breguet merged, as did Thomson and Brandt in electronics. At the same time, an official report into the running of public enterprises, the Nora Report, was published. This advocated a much larger degree of self-management, a reduction in public subsidies and investment and a lowering of prices for the consumer. The report divided opinion, with the unions and those on the left seeing it as the beginning of the end of the concept of public service. It was not long before the Confédération Générale du Travail (CGT) and the Confédération Française Démocratique du Travail (CFDT) unions withdrew from the Modernization Commissions of the Plan on the grounds that the plan was no longer trying to satisfy the needs of the population and the general interest but only satisfied the needs of private industry.

As the character of economic planning changed to reflect narrow political rather than economic and social criteria, it became more sophisticated technically with the use of new computer modelling and warning lights ("*clignotants*"), to signal if inflation was knocking targets off course. But with stable government and continuous economic growth, business increasingly ignored civil servants and also became less interested in the planning process. By the time of the fifth plan (1966–70), industry was questioning the usefulness of the national planning institutions themselves.[34]

The preparation of the sixth plan took more than four years to complete, with at least 5,000 contributors. Work began in 1966, but the plan was set back by a year due to the eruption of a general strike in May 1968. This was the largest ever experienced in France, mobilizing more than twice as many people as the great general strike of 1936 that had led to the Matignon reforms. Among the many reasons for workers' anger were rising prices that had wiped out increases in incomes, a rise in unemployment and the fact that working hours were among the longest in Europe, regional disparities that were bad and getting worse, while some areas (including Nantes, where the first strike broke out) were starting to suffer. Entry-level wages for young workers were low and recent reductions in social security benefits had hurt workers economically and underlined the arrogance and insensitivity of the government's approach to dealing with workers.[35]

The strikes were brought to an end by the Grenelle Agreements negotiated between the state, employers' organizations and workers, under which the minimum wage, the SMIG, was increased by 35 per cent. Whatever the shock to the political establishment and the system of planning that the events of 1968 brought about, it has been claimed that the sixth plan "was prepared in a climate of opinion which acknowledged that the Plan had an important role to play".[36] There were increasing calls for more openness in the technical preparation phases and for more time to be devoted to considering deeper structural analyses with greater discussion of social and regional problems.

De Gaulle's response to the strikes was to call a referendum for regional reform in April 1969 (see Chapter 4). When it was rejected by 52.4 per cent of the voters, he resigned as promised. His successor, Georges Pompidou, devalued the franc, lifted the veto on Britain's application to join the EEC and presided over the decision by the Bank of France in 1971 to extend the liberalization of the banking and financial system. With his prime minister, Jacques Chaban-Delmas, he ushered in the "New Society" with a fourth week of paid holidays, the wider roll-out of the 40-hour week, a new way of calculating the minimum wage (SMIC), which was to be linked not only to increases in prices but also to productivity, wages indexed to the rate of economic growth above inflation, and wages that were formerly paid by the hour or week now paid on a monthly basis. The plan was retained but, despite the huge effort that had gone into preparing the sixth plan that was to cover the period 1971–75, it contained very few numerical targets compared with earlier plans.[37] Pompidou saw growth, industrialization and prosperity as the answer to the grievances that had erupted in 1968, themselves the result of an over-extended austerity policy. His goal was for industrial production to double in ten years, to enable France eventually to overtake Germany as an industrial power.[38] In a report commissioned by the French government before the 1973 elections, the Hudson Institute happily predicted that by 1985 France could have overtaken even the United States in terms of GNP per capita.[39] The merger mania continued, but at a slower pace. The non-ferrous metals firm Ugine-Kuhlmann merged with the chemical firm Péchiney; Pont à Mousson merged with Saint-Gobain; Berliet merged with the truck maker Saviem; Agache-Willot took over the textile firm Boussac Frères; Peugeot merged with Citroën and together they went on to buy Chrysler-Europe; Elf-Erap merged with the Société Nationale d'Aquitaine to form the Société Nationale Elf-Aquitaine, of which 70 per cent was owned by the French government.[40]

However successful the mergers may have been in furthering the competitiveness of individual sectors of the French economy, any benefits were undermined when the entire international monetary system was rocked by the decision of the United States to suspend the convertibility of the dollar into gold. This was to mark the end of the Bretton Woods system and any hope of creating an international monetary system based on stable exchange rates and international cooperation. France, in converting dollars into gold in order to put pressure on the dollar from 1964 onwards, is considered to have overplayed its hand, pressing too hard for a return to something more like the Tripartite Agreement of 1936.[41] At subsequent talks between Richard Nixon and Pompidou in the Azores in December 1971, Nixon agreed to devalue the dollar in terms of gold but not to restore its convertibility immediately.[42] This was followed by a multilateral meeting at which countries that were running trade surpluses, such as West Germany and Japan, agreed to revalue their currencies. Under the Smithsonian Agreement all currencies were then allowed to fluctuate by as much as 2.25 per cent on either side of their par value, compared with fluctuations of 1 per cent under the previous rules. But since this new flexibility created operational problems for the common pricing structure of the CAP, it prompted an agreement among the six member states of the EEC on 7 March 1972 to set lower limits of 1.125 per cent on either side of the par value for their currencies. This was only very slightly higher than the limits that had operated under the fixed-exchange system of Bretton Woods. This closer arrangement, known as the "snake", was joined by the United Kingdom, the Republic of Ireland and Denmark on 1 May 1972. But, despite monthly interventions of the central banks to maintain these parities, the system did not last. On 23 June 1972 the UK left the snake and allowed the value of sterling to float. Pressure built up against the dollar, and on 12 February 1973 the main international players reached an agreement to devalue the dollar in terms of gold, although a number of them refused to fix a value for their own currency. By 11 March 1973 the few countries left in the snake, West Germany, France, the Benelux and Denmark, decided to increase the margin of fluctuation in the snake from 1.125 per cent to 2.25 per cent but to end any attempt to fix a rate with the floating currencies, which now effectively included the dollar.

The devaluation of the dollar (from a rate of 35 to 42.2 per ounce of gold over two years) and every likelihood of it declining further had implications for the price of internationally traded commodities that were priced in dollars, with oil being the most important example. In November 1973 the Organization of Petroleum Exporting Countries (OPEC) took action to correct the loss of real income by quadrupling the price of oil. France was particularly badly hit, since it was in the process of switching from coal to oil, while its nuclear energy programme, begun in the 1950s, accounted for only 1.8 per cent of national energy use by 1973. Worse still, when France had, following Algerian independence in 1962, lost its rights to the oil fields in the Sahara (which they had started to exploit in 1956), the publicly owned oil companies had turned to the Middle East for almost all their imports of oil.[43] France reacted to the inflationary shock by leaving the snake in January 1974 and allowing the exchange rate to float rather than increase interest rates.

THE ECONOMIC MODEL IN TRANSITION 1974–83

Pompidou's sudden death in 1974 brought the long era of Gaullist rule to an end. It also marked the end of the long period of economic growth that had begun in 1945. This section analyses how French governments, both Liberal and Socialist, reacted to the challenges of slower growth following the first recession of the postwar period, rising energy prices and the collapse of the international monetary system of Bretton Woods. As the European and world economy also moved into recession, it was a new president, Valéry Giscard d'Estaing, who had to meet the challenges. The changes made to the management of the domestic economy under both de Gaulle and Pompidou had left him without many of the tools necessary to meet those challenges. Under the presidency of Giscard d'Estaing, public spending on nuclear power and public transport was increased, only to be followed by a programme of public spending cuts by his prime minister, Raymond Barre. The rise in mass unemployment that resulted from those austerity policies propelled the Socialist president François Mitterrand into power. His reflationary programme based on nationalizations and increased social spending produced the worst foreign exchange crisis since the end of the Second World War.

While it was easy to blame the inflation of the 1970s on the oil price hike, it is now argued that the inflation was a symptom of the poorly controlled changes to the credit policy in the 1960s that in turn undermined the interventionist policies that had been followed quite successfully in the late 1940s and 1950s.[44] This was particularly true of planning and credit policy. As private investment all but dried up after the recession of 1974–75, despite the government's refusal to raise interest rates, the government tried to compensate by spending on a number of high profile public sector projects, with nuclear energy, defence, aeronautics and electronics benefiting most. As in the case of EDF and SNCF, some of these new investments were to weigh heavily on the public purse up to 2018 and beyond. The choice of recipients, both public and private, of state investment is considered to have been ill-judged.[45] In 1976 six private companies (Empain-Schneider in nuclear energy installations, CGE in telecommunications, Thomson-CSF in military electronics, CII-Honeywell-Bull in computers and SNIAS and Dassault in military aviation) received half of the total subsidies.[46] The projects included: extending the Paris metro into the suburbs with a new double-decker train system, the Réseau Express Régional (RER), which had been started in the late 1960s; building a new high-speed train, the Train à Grande Vitesse (TGV), linking Paris with Lyon and a number of other cities in France; a renewed public commitment to the aircraft industry buoyed up by the promised commercial success of Airbus and the technological success of Concorde as well as a recognition of the need to increase exports of military aircraft to earn the foreign exchange required to pay the enlarged oil bill; and, finally, the construction of a new generation of nuclear power stations to limit French dependence on imported energy.

At the same time older industries such as steel, mechanical engineering and textiles were particularly badly affected by the international recession, with the steel industry shedding 55,000 employees between 1973 and 1979, thereby reducing the workforce to 105,000.[47] The two giants Sacilor and Usinor were only saved from bankruptcy by huge state loans, making the state the main shareholder. Others were left to fail. Indeed, as the crisis continued, it was the small and medium-sized firms that performed better than many of the large ones which had merged in the 1960s and early 1970s, although these firms were not large enough to absorb those made redundant or who were looking for work for the first time.

Recognizing the need for greater policy coordination to promote economic recovery, the French and German governments agreed on an arrangement to replace the "snake" with one that would both stabilize exchange rates and promote economic growth. The main innovation of what became the European Monetary System (EMS) was the creation of an artifical unit of account, known as the European Currency Unit (ECU), which was composed of all the members' currencies in differing proportions. Each currency was allowed to fluctuate against the ECU by ± 2.25 per cent before corrective action, agreed collectively, was taken. The burden of adjustment was to be placed on both the surplus country and the deficit one, with realignments occurring as frequently as necessary (see Chapter 6).

The first test of the new arrangement came almost immediately, when the price of oil doubled, throwing the developed economies into another recession. The cost to the French economy of maintaining the parity of the French franc against the Deutsche Mark was rising unemployment (it was to reach 2 million in November 1981) and sluggish growth. The cost to Giscard d'Estaing was defeat in the presidential elections.

In May 1981 it was the Socialist François Mitterrand who was elected president. In the subsequent legislative elections a coalition of Socialists and Communists won a majority of seats in the national assembly: the first time that the Socialists had held power under the Fifth Republic, and the first time that the Communists had been in government since May 1947. Following the strikes in 1968 that had taken the Communist party and its trade union, the CGT, by surprise, they had changed their strategy.[48] Over a decade of continuously high rates of economic growth had caused them to abandon their belief in the inevitability of a revolutionary crisis and end their self-imposed isolation. This recognition had led them in 1972 to agree to a common programme of policies with the Socialists (now renamed as the "Parti Socialiste" (PS), abandoning the international dimension of the SFIO). That programme was based on extending the national ownership of industry and banking, begun in 1944–48, to bring about the nation's control over the wealth it created and moving towards greater decentralization of economic decision-making.

However, the economic situation that faced them in government in 1981 was very different from that of a decade earlier. Confronted with rapidly rising unemployment, Mitterrand embarked on an expansionist policy based on stimulating domestic demand through an increase in social payments, as well as implementing a programme of extensive nationalizations. It was his conviction, shared by his prime minister, Pierre Mauroy, that by targeting state-led growth, aided by an expansion of the nationalized sector, they would be able to restrict imports and expand exports.

With many experts predicting an upturn in the world economy in 1982 the government immediately granted an increase in wages and pensions: the minimum wage was increased by 10.6 per cent, family allowances and the housing subsidy increased by 50 per cent, and old-age pensions by 62 per cent. In addition, the working week was shortened by one hour to 39 hours without loss of pay, and workers were also given a fifth week of paid holidays. To pay for the new measures the public sector deficit was to be increased, higher taxes imposed on employers and a new wealth tax introduced. The centrepiece of the legislation, however, was the programme to extend the nationalizations of 1944–48 by taking into public ownership a number of industries and banks. The industries in question were Thomson (electronics and communications), Péchiney (chemicals), Compagnie Générale d'Électricité (CGE), Saint-Gobain (glass, paper and textiles) and Rhône-Poulenc (textiles and chemicals). In addition, the state took a majority share (51 per cent) in some other key companies, including the arms manufacturers Matra and Dassault, as well as in the French subsidiaries of the telecommunications multinational ITT, Roussel-Uclaf (pharmaceuticals) and CII-Honeywell Bull (computers). The nationalization of the steel industry, which had been carried out in all but name by Barre, was now made official. The private investment banks Paribas and Suez were taken into public control, as were more than 30 other banks (including small local ones) and financial services groups.

All the newly nationalized companies were considered by the left to have failed to match international competition due to a lack of investment. Despite the recent mergers they were still smaller than their main competitors in the United States, Britain, Japan and Germany and had lost market share both domestically and externally. The main objective of nationalizing them was to regain the domestic market by cutting foreign trade to less than 20 per cent of GDP and expanding domestic production. But if the nationalization programme was the means of protecting France from competition within the EC and the wider world, it was, according to one historian, "spectacular because it left out the two main water supply companies operating within France, the Générale des Eaux and Lyonnaise des Eaux, but touched groups involved in European and world-wide competition".[49] The emphasis was clearly on nationalization rather than national planning. The official eighth plan (1981–85) was shelved in favour of an interim one covering 1982–83, but in fact the preference was for planning to be at a regional rather than national level (this is explored in Chapter 4).

The expected upturn in the international economy did not happen, as other countries reacted to the second oil price rise by deflating domestic demand, thereby thwarting French hopes of expanding exports. At the same time, since the increase in domestic demand was met from imports rather than from domestic production, the trade deficit worsened. The franc was devalued three times within the EMS between October 1981 and March 1983. The third devaluation within two years was taken as proof that the government's policy was not working by those economists within the Bank of France and the CGP who had been arguing since the mid-1970s that it was state controls that were holding back private investment. They maintained that if the Paris stock exchange were liberalized and open to international finance, foreign investors would revive investment in the French economy. Jacques Delors, a former employee at the Bank of France and now Minister of Finance, took the opportunity to dismantle many of these controls and to pursue a less expansionist policy that would be more in line with that of other members of the EMS. When he became president of the European Commission in 1985 Delors extended the liberalization measures to the European Community as a whole, as part of the European Single Market programme.

THE LIBERAL MODEL OF REDISTRIBUTION, 1983–2018

This final section analyses how the French state prioritized the interests of the service sector over much of industry by promoting the liberalization of services within the European single market, followed by the introduction of a single currency and the privatization of many publicly owned companies. National planning was gradually abandoned, but, unlike governments of other developed economies, French governments on both the right and left increased taxes to redistribute income and reduce inequality between regions and households. (The financial crisis of 2008, which slowed down the growth of services, combined with the strict controls over public spending enforced by the European Central Bank, challenged the sustainability of this political choice.)

In the years after 1983 the last remnants of the postwar interventionist economic model were dismantled as France embraced the liberal agenda of the single market and the single currency. What was left of the system of preferential credit controls and industrial policy was abandoned as bank lending was replaced with equity financing. The Communist party was the biggest casualty of the change in economic policy-making. In elections in 1986 it scored its worst result since 1932, winning only 35 seats. The Socialists remained the largest single party but lost out to an alliance of the two right-wing parties, the Rassemblement pour la République (RPR) and Union pour la Démocratie Républicaine (UDR). The biggest victor was a new party on the extreme right, the Front National (FN), led by Jean-Marie Le Pen, which won 9.8 per cent of the national vote, although in cities such as Marseille and Perpignan it won 25 per cent of the vote.

Privatizations

Under a period of cohabitation in which the Socialist president, François Mitterrand, shared power with a government of the right under Jacques Chirac, many of the recently nationalized firms were privatized. The reasons for privatizing some sectors more quickly than others were influenced by many factors, including the size of firms in the sector, the length of time they had been in public ownership, whether they were regulated at a European level, whether or not they were profitable (while it was easier to sell a well-run profitable company it was more acceptable politically to privatize a poorly run one), the degree of unionization (the CGT was always opposed) and, ultimately, timing.

The smaller companies and the industrial firms nationalized in 1982 were privatized quickly and usually by government decree, but the larger ones went through a very long and often arduous process requiring acts of parliament as they all had hundreds, and sometimes thousands, of subsidiaries. An evaluation commission (Commission des participations et des transferts) was set up in 1986 to estimate the lowest value of the companies being sold. The Minister of the Economy then decided on the actual sale price, higher than the floor estimate, and the method of sale, whether on the stock market to a single investor or a group of investors or by auction. The proceeds of the sale were then placed in a special account that could be used when the state-owned companies needed fresh capital or loans.[50]

Saint-Gobain was the first company to be privatized in 1986, followed by the Compagnie Générale de Construction Téléphonique (CGCT) and the CGE in 1987. In the service sector, the television channel TF1 and the advertising and marketing firm Havas were sold, and in banking and insurance it was Paribas, the Compagnie Financière de Suez, Société Générale, Crédit du Nord and Crédit Commercial de France that were privatized, followed by the industrial conglomerate Matra in 1988.

The six largest industrial groups nationalized in 1982 (CGE, Saint-Gobain, Péchiney, Rhône-Poulenc, Thomson and Bull), several of which had been losing money before their nationalization, were all profitable by 1985, partly because the state had pumped in 45 billion francs to recapitalize them. In 1990, a report by the official accounting office, the Cour des Comptes, showed that when the costs of nationalization and recapitalization were set against dividends and privatization income there was no net impact on government finances.[51]

Mitterrand's re-election as president in 1988 on a commitment neither to nationalize nor to privatize (ni-ni), put a temporary halt to the programme of privatizations, although under the Socialist governments of Rocard, Cresson and Bérégovoy some of the state's shares in a number of companies (Bull, Total, Elf-Aquitaine and Rhône-Poulenc) were sold. In the second period of cohabitation under Mitterrand (1993–95) the privatizations resumed. Under the Balladur government the list included some shares in the state flagship company, Renault, as well as the remaining shares in Elf-Aquitaine, Rhône-Poulenc and the Banque nationale de Paris.

Under the presidency of Jacques Chirac more shares in Renault were sold, along with the remainder of the shares held by the state in SEITA, Usinor, Péchiney, AGF and Total. By December 1996 only a few groups that had been in public ownership for 60 years remained: Aérospatiale and SNECMA, Air France and Air-Inter, SNCF, Thomson-CSF, Charbonnages de France, EDF, Gaz de France, the CEA subsidiaries and France Télécom (formerly the Direction générale des Télécommunications).

In the third and final period of cohabitation (1997–2002), under the Socialist government of Lionel Jospin, shares in Air France, GAN, CIC, Thomson-CSF, Crédit Lyonnais, Matra-Aérospatiale, COFACE and Hervet were all sold. In 2002–05 under the Raffarin government Crédit Lyonnais, France Télécom, Renault, Dassault and Thomson were privatized. By 2014 the state held majority shareholdings in Nexter (100 per cent), La Poste (100 per cent), France Télévision and other media (100 per cent), EDF (84.5 per cent), Française des Jeux (72 per cent), DCNS (naval and energy industry: 63.5 per cent), Paris Airports (50.6 per cent), the Imprimerie Nationale and the main food market in Paris, the Marché international de Rungis. The state was a minority shareholder in a number of other companies, including Renault, GDF Suez, Areva, Thales, Safran, Orange, Air-France-KLM, Airbus and Eramet, but with no power of control over their affairs.

Towards a new protectionism?

One major concern of the government throughout the privatization process was to retain control of the companies while selling their share capital, or, at the very least, to prevent the privatized companies from falling into foreign hands and ultimately lead to asset stripping. Indeed, this did happen when the Canadian firm Alcan bought Péchiney in

2003. At the time Péchiney was the world's fourth largest producer and developer of aluminium products, employing 34,000 people and operating 320 manufacturing and sales facilities in 50 countries. Alcan proceeded to transfer to Quebec much critical technology, leaving the French firm at the mercy of Rio Tinto when the latter bought Alcan in 2007. The government of Dominique de Villepin, having previously tried to reinvigorate French economic competitiveness and boost innovation by offering research funds and tax incentives to sectors including neurosciences, nanotechnology, health, secure communications systems and aeronautics, now simply outlawed some foreign mergers or acquisitions. After the 2008 financial crisis, President Nicolas Sarkozy went further and set up a strategic investment fund to protect French firms considered critical to the economy. Although it had a capitalization of €20 billion, the French fund paled alongside the sovereign wealth funds of Norway or Qatar with which it was sometimes compared. Nor was it clear what the precise purpose of Sarkozy's strategic investment fund was: whether it was designed to support firms that could not raise enough finance to survive or whether, in the words of its director, Jean-Yves Gilet, it should focus on successful profitable companies that had a track record of social responsibility.[52] Questions were asked when the fund was used to buy back a 10 per cent shareholding in Alcan in 2010 when the American fund Apollo had acquired 51 per cent of the company, and two years later when it invested €30 million to bail out the chemical firm Novasep, which was in financial difficulty.

But it was the generally poor performance of the whole economy under Sarkozy that brought the Socialists back into power in May 2012. President François Hollande based his recovery strategy on the introduction of a number of new spending initiatives as well as trying to stimulate investment. The former included measures such as hiring 60,000 new teachers, creating 150,000 new jobs for young people, increasing the minimum wage and restoring retirement from the 62 years of age that Sarkozy had introduced to 60 years of age. These measures were to be funded in part by raising the marginal rate of income tax on those earning more than €1 million to 75 per cent, and increasing the rate of corporation tax on large firms. Although tax receipts as a proportion of GDP grew, from 42.1 per cent in 2009 to 46 per cent in 2014, the public debt continued to rise, reaching almost 100 per cent of GDP in 2015, well above the 60 per cent limit set by the European Central Bank (see Chapter 6 for further discussion). By that time public sector employment, at 778,000, represented 3 per cent of the workforce compared with 10 per cent in 1985. The majority of the public sector workers (85 per cent) were employed in the post office, the railways, EDF, the Paris metro, RATP and Paris airports.

The method chosen by the Socialist government to stimulate investment was to merge the strategic investment fund, set up by Sarkozy, with two other funds, Oseo and CDC Entreprises, to create a public investment bank (BPI). The idea was that this public bank would be a single point of contact for firms in need of financing, offering access to a range of financial instruments including both loans and the opportunity to issue shares to the state-owned bank.[53] The capital of the new bank was held jointly by the state and the Caisse des dépôts in a complicated structure that was less than transparent. As the Cour des Comptes commented in 2016, the BPI proposed to mobilize €2,400 million to finance its activities between 2017 and 2019 without it having demonstrated that it had the funds to cover such a commitment: a view not shared by either Michel Sapin, the Minister of Economy and Finance, or Nicolas Dufourcq, the general director of BPI. In response, the Cour des Comptes called for a more realistic discussion to ensure that objectives matched the availability of funds.[54]

It was a polite rebuke in the midst of an economic, social, political and cultural crisis that propelled Emmanuel Macron into power in May 2017. Claiming to be breaking the mould of French politics by creating a new political movement, La République en Marche (LREM), bringing together people with little experience of party politics, his focus was on reforming the social model in order to reduce labour costs while reaffirming France's commitment to remaining in the European Union. In April 2018, the government sent the details of a stabilization programme to the

EU in which public expenditure was to fall to 52.5 per cent of GDP in 2021, thereby reverting to the level of 2007.

According to left-leaning think tank the Observatoire français des conjonctures économiques (OFCE), in 2018 the French economy seemed ready to continue the recovery that had begun at the end of 2016. External conditions were favourable, with low interest rates, the end of austerity in the eurozone and oil prices, expressed in euros, stable.[55] Demand for French exports should therefore have been high. Domestic conditions were also judged to be favourable. The financial position of firms was set to improve due to the further transfer of employers' contributions to social security to the public purse via the CSG tax, while the budget deficit was to be reduced by imposing a number of "green" environmental taxes. While it was expected that household purchasing power would suffer initially from these higher indirect taxes, it was to improve subsequently as direct taxes were reduced. It was expected that investment would continue to grow due to rising profits, low interest rates and dynamic demand. Unemployment was expected to fall as new jobs were created. No one predicted the outrage that the imposition of the first green tax on fuel would cause throughout rural France in autumn 2018. No sooner had the protests by the *gilets jaunes* (named after the high-visibility yellow vests required by law to be worn by all drivers) died down than the public sector workers, quite predictably, staged continuous strikes in opposition to the plans to merge their separate occupational pensions into a single one. And no one predicted that, while attention in France was focused on the strikes, an airborne virus spreading in China in December 2019 would engulf the entire world in an unprecedented pandemic. In the face of the supply problems that quickly arose, together with a growing recognition of the enormity of the tasks of reviving the economy after its shutdown during the pandemic, President Macron spoke of the possibility for the state to develop a plan to rebuild a stronger economy that would be independent in critical areas of agriculture, industry, technology and health and better able to cope with crises in the future.[56]

CONCLUSION

One of the most marked changes in French economic policy-making after the Second World War was the replacement of the laissez-faire economic liberalism of the Third Republic with a new form of state intervention in the economy. This was designed to make economic policy-making more democratic and deliver greater security to a majority of the population. What became known as the French model of economic policy-making was, as in other European countries, based on the nationalization of the key sources of energy, transport and credit, as well as the creation of a welfare state. Where France differed was in the introduction of a system of indicative planning that was designed to direct investment into key priority sectors. Where planning was least successful was in forecasting and controlling the growth of demand, both in France and in its main trading partners. It was to address this problem that the French government agreed to participate in a common market in western Europe when it signed the Treaty of Rome in March 1957.

By the mid-1960s it was clear that the consensus which had underpinned the interventionist model of economic policy-making forged after the Second World War had been broken. Although the nationalized sector remained intact and the CGP continued to publish five-year plans, the third arm of the model, that of credit control, had been severed. With little means of controlling private investment and an unwillingness or inability to control consumption, inflation became more of a continuous problem. When measures to control inflation resulted in mass unemployment in the 1970s and when attempts to reduce unemployment failed to stimulate private investment, hopes were vested from 1983 onwards in attracting foreign capital into expanding the successful service sector of the economy. When the tenth national plan was published in January 1989 the importance of liberalizing services within the single market of the EC was stressed. The decision to cede all control over the exchange rate by replacing the franc with the euro reflected an aspiration that foreign investment would be attracted by the stability of the common currency. The eleventh plan (1992–96) contained no targets at all, with the only concrete measures being a contract signed every five or six years with the regions in the areas of transport and education. In March 2006 the Commissariat général au Plan was finally dismantled, to be replaced in the Rue de Martignac in Paris by a Centre for Strategic Analysis, which in turn became a Commissariat général à la Stratégie et à la Prospective with no powers at all. Concern that foreign investment could result in asset stripping rather than boosting the competitiveness of the French economy led prime minister Dominique de Villepin to introduce a scheme in 2005 to promote research and development by offering research funds and tax incentives to a number of sectors including neurosciences, nanotechnology, health and secure communications systems as well as aeronautics. Subsequent initiatives to direct investment into strategic sectors paved the way for President Macron to revive the idea of planning the recovery of the economy after the pandemic to make it more resilient in the future.

In the next chapter we will analyse the performance of the French economy over the entire postwar period under the changing economic models of policy-making.

3

Growth and structural change in the French economy, 1945–2018

We have seen in the previous chapter that one of the purposes of the postwar reforms was to democratize economic policy-making in France in order to provide a wider range of groups with the economic security that governments of the Third Republic had failed to deliver. This was to be achieved by changing the structure of the economy according to a national economic plan. While the new postwar state was committed to intervening in the economy rather than continuing the combination of economic liberalism and protectionism that had failed to guarantee the living standards even of the agricultural sector under the Third Republic, the instruments and objectives of such an intervention changed over time.

What is clear is that there was nothing automatic about the way in which the French economy caught up with the more technologically advanced economies after the Second World War. The aim of this chapter is to analyse and, based on national accounts, measure how well the French economy performed over the whole period 1945–2018, before focusing on the performance in each of the four sub-periods identified in Chapter 2.

OVERVIEW OF THE PERFORMANCE OF THE
FRENCH ECONOMY, 1945–2018

Growth

In contrast to the behaviour of the French economy in the nineteenth century and in the interwar period that had led historians to conclude that for better or worse France was following its own path to economic development, after 1945 it participated fully in the boom experienced across western Europe. Growth rates averaged 5 per cent per annum over the period 1950–73 compared with 1.5 per cent in the period 1870–1913. By 1973 per capita GDP was above that of the United Kingdom and was closing the gap with the United States, the technological leader (up from 48 per cent in 1950 to 73 per cent in 1973).[1]

The postwar boom came to a sudden end in the international recession of 1973–75 but it hit the French economy later and was of shorter duration than the OECD average. Along with the rest of the developed world, the French economy suffered a second recession in 1992–93 and a

Figure 3.1 Annual changes of GDP in France, 1950–2018 (by volume)

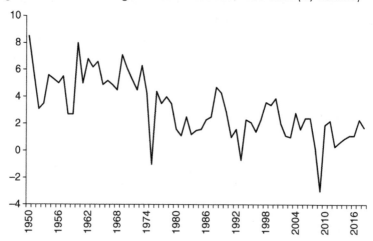

Source: INSEE, *Les comptes nationaux,* 2019

third in 2008–09. The third recession, while much more severe than the first or the second, was nonetheless not as bad as the OECD average, and by 2011 French GDP had rebounded above its 2008 level. But the recovery proved short-lived, and following a further contraction in 2012 growth rates averaged little over 1 per cent per annum, below the OECD average, before falling again after 2016.

Structural change

Since 1945 the structure of production and employment in the French economy has changed dramatically. Employment in agriculture declined from over 6 million people in 1945 to no more than 670,000 in 2018. As an indication of the improvement in the produtivity of French farmers, in 1946 they represented 36 per cent of the active population but contributed only 17 per cent of value added, whereas in 2016 they were no more than 2.8 per cent of the labour force and contributed 1.6 per cent of value added. As productivity improved, France moved from being a net importer of food and agricultural products to being a net exporter after 1980. Over the same period employment in industry and construction first of all expanded from 32 per cent of the total in 1946 to reach almost 40 per cent by the end of the 1960s, before contracting in the 1970s. By 2016 it employed 20 per cent of the labour force while contributing just under 20 per cent to value added, down from 33 per cent of value added in 1950. There were also great changes in the service sector. Traditionally this was a very diverse collection of activities ranging from distribution and retail, public service and domestic service to finance. Apart from public and domestic service, most jobs in the sector were linked to the manufacturing industry. However, in the 1980s, as manufacturing in the traditional sectors of textiles, steel and mechanical engineering declined, new marketable services independent of industry began to appear. By 2016 the service sector, marketable and non-marketable, was employing about 76 per cent of the work force while contributing almost 80 per cent of value added.

Table 3.1 Value added by sector, 1950–2016 (%)

	1950	1960	1970	1980	1990	2000	2010	2016
Agriculture, fisheries & forestry	17.5	12.1	7.5	4.0	3.5	2.3	1.8	1.6
Industry	27.7	27.4	24.6	23.2	20.6	18.4	13.5	14.0
Food processing	5.8	3.9	3.6	3.5	3.2	2.7	2.2	2.2
Capital goods	3.6	3.9	3.8	3.4	2.9	2.7	1.6	1.6
Energy	2.2	2.2	2.2	3	2.9	2.7	2.3	2.7
Vehicles	1.4	1.9	1.7	1.6	1.5	1.5	1.2	1.4
Construction	5.1	6.6	7.9	7.5	6.3	4.9	6.0	5.5
Marketable services	36.5	39.6	44.3	45.7	50.2	53.5	56.1	56.1
Trade, hospitality & transport	21.1	20.3	18.9	18	18.5	18.1	17.9	17.6
Financial services	2.2	2.7	3.4	4	4.8	4.1	4.5	4.1
Real estate	3.6	5.3	7.8	7.7	9.6	11.4	12.8	13
Non-marketable services	13.1	14.3	15.7	19.5	19.4	20.8	22.5	22.7
Total	100	100	100	100	100	100	100	100

Source: INSEE, Tableaux de l'économie française 2018.

Investment

These structural changes in the economy were accompanied by higher rates of investment, which peaked in 1973, a level that was not regained in any of the subsequent years. Private investment did not follow the public investment programmes of the 1970s and early 1980s. The recovery in the late 1980s was short-lived, and it was not until after 1997 that rates of investment grew over a sustained period. Investment fell following the financial crisis of 2008–09, but started to recover after 2014.

Table 3.2 Employment by sector, 1946–2016 (%)

	Agriculture	Industry & construction	Services
1946	36	32	32
1968	14.6	38.9	46.5
1979	8.6	35.3	56.1
1993	5.1	27.7	67.2
2000	4.3	22.7	73
2016	2.8	20	75.8

Sources: Mouré, "The French economy since 1930", 373; Dormois, *French Economy in the Twentieth Century,* 126; INSEE, Tableaux de l'économie française 2018.

Figure 3.2 Rates of investment, 1946–2019 (base 2014) (%)

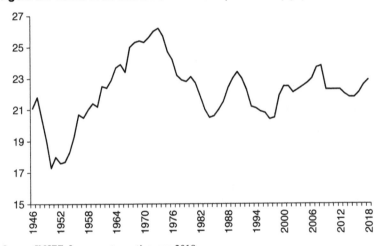

Source: INSEE, Les comptes nationaux, 2019.

Foreign trade

The structural changes in the French economy were accompanied by higher levels of foreign trade, as tariffs and other barriers to trade were reduced as part of the liberalization measures of the EEC/EU and GATT/WTO. However, even though France ranked as the world's fourth largest exporter of manufactured goods by the mid-1970s, those exports were not rising quickly enough to cover the trade deficit in energy, particularly after the escalation in the price of imported oil in 1973. The combination of a second rise in the price of oil in 1979 and the domestic expansion programme of the Socialist government in 1981–82 produced the worst foreign exchange crisis in the entire postwar period. During the 1980s exports from the service sector began to overtake those of manufacturing, with France second only to the US as an exporter of services at that time. For a 14-year period after 1991 France enjoyed a trade surplus based on a slimmed down industrial sector and a greatly expanded service sector. It was seen as a golden age of international trade, marked finally by the creation of the WTO in 1995 (almost 50 years after the American Congress had vetoed the creation of an international trade organization).

Figure 3.3 Rate of cover of imports of goods and services by exports, 1949–2019 (%)

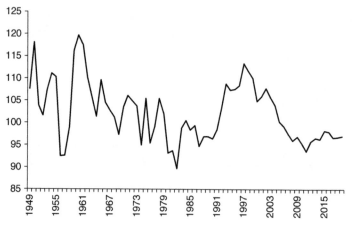

Source: INSEE, Les comptes nationaux, base 2014.

Two years before the subprime crisis in the United States plunged the world into recession, the French balance of trade in goods and services moved into deficit and stayed in deficit. What this meant was that the trade surplus in services, evident since the 1980s, was no longer able to cover the deficit in goods (of which energy imports weighed heavily). From 2013 onwards France began to run a slight deficit in trade in services in addition to the trade deficit in goods. By 2018 France had fallen from second to fourth position in the world as an exporter of commercial services.[2] It had also fallen from fourth to seventh position in the world as an exporter of goods.[3] In 2017, the biggest trade deficits were recorded with China and Hong Kong, Germany, the Netherlands, Italy and Belgium, while the biggest trade surpluses were recorded with the Middle East, the UK, Africa and Switzerland.

Figure 3.4 Trade in services, 2000–16 (billion euros)

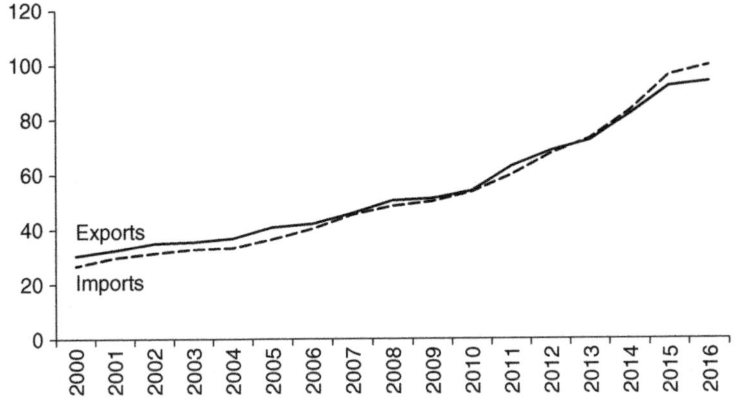

Source: Matas, *Panorama du commerce extérieur.*

Birth rate

In sharp contrast to the nineteenth century, when France had singularly and precociously restricted its birth rate long before other countries, after 1945 this behaviour changed. In line with other European countries the French experienced a baby boom after the Second World War, although this was greater and lasted longer than elsewhere apart from the Republic of Ireland. By 1975 the population was 54 million, an increase of 12 million over 30 years, rather longer than de Gaulle had called for in 1945.[4]

Forty-five years after 1975, the population had increased by a further 11 million. With a median age of 42, in 2019 France had a slightly younger population than the European average of 43.[5] However, as Table 3.3 shows, it has a smaller proportion of the population of working age (20–59 years of age) than it has had at almost any time since the beginning of the twentieth century, as well as the smallest proportion aged under 20 and the greatest proportion aged over 60 and over 75.

Table 3.3 Structure of the French population, 1901–2018

	Under 20 (%)	20–59 (%)	60 and over (%)	Of which over 75 (%)	Total (millions)
1901	34.3	53	12.7	2.5	38.5
1910	33.6	53.7	12.7	2.5	39.1
1920	31.3	54.9	13.8	2.8	38.4
1930	30.1	55.7	14.2	2.9	40.9
1946	29.5	54.4	16	3.4	40.1
1950	30.1	53.6	16.2	3.8	41.6
1960	32.3	51	16.7	4.3	45.5
1970	33.1	48.9	18	4.7	50.5
1980	30.6	52.4	17	5.7	53.7
1990	27.8	53.2	19	6.8	56.6
2000	25.6	53.8	20.6	7.2	58.9
2010	24.5	52.7	22.8	8.9	62.8
2018	24.1	50	25.9	9.3	65.0

Source: INSEE, Tableaux de l'économie française 2019.

Following the high birth rates of the 1950s and 1960s, the population expanded at a slow but steady rate between 1975 and 2009. Since 2009 the birth rate has been falling gently.

Until the first cohort of the baby boom generation reached working age, the French economy faced a labour shortage. Unlike the period after the First World War, when France was as large an immigrant country as the United States, after 1945 the government was unable to recruit enough migrants to meet demand. It was only after 1955 when the government restored immigration to private channels that the numbers picked up. Following the recession of 1974–75 the numbers declined sharply and did not return to those of the peak period 1955–70.

Figure 3.5 Growth rate of the French population, 1946–2018 (live births per 1,000 inhabitants)

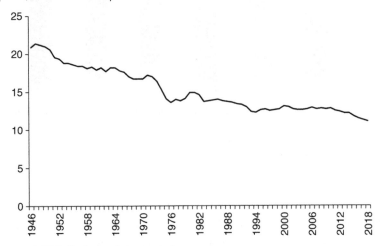

Source: INSEE, Évolution de la population.

Unemployment

In 1975 unemployment reached one million. This represented a landmark figure for the French, since the high proportion of underemployment in agriculture in the 1930s had shielded them from the very high numbers experienced in other developed economies in that decade. Unemployment continued to rise after 1975 and peaked in 2015 at 3.052 million (10.4 per cent of the active population).[6] Although not as high as in Italy or Spain, unemployment in France was well above the rates experienced in Germany or the UK and called into question the sustainability of the French economic model as it had developed since 1983.

Figure 3.6 Unemployment in France, 1980–2018 (in thousands)

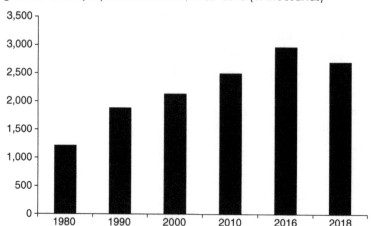

Source: INSEE, France, portrait social, Édition 2019; Wieviorka, *La France en Chiffres.*

THE ECONOMY UNDER THE FOURTH REPUBLIC, 1945–58

Between 1945 and 1951 GDP grew rapidly, averaging 8.7 per cent per year. This compared very favourably with an annual average growth rate of 1.9 per cent over the period 1896–1913 (*La Belle Époque*), and 1.5 per cent over the period 1913–29 (the growth years of the First World War and 1920s).[7] However, since the government refused to stabilize the currency until levels of production had recovered at least to those of 1938, inflation averaged 28.3 per cent over the period 1945–51.

Under the Monnet Plan the priority was not to reconstruct but to restructure and modernize the economy to make up for the lack of investment, particularly in heavy industry, over a 15-year period. An awareness of just how far the French economy had fallen behind other major economies during the 1930s and the Second World War explained the scale of the planners' ambition. As a first step in such a huge undertaking a small number of sectors were identified as priorities for investment. However, it was only in petroleum products that the results by 1950 measured up to their planned objectives; industrial production in general had not regained the interwar peak level achieved in 1929. The more modest objectives set out in the revised 1948 plan were largely achieved by 1952, with levels of industrial production 12 per cent above 1929.

Table 3.4 Objectives and results in the priority sectors of the first modernization and equipment plan

	Unit	1929	1938	1950 (obj.)	1950 (act.)	1952 (obj.)	1952 (act.)
Coal	Million tons	55	47.6	65	52.5	60	57.4
Electricity	Billion (US) kWh	15.6	20.8	37	33.1	43	40.8
Petroleum products	Million tons refined	0	7	8.1	14.5	18.7	21.5
Steel	Million tons	9.7	6.2	11	8.7	12.5	10.9
Cement	Million tons	6.2	3.6	13.5	7.2	8.5	8.6
Tractors	Thousands	1	1.7	50	14.2	40	25.3
Nitrogeneous fertiliser	Thousand tons	73	177	320	236	300	285

Source: Commissariat général au plan, *Rapport sur la réalisation du plan de modernisation et d'équipement de l'Union française*, année 1952.

Between 1947 and 1953 investment in the economy as a whole grew at an average annual rate of 5.2 per cent. Of this, 62.1 per cent was funded by the state.[8] To ensure that the investment identified as a priority by the planners would in fact take place, since not all the priority sectors had been nationalized, it was decided to create a special fund in the Treasury, the Fonds de Modérnisation et d'Équipement (FME), into which the counterpart in French francs of the dollar loans and grants provided by the United States under the Marshall plan were lodged. Over the period 1948–52 the funds in the FME covered 14.7 per cent of the total investment in metropolitan France.[9]

Although growth of GDP averaging 4.2 per cent per annum between 1952 and 1959 was lower than in the immediate postwar years, it was nonetheless at a historically high rate. At the same time, inflation was more controlled, rising at 3.3 per cent per year on average. Because the growth in GDP was achieved with very few additions to the labour force from outside France, productivity rose at 4.3 per cent per annum, having been little more than 2 per cent per annum between 1896 and 1938.[10]

Over the longer period of 1949–63, the average investment ratio (the proportion of GDP taken by gross fixed capital formation) was over 20 per cent as compared with 14.9 per cent on average between 1896 and 1913, and 16.1 per cent between 1922 and 1938. The most important part of the postwar investment ratio was the rapid increase in capital equipment produced by the mechanical and electrical industries.[11]

Unlike previous periods of growth such as in the 1890s and 1920s, the growth after 1945 was achieved with few additions to the labour force. Not only were rates of immigration under the Fourth Republic lower than after the First World War, they were lower than the new ministry for population (created by decree on 24 December 1945) hoped for. In line with the natalist policy articulated by de Gaulle in 1945, immigration was viewed by many not only as an economic issue but also as a demographic one, although they saw the two as closely linked.[12] The loss of 1.5 million young men during the First World War had skewed the age profile of the French population, while the depressed economic conditions of the 1930s had caused the number of migrants to shrink. Postwar calculations showed that, in order to have an age structure similar to that of the British population, France would need to accept 5,490,000 people, of whom 4,350,000 would be adults. To have an age structure ressembling that of the Netherlands the numbers would have to be even higher: 14,390,000, of whom 9,760,000 would be adults. Figures on this scale raised questions of assimilation, housing and food supplies even if the migrants could be found. The national immigration office, set up on 2 November 1945, thought that it would be possible to sign a bilateral agreement to import labour from Italy, its preferred choice of country on cultural grounds, and also because it was thought to have a supply of people willing to work in France. When this turned out not to be the case, it extended the invitation to Germany and Belgium but with similarly disappointing results. Finally, on 20 September 1947 it was decided that Algerian Muslims should be given French citizenship, with full freedom of movement to metropolitan France for the first time.[13]

Between 1950 and 1955 the number of Algerians who went to France was 868,000 (although 714,000 returned to Algeria). They were joined by just over 80,000 Italians and a small number of other western Europeans. Between 25 per cent and 33 per cent worked in agriculture; initially, 25 per cent worked in the mines and 30 per cent in construction. From the perspective of the ministry for population the results for the ten years after 1945 were very disappointing indeed.[14]

Set against the natalists in the ministry for population were the economists in the planning commissariat, who at that time included Jean Fourastié. In the 1930s Fourastié, along with Colin Clarke and Allan Fisher, had been the first to explain economic development in terms of a sectoral shift in employment from agriculture to industry and then to services. In doing so they were challenging the view, popular in France since the late nineteenth century, that with similar numbers of people employed in each of the three main sectors France had achieved a perfect balance and harmony in its economy. It was a static view that, to Fourastié, ignored the role played by technology in changing the distribution of labour and promoting economic development.[15] Investment in new technology was to become a mantra for the planners. It led them to argue that, in comparison with the ministry for population's target of importing between 5 and 14 million people, the growth targets of the Monnet Plan could be met by importing between one million and 1.5 million people. But at the same time they argued that if the productivity of domestic labour could be raised by 35 per cent in agriculture and 25 per cent in industry, the 1950 targets could be met without needing to import any migrant labour at all.[16]

Agriculture

The low productivity of French agriculture had been a major problem for policy-makers throughout the Third Republic. Jules Méline's solution to the lack of competitiveness of the sector had been to protect it from cheaper imports. However, the tariff of 1892 had failed to stop the decline in living standards and failed to address the country's continued dependence on imports, even of basic foodstuffs such as wheat, in some years. The price support mechanisms set up by the Popular Front government were no more than an emergency measure to address the widespread poverty and misery in the countryside in the 1930s, but did not tackle the long-standing issue of the low productivity of French peasants. The Vichy planners, while recognizing the need to modernize and expand French industry, were not prepared to alter the structure of employment in the agricultural sector, believing that a large agricultural labour force was essential for social and political stability. Jean Monnet's plan also focused primarily on expanding and modernizing French industry but, in thinking about how agriculture could contribute to the plan, Monnet turned to the agronomist René Dumont for advice.[17] Dumont had been marginalized in the 1930s for his views on how agriculture could be modernized, but now with the chance to express his ideas, he argued that agriculture could supply one million workers for industry if the number of tractors were dramatically expanded beyond the 34,000 in use in 1939. He convinced Monnet that agricultural machinery should be selected as one of the priority sectors of the plan. However, the planners were much more cautious about the numbers of workers who could be persuaded, rather than forced, to leave agriculture, particularly at a time of food shortages. Over the period 1946–50 they hoped to cut the numbers working in the sector from 6,600,000 to 6,250,000 by encouraging 250,000 former prisoners of war not to return to farming, as well as persuading about 100,000 others to move into industry. The food crisis caused by a disastrous harvest in 1947, which obliged the French government to import wheat from the United States and negotiate a dollar loan to pay for it before Marshall aid became available, convinced the planners that more was needed to modernize French agriculture than simply increasing the number of tractors. The size of farms needed to be increased, along with the use of more fertiliser and better seeds, more irrigation, better education and more financial help from the government. In recognition of some of the issues involved, the share of public funds in agricultural investment rose from about 4.5 per cent in 1947 to 7.5 per cent under the revised plan.[18]

The increased public support marked the beginning of what was termed the "silent revolution" in the French countryside.[19] A combination of increased demand for labour in industry, construction and services and subsidies for investment in a wide range of agricultural products and methods led to rapid improvements in the productivity of agriculture. By 1950 the numbers working in agriculture and forestry had fallen by over one million, so great was the demand for labour elsewhere in the economy.[20] Under the second plan, an annual reduction of 50,000 was seen as possible, but in fact almost three times that number left every year. Under the third plan, the estimate was revised upwards to 80,000 per year, which was once again an underestimate. Altogether, over the 20 years between 1949 and 1969, 2.7 million people left agriculture, while production expanded on the same area of cultivated land.

Although the numbers leaving the land contributed to a rise in the productivity of those who remained, it was the case that many of those who stayed (particularly the young) were more open than previously to the idea of investing in machines and fertilisers, attending agricultural colleges and borrowing from the specialized agricultural bank to fund new modern methods of farming. Offered loans at subsidized rates by the Crédit Agricole, peasants overcame their religious scruples and flocked to an institution that had previously been shunned as representing an arm of the secular state. The Crédit Agricole grew in size to become the third largest bank in the world.[21] Spurred on by the increase in the demand for food as incomes rose, those who borrowed the most were the wine growers in the south of France, who saw an opportunity to expand the production of wine for everyday consumption (much of which had come from Algeria), producers of pork, for which demand was growing more rapidly than for beef, and most particularly the young.

At the same time the number of tractors in use did expand, rising from 34,000 in 1939 to 120,000 by 1950. Of these 8,549 were made by Renault (which had adapted its tank production to the manufacture of tractors after the First World War), but over 100,000 had to be imported from the United States. By 1964 there were 953,000 tractors in use. For many former prisoners of war who were unpersuaded to abandon farming on their release, the experience during the war of working on German farms, where the use of fertiliser was nearly four times higher than that in France (23.6 kg of nitrate fertiliser per hectare in Germany compared with 6.6 kg in France), was also instumental in changing habits. As a result, the use of fertiliser increased almost sixfold between 1946 and 1964. Together with the expansion of tractors and fertilisers, there were also improvements in irrigation and in the selection of seeds.[22]

But, despite the large numbers leaving the land, the small family farm still dominated in the 1950s. With their horizons limited to the domestic market or even closer to home, less than 4 per cent of total production was exported, while imports equated to over 10 per cent. To encourage further investment and productivity improvements, the government recognized that it needed to overcome the fear that increased production would lead to a fall in prices on the domestic market and to unsold produce while prices of manufactured inputs such as fertiliser and machinery continued to rise. Giving in to pressure, the government agreed to index agricultural prices to industrial ones. But this raised the issue of how to dispose of any surpluses created as a result, which were not competitive on the international market. A further issue was the impact on the trade balance of the subsidized investment in agriculture. While the French chemical firms such as Péchiney-Ugine-Kuhlmann, Saint-Gobain-Pont-à-Mousson and CDF-Chimie benefited from the huge and continuous expansion of demand for fertiliser, most of the tractors and other agricultural machinery had to be imported, mainly from the United States and Canada, thereby adding to the trade deficit.

Industrial modernization

However momentous the changes made in agriculture after 1945, they were made largely in response to the increased demand for labour in industry, which could not be met through the traditional channels of importing labour. What drove the changes in industry was the high rate of investment, much of it publicly funded, designed to change the structure of production to align the French economy more closely with that of other major economies. An expansion of steel production was central to the economic and security objectives of the Monnet Plan and was one of the priority sectors selected. Having reached a maximum output of 9.7 million tonnes in 1929, steel production had fallen to 6.1 million tonnes by 1938 at a time when German production was over 22 million tonnes. At the same time, labour productivity in the French steel industry was much lower than in the German industry (53 tonnes of steel per man-hour in France against 90 tonnes in Germany in 1937).[23] The postwar planners attributed this poor performance to the fact that the French steel industry was composed of a large number of small, inefficient firms operating within a highly restrictionist cartel, created to avoid problems of overcapacity. None of the firms had the financial resources to invest in new technology, particularly that of the wide strip mill first developed in the United States in the 1920s and then adopted in Germany, the UK and the Soviet Union in the 1930s. These mechanized wide strip mills replaced manual rolling processes and were essential for the production of low-cost steel sheets necessary for the mass production of cars and the new generation of electrical consumer durable goods, such as refrigerators and washing machines, as well as office equipment.[24] Under the occupation the Germans had forced the French steel firms located in the north and east of France, the Forges et Aciéries de Denain-Anzin (founded in 1834) and the Forges et Aciéries du Nord et de l'Est (founded in 1881), to amalgamate their production. After the war, with the French Communist party and its affiliated trade union, the Confédération Générale du Travail (CGT), calling for the nationalization of the steel industry, these two firms offered to cooperate with the planners in order to remain in private hands, even if this meant merging and investing in the new technology of the wide strip mill. A further inducement was the prospect of benefiting from state aid under the Marshall Plan. On 1 July 1948 the firms formally merged to become the Union Sidérurgique du Nord (Usinor). The merger, together with pressure from Renault, the recently nationalized car firm, for cheaper sheet steel, caused the steel firms in Lorraine, led by the de Wendel group, to amalgamate in December 1948 to form Société Lorraine de Laminage Continu (Sollac) and also to invest in wide strip mills. Although the output targets set by the Monnet Plan for crude steel (12 million tonnes in 1950 with a further target of 15 million tonnes by the mid-1950s) were not met as quickly as hoped, the plan was successful in overcoming the resistance of the steel firms to invest and to expand production. Output from the wide strip mills in France was second only to that in Germany over the following 50 years. By 1968 France had overtaken the UK in the output from its wide strip mills.

Table 3.5 Comparative output from wide strip mills, 1948–98 (Europe-wide strip mill output, in millions of metric tonnes).

Year	UK	West Germany	France	Italy	Belgium	The Netherlands
1948	1.02	0	0	0	0	0
1958	3.3	1.5	2	0.9	2	0.8
1968	4.9	10	6	3.8	5	1.7
1978	5.46	14.09	10.29	5.62	6.6	3.45
1988	6.5	17.58	9.69	7.6	8	2.92
1998	7.23	20.69	11.24	8.22	10.5	4.34

Source: Ranieri & Aylen, "The importance of the wide strip mill and its impact", 44.

Electricity

Investment in the wide strip mills of the steel industry, together with investment in the nationalized electricity industry, stimulated the expansion of electrical consumer goods industries, which in turn increased the demand for electricity. The production of hydroelectricity was one of the few sectors of the economy to have expanded in the 1930s, when investment in dams was important for supplying electricity to those areas of France unconnected to the emerging national grid network. It remained an important and traditional source of electricity in France, providing around half of French electricity output in the early postwar years compared with barely 2 per cent in the UK.[25] Under the first postwar plan for electricity, investment in new generating capacity was split roughly between thermal and hydro.[26] Marshall aid was used by EDF to tap the hydroelectric potential of the Alps, Pyrenees and the Massif Central by building dams across major rivers. As many as 48 hydroelectric power stations were built between 1949 and 1957, including the major ones of Génissiat, Donzères Mondragon, Ottmarsheim, Tignes and Roselend, some of which had been started before the Second World War.[27]

However, persuaded by the Americans in the Economic Cooperation Agency (ECA) of the cost advantages of substituting oil for hydroelectricity, the French began to import oil and on such a scale that by 1960 it accounted for one third of French energy use. But, with concern that this increased the dependence of the economy on foreign sources of energy (the Middle East for oil and the United States for coal), interest in producing nuclear energy grew. Thanks to its colonies in Madagascar, Gabon and Niger, France had about 3 per cent of the world's reserves of uranium at that time.[28] Since 1947 the nuclear energy commission (CEA) had been carrying out research into the production of nuclear energy according to the natural uranium–graphite–gas method, but the technical and financial costs were considerable.[29] When the American government refused to sell the cheaper technique using enriched uranium to the French, EDF reluctantly agreed that the first nuclear power station, to be built at Chinon in 1957, would have to use the more expensive method developed by the CEA. It was known that the British were using the same method for the same reasons, and it had the added advantage of producing the plutonium needed for the French atomic bomb.[30]

Investment in electricity also benefited the railways. In 1938, when the SNCF took over from the private companies running the railways, only 3,340 km of lines had been electrified. Under a programme of investment in the first and second plans both the rolling stock and lines were modernized, and 6,890 km (32 per cent) of lines were electric by 1960.[31]

Foreign Trade

If the switch to importing oil was planned, this was not the case for the rest of the foreign trade sector. We have seen that it was in trade that the plans were least able to forecast and control the growth of demand. Given the rising demand for imports, the measures to reduce quantitative restrictions on trade within OEEC were suspended in 1952 and a temporary surcharge imposed to safeguard the balance of payments. At the same time every effort was made to encourage exports. The various measures worked such that by the mid-1950s a pattern of trade had been established that was to last beyond the mid-1970s. With demand for the products of mechanical engineering, electrical engineering and transport equipment expanding to meet the needs of France itself as well as West Germany and Italy, labour was drawn to these sectors not only from agriculture but also from the textile, clothing and leather industries, where demand in the traditional markets of the colonies was rising much less rapidly. Strict controls over the allocation of credit ensured that credit for investment went into those sectors where exports were expanding rather than into those satisfying a protected domestic or colonial market. As a result, employment in the traditional textile industry fell from 26.5 per cent of the active population in 1952 to 21.4 per cent in 1959. Many people also moved into the construction and service sectors, where demand was also rising. Controls over the allocation of credit kept inflation in check, at least until 1956, when the cost of the war with Algeria, together with the decision to participate in the liberalization of trade within a common market of the ECSC countries, necessitated a devaluation of the franc (see Chapter 6).

Domestic trade

One sector that was squeezed in the 1950s by the new direction of state intervention was that of domestic distribution. Although Paris may have been home to the first department store in the world, throughout rural France the small specialist shop, with its high profit margins on which it paid as little tax as possible, predominated. Hit by the new tax on the self-employed introduced in 1948 and enforced with vigour in the early 1950s, the sector rallied to support a particularly vociferous father of five, Pierre Poujade, the owner of a small book and stationery shop in south-west France. In 1953, as de Gaulle wound up his political party, the RPF, Poujade created a new political party, the Union de Défense des Commerçants et Artisans (UDCA), on a platform to repeal the tax on the self-employed. Although it recruited around 800,000 members (including Jean-Marie Le Pen, founder of the Front National in 1972) and won 42 seats in the parliamentary elections of 1956, it failed to prevent the opening of the first supermarket in France in 1957. Active supporters of de Gaulle and of retaining Algeria as part of France, the UDCA was partially repaid when de Gaulle abolished the tax on the self-employed when he returned to power.[32] This did little to stop the expansion of the supermarket and the emergence of the hypermarket, but it did enable the small specialist shop to survive in an uneasy coexistence with them. Although it did not halt the spread of tax resistance in subsequent decades.[33]

THE ECONOMY UNDER GAULLISM, 1958–74

In the period 1958–74 the French economy grew even more rapidly than in the 1950s, averaging just under 5.7 per cent per annum. Investment was higher than the earlier period after many of the controls on credit for investment were removed. The supply of labour was also higher due to the effects of a higher birth rate and the fact that after 1955 the government had abandoned its attempts to organize the recruitment of migrant labour, returning immigration to private channels. Having averaged

66,400 per year over the period from 1946 to 1955, immigration jumped to 248,000 per year in the period from 1956 to 1967.[34] From the early 1960s the increase in migrants coincided with the arrival onto the labour market of the first of the baby boom generation born after the Second World War. After over a century of relatively slow demographic growth France had experienced an increase in the birth rate from 1942 onwards, at a time when the Vichy state was extolling the virtues of family, work and fatherland over the republican principles of liberty, fraternity and equality. Since there was little new in such right-wing exhortations, a more plausible explanation is that it was the introduction in 1945 of a new method of income splitting for the purposes of calculating income tax liability, known as the family quotient, that, as we shall see in Chapter 5, played a greater part in encouraging a higher birth rate. Anecdotal evidence of the link between the tax rules and the birth rate is provided by Guy Delorme, a high ranking civil servant in the Ministry of Finance. On a family summer holiday in 1967 with his friends, a married couple with three children, and perfect examples of what he called the "provincial bourgeoisie", he was asked whether reports in the press that the government was considering the abolition of the family quotient system were true. With the couple having been reassured that such reports were without foundation, a fourth child appeared in the family the following summer.[35]

Although de Gaulle had been brought back to power in 1958 to deal with the crisis in Algeria, he also faced a foreign exchange crisis that had already forced a devaluation of the franc and a loan from the IMF. Advised by Jacques Rueff in 1958 that the problem stemmed from the fact that France had been living beyond its means under the Fourth Republic, de Gaulle cut demand by ending the cross indexation of agricultural and industrial prices and devaluing the currency a second time. Agriculture, he argued, would have to become more competitive internationally by increasing mechanization, accelerating the rural exodus and merging farms to increase their size. However, confronted with roads and railway lines blocked by tractors, potatoes dumped in town centres, telephone lines cut and all the other forms of protest peasants could organize, he quickly backed down and turned instead to negotiating guaranteed prices and markets for French agriculture in the EEC.[36] It was only in certain products, mainly wheat, that France had a surplus at the beginning of the 1960s: overall it had a trade deficit in agricultural products until the 1980s.

Table 3.6 Top 20 French firms, 1960

	Annual turnover (million francs)	Size of labour force
Renault	19,500	61,000
CFP	18,600	6,000
Citroën	12,600	25,000
Simca	12,240	25,000
Peugeot	10,140	20,000
De Wendel	9,720	22,500
Esso Saf	9,360	6,500
Usinor	9,060	19,300
Michelin	9,000	40,000
Lorraine-Escaut	8,100	29,000
Sidelor	8,040	29,000
Shell française	7,800	5,000
Antar	6,960	3,300
BP française	6,600	5,600
Sud Aviation	6,000	23,200
Saint-Gobain	5,940	23,000
Mobil Oil française	5,820	3,800
Péchiney	5,760	7,000
Ugine	5,640	12,300
CGE	5,520	15,000

Source: Eck, *Histoire de l'économie française depuis 1945*, 94.

It was the same argument for industry. Rather than continue the policy of governments under the Fourth Republic of raising living standards while channelling the direction of investment into those sectors where demand was increasing most rapidly, Gaullist policy was to remove controls over investment while restricting consumption. Rather than continue to change the structure of the economy, the focus of policy was to address the small size of French firms, a factor that was held responsible for their lack of competitiveness. With the exception of the nationalized company Renault, which employed 61,000 workers in 1960, and Michelin, which employed 40,000, no other French company even employed as many as 30,000 workers at that time.

Apart from a number of technologically advanced projects in aircraft, space research and computers that were publicly funded, the choice of most investment was left in the hands of banks, which were now increasingly freed from state controls, or of family firms to fund from their own resources.

Publicly funded investment projects

One such technologically advanced project was led by the French aircraft industry. Since its nationalization by the Popular Front government in 1936, the French airframe firm soon to be called Sud Aviation had had a notable triumph with building the first successful commercial jet aeroplane, the Caravelle, which entered the market in the mid-1950s. Coming on the heels of the succession of crashes that had grounded the British jet, the Comet, the Caravelle marked the return of French aviation to the international stage and left the British looking for a way to re-establish their industry. British engineers and civil servants thought that beating the United States to build the world's first commercial supersonic aircraft was the answer. To build it with the French would reduce the cost and might open the door to British membership of the EEC: a policy that the British Conservative government had belatedly concluded was necessary to kickstart the economy. The appeal for de Gaulle and his government of cooperating with Britain was twofold. First, it would keep the team of skilled engineers in Sud Aviation in Toulouse employed until a successor to the Caravelle was found. Second, if each country built the entire aeroplane it would give the French aero engine firm, SNECMA, the technological skills that it so badly needed. Unlike the airframe industry, which had benefited from the amalgamation and nationalization of a number of smaller firms to become what would eventually be a world leader in aviation, the same had not worked in the case of aero engines. The nationalization of the main firms, Gnôme et Rhône and Hispano Suiza, after the Second World War had not led to any technological breakthroughs. The engine for the Caravelle was built under licence. What was needed, de Gaulle thought, was for the French nationalized firm to work with and learn from the leaders in the field. British membership of the EEC was not necessary for such a joint venture to take place, nor was commercial success the driving objective of building Concorde with the British. Thus, as well as vetoeing the British government's applications to join the EEC, de Gaulle also opposed its request to abandon or delay the construction of Concorde in order to make budgetary savings. Indeed, in 1963 the French economy was facing similar inflationary problems to those in Britain. Following the return of 800,000 European settlers (*pieds noirs*) from Algeria and the arrival of the first generation of baby boomers onto the labour market, the French economy was overheating to such an extent that the fourth plan was suspended while the economy was stabilized.[37] Investment in Concorde was not cut, however. But lessons were learned and the successor to Concorde, Airbus, involved West Germany and other European partners and was designed from the out-set for a growing mass market for air travel. The first airbus, the A-300, went into service in 1974, a most unpropitious time right in the middle of a severe international recession with the price of fuel at an all-time high. It was not until the early 1980s that demand picked up and Airbus gradually became a rival to Boeing in the international market, with the French publicly owned company Aérospatiale, based in Toulouse, at the centre of a successful European consortium. The production of Airbus together with that of the privately owned firm Dassault Aviation, which specialized in fighter jets commissioned by the French and many other governments world-wide, meant that French aircraft was to become one of the leading export sectors of the French economy.[38]

Other publicly funded projects took even longer to deliver results. In 1960 France launched a programme into space research and later became the technical leader of the European Space Agency (ESA), based in Paris. In 1979 its first space rocket, Ariane, was lauched from Kourou in French Guiana and the site, near the equator, was subsequently leased to countries across the world for lauching telecommunication satellites into space. Although the ambitions to compete with the United States in developing commercially successful computers was not achieved, the first microprocessor-based computer in the world, developed in the 1970s, was French. The French went on to develop a system for downloading information by telephone or television and, by supplying a free device, the Minitel, to five million people, France was, by 1989, the most wired country in the world.[39] It may have been a good idea but the method of implementing it represented a huge waste of public money.

Privately funded investment

However, the policy of leaving most investment decisions in the hands of the private sector was no more successful in changing the structure of production begun under the Fourth Republic. Notwithstanding the changes made since 1945, by the beginning of the 1960s the French economy was still specializing in lines of production for which demand was growing most slowly. These included agricultural products, traditional consumer goods such as textiles and clothing, as well as intermediate goods such as steel, construction materials, glass and chemicals (including pharmaceuticals). It was particularly weak in equipment industries, where German specialization was strongest. The industries equipping both firms and households made up for some of their initial backwardness and lack of competitiveness over the decade between 1960 and 1971, so that by 1971 the share in exports of the

French mechanical and electrical industries had reached the average for the EEC countries. At the same time, the initial advantages that France had enjoyed in intermediate and consumer goods industries owing to protection in both the domestic and colonial markets disappeared when faced with competition within the EEC. The consumer goods industry, particularly textiles, which had been considered one of the strongest points of the French economy, with a trade surplus equal to 7 per cent of production in 1959, soon lost this surplus when protection was removed. Similarly, intermediate goods industries, most of which had a strong export performance in the early 1960s, grew slowly and lost market share. Overall, the trade balance of the sector declined from a surplus equal to 5.7 per cent of production in 1959 to a deficit equal to 4.3 per cent in 1972. Another potential weakness was in the energy sector, as imported oil gradually replaced domestic coal. From covering 48 per cent of domestic consumption in 1963, domestic coal covered 19 per cent ten years later, while oil, 95 per cent of which was imported, covered 65 per cent, up from 37.7 per cent in 1963. While this was a deliberate policy choice based on the assumption that the price of oil would continue to be much lower than that of coal, it left the balance of payments vulnerable were this to change. Imports of intermediate goods, equipment goods and consumer goods all grew by much more than exports between 1959 and 1972.[40] In the late 1960s the external account moved into deficit for the first time under the Fifth Republic. It could not have been unexpected.

Growth rates accelerated in the 1960s as the rates elsewhere in western Europe slowed down, but inflation was less controlled. Rates of investment were higher, but these came at the price of more slowly growing living standards. The focus on uncontrolled private investment and publicly funded technologically advanced projects played a part in the political upheaval of 1968. The Grenelle Agreements that restored social peace after May 1968, together with the devaluation of the franc in 1969 implemented by President Pompidou, increased domestic demand while giving a competitive edge to French exports. As a result of the boost to domestic demand and investment, while other European economies had already been slowing down in the years before the June 1973 oil price hike that plunged the world into recession, the French economy grew at a rate of 5.6 per cent per annum between 1969 and 1973.

Table 3.7 Growth of value added, exports and imports, 1959–72

	Annual average growth rate (%)		
	Value added	Exports	Imports
Agriculture	7	18.6	4.9
Food industries	9	9.8	9.9
Energy	9.8	8.7	9.9
Intermediate goods	9.6	10.9	14.4
Equipment goods	11.5	14.4	22
Consumer goods	9.5	10.1	14.2
Housing	14.8		
Transport and telecommunications	10	7.9	
Building and public works	12.4		
Services	12.8		
Internal trade	9.2		
Whole economy	10.5	12.2	13.6

Source: INSEE, Fresque historique du système productif, 19.

FROM RECESSION TO U-TURN, 1974–83

Less dependent on the international economy than many other developed countries, France was initially less affected by the international recession that started in Japan and West Germany in the fourth quarter of 1973 and reached France in the third quarter of 1974. Between then and the third quarter of 1975 the French economy contracted by 10 per cent, but the recession, the first since the war, was shortlived and the economy grew at 3.4 per cent per year between 1975 and 1979. But, as the decade closed, industrial production, far from having doubled over the previous ten years as Pompidou had hoped, was no more than 35 per cent greater than in 1970.[41] It was the service sector that, together with housing, had recorded the fastest rates of growth between 1959 and 1972, and continued to expand.

Table 3.8 Comparative rates of growth of GDP (volume)

	Before the recession		After the recession	
France	1960–73	5.4%	1975–79	3.4%
UK	1960–70	2.8%	1975–79	2.1%
Italy	1960–70	5.3%	1975–79	2.9%
Japan	1960–73	10.0%	1975–79	5.7%
West Germany	1960–70	4.3%	1975–79	3.7%
USA	1960–66	4.8%	1975–79	4.2%

Source: INSEE, La crise du système productif, 26.

From its outset, the global recession that followed the quadrupling of the price of oil in 1973 exposed the fragility of the French balance of payments. Forty per cent of the French supply of electricity came from oil, compared with 15 per cent in Germany and 26 per cent in the UK.[42] About 75 per cent of the French oil supply was imported. In 1974, even though France had a surplus in its trade in food, agricultural products and manufactures, as well as a very small surplus in services, largely due to tourism, together these were not enough to cover the deficit in its trade in oil, gas and electricity. Understandably, the largest trade deficit in 1974 was with Saudi Arabia, but the next most important one was with West Germany. The problem was worsened by the fact that, following the recession of 1974–75, the fastest growing markets shifted from western Europe to the oil-producing and other developing economies, where the greatest demand was for equipment goods, electronic goods and armaments. But, since the size of the developing markets was much smaller than those they replaced, France, like the rest of the developed world, had to find a way to reduce its imports and expand its exports. The political turmoil in the Middle East provided a growing market for French exports of armaments.

Rising prices and the contraction of markets in western Europe left those sectors that had grown most slowly in the 1960s even more exposed. This was particularly true for family firms, which had traditionally relied on their own profits to fund investment. Having seen their reserves depleted in the 1930s and the Second World War and losing market share in France and the former colonies, they found it increasingly difficult to cover the rising cost of employing labour, particularly after the Grenelle Agreements. The level of self-funding of private investment began falling from 56 per cent of productive investment in the mid-1960s to less than 40 per cent in 1975–76. Despite changes in the reserve ceilings required of French banks by law, the banks were reluctant to lend to unprofitable firms. The government was equally reluctant. Starting with the textile firms based in northern France around Rouen, the banks gradually withdrew their credit. During the ten-year period 1974–84, France experienced a record number of bankruptcies, a contraction of its share of international trade and one of the world's steepest declines in employment in its industrial sector.[43] Big names such as the commercial vehicle producer Titan-Coder disappeared in 1974, followed by the textile firm les Ateliers Roannais de Construction Textile (ARCT) in 1975, the watch and clock company Lip in 1976, Manufrance, the first French mail order firm specializing in shotguns and bicycles, in 1977–80, the textile company Boussac in 1978, and the machine tool makers Forest in 1979.

Rather than prop up declining sectors, the government took the decision to reduce the dependence of the economy on oil by switching to nuclear energy. Although work had started on building a nuclear reactor in the 1950s, nuclear energy was much more expensive to produce than oil or coal. In 1962 the first nuclear power station, Chinon 1, was producing 68 megawatts (MW) of nuclear energy; in 1965 Chinon 2 produced 200 MW, and in 1967, when the third reactor produced 300 MW, it was decided that the electricity generated from the nuclear reactor could be put on the French grid for the first time. At the same time EDF decided that, by teaming up with the three firms Creusot-Loire, Alsthom and CGE, they could create a techno-nuclear industry and start to export French nuclear technology. It also decided to create a company, Framatome, to make nuclear reactors using the pressurized water reactor (PWR) method, under licence, in partnership with the French firm Schneider (which had bought the licence for making PWRs developed by the American firm Westinghouse in 1958). In that same year, 1967, EDF agreed to build its first nuclear power station with the Belgians at Chooz on the River Meuse. Whereas de Gaulle, in his determination for France to be independent of the United States, had backed the more expensive natural uranium–graphite–gas method developed by the CEA, Pompidou backed the PWR method instead. As a result, the CEA withdrew from the production of nuclear energy altogether, leaving Framatome as the only constructor of boilers for nuclear reactors in France. In 1970 the French government set up an experimental supergenerator factory, Phenix, and the following year, in partnership with the British, set up a company, United Reprocessors, with a view to controlling the supply of nuclear energy in Europe. In 1972 Framatome started to build its first nuclear power station at Fessenheim on the Rhine in Alsace but, given the time lag between the installation and production of nuclear energy, its share of French energy consumption was negligible before the 1980s.

When the United States set up the International Energy Agency in 1974 in order to strengthen the cooperation among the OECD members and reduce their dependence on imported oil, the French government refused to join. Instead, it decided to commission Framatome to build 13 nuclear power stations of 1,000 MW each, over six years, to be followed by a further five power stations, to raise its nuclear capacity to 55,000 MW by 1985. In the words of one French economic historian "it was the greatest industrial gamble taken by the French since the Monnet Plan".[44] But, unlike the Monnet Plan, it was ill-judged and saddled the French economy with a problem stretching far into the future.

By the end of 1985 France had reached a nuclear capacity of 39,000 MW, with nuclear energy supplying 70 per cent of its electricity consumption. But, in that same year the price of oil collapsed by 50 per cent, reflecting a reduction in the demand for oil and the depreciation of the dollar. Following a major accident at the nuclear power station in Chernobyl in May 1986, which led many countries to close their nuclear industry completely, the director of the commission set up to evaluate the risks in the nuclear industry in France publicly stated that the radioactive cloud from Chernobyl had not crossed the French border. Suitably reassured, public support for nuclear power remained high in France. What criticism there was, was mainly that the nuclear construction programme in the 1970s may have been at the expense of the modernization and competitiveness of much of the manufacturing industry, leading to a trade deficit in manufactured goods.[45] On the other hand, according to an OECD study published in 1984, the cost price of coal per KWh in France was 80 per cent above that of nuclear power, and as a result France was able to export electricity derived from nuclear power to the UK, West Germany, Switzerland and Italy.[46] By 1994 almost 78 per cent of French electricity came from nuclear power.

Table 3.9 Rate of growth of gross investment, 1960–79 (in 1970 prices) (%)

	France	UK	Italy	Japan	FRG	USA
1960–73	7.4	4.5	3.8	14	4.3	4.3
1975–79	1.6	–0.6	1.2	6.9	5.7	6.7

Source: INSEE, La crise du système productif.

As well as funding the expansion of nuclear energy, in the 1970s the government, as we have seen, also commissioned large infrastructure projects such as the TGV and the extension of the Paris metro to the suburbs (RER). But the public investment failed to stimulate private investment, which was disguised at the time by the fact that prices were rising rapidly. As a result there was no investment, either public or private, in the sectors where global demand was expanding, such as electronics, information technology, data processing and medical imaging equipment. At a time when West Germany,

Japan and the United States were adjusting to the changes in the international economy and increasing their investment, rates in France and also in the UK and Italy were considerably lower. Finally, in an effort to stimulate private investment, the French government passed the Monory Law of 13 July 1978, whereby people were encouraged to move their savings out of banks and into the stock market by exempting from tax any income made from the sale of shares: a policy that was very divisive politically.

At a time when 700,000 people, many of whom were women, were entering the labour market for the first time, it was the one million new jobs in services that prevented the unemployment figures from rising to nearly two million. However, of the new jobs in services, 797,000 were in services to individuals, particularly in health care, and many were part-time, while 297,000 were in services to firms.[47] The situation in West Germany was quite different. There the active population had fallen by 762,000 over the period 1973–78, and although more people lost their jobs in manufacturing and construction, few new jobs were created in services.

Table 3.10 Evolution of the active population in France, the UK and West Germany, 1973–78 (in thousands)

France	UK	West Germany
709	783	−762
97	−88	−1,501
−464	−64	−346
−505	−762	−1,336
−326	−574	−797
1,062	740	181

Source: INSEE, La crise du système productif.

By 1980 unemployment was beginning to fall in West Germany, whereas it continued to rise in France. The Socialist/Communist government elected in 1981 intended to reduce unemployment through a programme of nationalization and Keynesian pump priming. The miminim wage was increased, paid holidays extended by one week to five weeks and the working week reduced to 39 hours. By nationalizing a very large number of banks and firms in the manufacturing sector the government hoped to direct investment into activities that could meet the enhanced domestic demand arising from greater social spending. The expectation was that imports would fall and exports would rise, thereby turning the trade deficit into a surplus. France by 1980 was starting to run a trade surplus in agriculture and food, to add to existing surpluses in professional and transport equipment, but it had a deficit in consumer goods and household equipment goods. In the short term the economy grew but, given the contraction in the industrial sector since 1974, the increase in demand could not be met from domestic production. Imports increased, and since other countries such as West Germany and the UK had cut demand in response to the second increase in the price of oil, there was no corresponding demand for French exports. The result was a deterioration in the French trade deficit and a succession of devaluations of the French franc within the European Monetary System (EMS). The devaluations increased the price of imports and the trade deficit. It was only in intermediate goods (chemicals, metals and mineral raw materials) that a trade deficit became a surplus.

Table 3.11 Comparative unemployment, 1960–80

	Number of unemployed (thousands)				Rate of unemployment
	1960–67	1967–73	1973–79	1980	in 1980 (%)
France	125.5	306	976.8	1,447	6.5
UK	416.4	664.3	1,116.3	1,646	6.8
Italy	1,053.1	1,192.5	1,430.6	1,698	7.6
Japan	619	633.8	1,054.8	1,145	2
West Germany	217.6	223.7	938.9	899	3.9
USA	3,691.9	3,981.6	6,339.6	7,496	7.2

Source: INSEE, La crise du système productif.

On the other hand, the trade in services continued to be in surplus mainly due to trade in technology, including nuclear, and to a lesser extent due to tourism, but it was not enough to balance the deficit in goods.

Table 3.12 Main categories of trade in goods, 1978–84

	Imports (in billions of francs)						
	1978	1979	1980	1981	1982	1983	1984
Agriculture	29.1	30.6	32	35.2	41.9	46.6	52.2
Food industries	30	32.5	36	42.3	49.1	56.2	64
Energy	71.1	98.6	151.7	186.3	201.6	194.4	216.6
Intermediate goods	94.9	120.4	143.1	151.8	171.4	186.3	219
Professional equipment	62.6	73.6	88.7	104.9	128	135.7	153.3
Household equipment	8	9.6	11	13.3	16.8	16.2	17.9
Transport equipment	24	29.4	34.5	40.1	53	58.7	61.1
Consumer goods	47.6	60.6	71.3	77.3	93.3	102.3	116.2
Other	1	1.8	2.5	2.4	2.5	3	3.9
Total	368.4	457.1	570.8	653.6	757.6	799.3	904.1

	Exports (in billions of francs)						
	1978	1979	1980	1981	1982	1983	1984
Agriculture	25.6	29.4	34.9	43.6	47.1	59.9	66.2
Food industries	31.7	36.9	44.7	55.1	58.7	64.5	75.6
Energy	9	14.7	18.8	25.3	23.7	26.1	29.3
Intermediate goods	94.8	115.8	134.9	153.5	168.9	190.2	228.6
Professional equipment	78	91.5	98.4	120.3	140.9	161.5	188.4
Household equipment	4.2	5	5.5	5.9	6.8	7.6	9
Transport equipment	49.9	59.7	62.4	67.2	73.3	83.1	94
Consumer goods	48.3	56.3	64.3	72.6	80.6	93.1	110.7
Other	3	5.3	5.8	6	6.1	8.7	12.1
Total	344.6	414.7	469.7	549.5	606.1	694.6	813.8

Source: INSEE, Tableaux de l'économie française.

While public investment restored the profitability of many of the nationalized companies and banks, it did not restore full employment. The decision taken in 1983 to relax restrictions on capital movements to encourage more foreign investment into the economy marked a clear break with tradition and led to an expansion of the service sector.[48]

TOWARDS THE SERVICE ECONOMY, 1983–2018

In comparison with the growth rates of GDP, which averaged nearly 6 per cent per annum over the "30 glorious years", the growth of GDP over the 34 years after 1984 averaged about 1.9 per cent per annum. Lower growth was accompanied by rising unemployment. The controversial decision to reduce domestic demand in 1983 in order to reduce imports continued the contraction in the manufacturing industry and the loss of jobs. Between 1980 and 1985 a further million people became unemployed, with the numbers rising from 1,445,000 to 2,429,000.[49] In 1984 the giant of French mechanical engineering, Creusot-Loire, declared bankruptcy, followed two years later by the last of the French machine tool industries, Intelautomatisme, and the last of the French shipbuilding industries, Normed. By 1986, the largest remaining company was Renault, with Peugeot not far behind. Four of the top 20 companies in France were foreign-owned. Indeed, in the mid-1980s firms with foreign participation accounted for 21 per cent of industrial employment, 26 per cent of industrial investment and 26 per cent of total sales, making France the most attractive country for inward investment in the manufacturing industry of the top five advanced economies.[50]

At the same time high interest rates encouraged an inflow of capital into Paris.[51] The aim of the government was now to make Paris into a major financial centre and the centre for trade in the ECU (the predecessor of the euro).[52] The stock market, la Bourse, started to implement an electronic trading system, the Cotation Assistée en Continu (CAC). Despite the foreign investment in industry, the structure of manufacturing production was slow to evolve and France continued to specialize in exporting transport equipment, including aeronautical, nuclear power technology and armaments. In the newer, expanding fields of computers and information technologies French firms were unable to challenge the dominant position of the large American and Japanese multinational firms in the international market. In the sectors where it had finally established a trade surplus, food and agricultural products, demand was growing much more slowly.

Table 3.13 Top 20 companies in France, 1986

	Annual turnover (million francs)	Size of labour force
Renault	131,060	182,400
Elf-Aquitaine	119,730	76,100
Peugeot	104,950	165,000
CFP	95,720	35,100
CGE	80,900	149,000
Saint-Gobain	77,720	140,100
Usinor-Sacilor	72,280	102,200
Thomson	62,200	104,500
Rhône-Poulenc	52,700	77,000
Michelin	46,330	118,600
Bouygues	41,940	59,000
Shell française	36,680	7,300
IBM-France	36,630	22,200
Péchiney	34,670	49,900
Aérospatiale	33,840	42,900
BSN	33,620	42,800
CEA-Industrie	30,960	31,900
Esso Standard France	27,450	4,400
Schneider	25,750	59,300
BP France	23,510	4,000

Source: Eck, *Histoire de l'économie française depuis 1945*, 94.

Services

By the mid-1980s services were starting to account for an ever larger share of the French economy. In addition to the traditional services linked to production, such as transport and distribution, there were an increasing number of marketable and non-marketable ones. INSEE included marketable services in its annual economic tables for the first time in 1984, but four years later it admitted that the sector was diverse and not well understood: it covered a wide range of activities, some of which served businesses and some private individuals.[53] There were four categories of marketable services:

1. Car repair and trade, including the sale of fuel.
2. Hotels, cafes, restaurants and catering.
3. The very heterogeneous services for firms (including salvage and reprocessing, holding companies, instruction and market research, rental and leasing, commercial property advertising, renting agents, finance and insurance), and a wide range of consultants (e.g. engineers, IT, architects, surveyors, lawyers, accountants, advertisers, caretakers, security guards, temporary staff including secretaries).
4. Services for individuals: health, recreation, cultural and sport, cinema, radio and television, theatre, recreational services, as well as dry cleaners, laundry, hairdressers, funeral services, industrial cleaning and decontamination.

Even if they were not well understood, the service industry seemed to mark the beginning of a new chapter in the economic history of France, when the country would finally shake off its protectionist past and fully embrace the global economy. The introduction of the European Single Market at the end of 1992 and the conclusion of the Uruguay round of GATT in 1994 (which for the first time included the liberalization of trade in agriculture, services and intellectual property) were hailed as responsible for what was called a golden age in global trade over the period

1990–2008. GATT rules were strengthened and placed on a firmer institutional footing through the creation of the WTO in 1995.[54]

Between the beginning of the 1990s and 2005 one of the striking characteristics of France's economic performance was the strength of its external accounts. This was helped by the fact that, after 1985, the deficit in energy trade had diminished as nuclear power began to replace oil and as the price of oil began to fall (in 1994 the energy deficit was back to its value in the early 1970s). The strong performance of its external accounts was also due to the impact on domestic demand, including the demand for imports, of the austerity policies followed by the French government to meet the criteria agreed under the Treaty of Maastricht for joining the single currency (see Chapter 6). In addition, the demand for French exports to Germany rose following its unification in 1990. It was not until 1997 that the French and European economies began a period of recovery, which lasted until 2001, when what was popularly known as the "dot-com bubble" burst in the United States and growth rates tumbled across the Western world. In France, the growth rates fell from 4 per cent in 2000 to 0.8 per cent in 2003 before bouncing back to 2.6 per cent in 2006 and 2.3 per cent in 2007.[55]

Nonetheless, over the period between 1997 and 2005 the French economy recorded a higher rate of growth than the average for the EU (3.6 per cent compared with 3.2 per cent) as well as the lowest rate of inflation and the strongest current account surplus. Investment, particularly in digital communications and Internet-related companies, which had been postponed since the early 1990s, now took off and with unemployment falling faster than elsewhere in Europe there was much optimistic talk of a return to full employment at last. In 1997 France Telecom was privatized, with the sale proving very attractive to investors. The CEO, Michel Bon (a former high civil servant, graduate of the ENA), who had been paid about €370,000 per year, was replaced by Thierry Breton (an electrical engineer, formerly CEO of Thomson), who earned €1.25 million in 2002.[56] He lost no time in cutting employment from 160,700 in 1996 to 141,000 in 2002, replacing many older civil servants with a new generation of younger, less skilled employees. Coinciding with the development of new services, particularly the mobile phone, sales per employee increased from €138,000 in 1996 to €194,000 in 2002.[57]

At the beginning of the new millennium France was doing better than either Germany or Italy, largely because domestic demand was higher due to higher taxes and redistribution (see Chapter 5) and higher levels of labour productivity due to the investment postponed in the 1990s. It was calculated that a French worker produced 12 per cent more than a British worker, 18 per cent more than a German worker and 22 per cent more than a Japanese worker. At the same time the French worked fewer hours than their competitors, and the cost of an hour's labour was 4 per cent lower in France than in Britain, 33 per cent lower than in Germany and 17 per cent lower than in Sweden.[58]

By 2000 the service sector employed 73 per cent of the active labour force: private services employed 45.1 per cent and accounted for 51.6 per cent of value added, while public services employed 27.9 per cent of the total and contributed 20.2 per cent of the value added.[59] By contrast, employment in industry was 22.7 per cent and value added was 25.4 per cent. Although over two million people remained unemployed and an increasing number of jobs were in the public sector, funded out of taxation, optimism was high. The French economic historian, Jean-Pierre Dormois, concluded his analysis of the French economy in the twentieth century by saying that

> France's strength remains with its now cut-down-to-size manufacturing sector, the most open to outside competition, and the best performing of its services, such as finance and the professions.... The way ahead is clearly to further open services to international competition, in which France is well equipped to score further points.[60]

The most successful categories of services where French firms were major players in the global market were: tourism, where the French hotel group Accor had a global presence; waste and water management, energy, transport services and property, where Veolia was dominant; insurance, where Axa was a global player; mass media, where Vivendi was strong; advertising, where Publicis ranked high; food services, where Sodexo was the largest firm; construction, including of airports, dominated by Vinci and Bouygues; and, finally, rail transportation, where Alstom (formerly Alsthom) was the main supplier.

But, while trade in services made a positive contribution to the balance of payments, it came from technical cooperation, large export contracts and tourism. Other services, such as transport and insurance, which were linked to the trade in merchandise, continued to run a deficit, as did patents. Nonetheless, in the first eight years of the new millennium more than one million new jobs were created in the service sector, which was seen by many as more than compensating for the loss of industrial jobs and, in any case, the losses in the more successful sectors of car production, energy and food processing were very much less than in the rest of the industrial sector (7 per cent, 4 per cent and 0.3 per cent respectively).[61]

The car industry

France had been the leading producer of cars in the world at the beginning of the twentieth century, having expanded by 28.4 per cent between 1904 and 1914. At that time there were 155 different firms, mostly family run, employing 100,000 people.[62] In the depressed years of the 1930s production was cut and firms merged, and by 1939 there were only 31 firms. Whereas French private car production had peaked in 1929 at 212,000, it declined in the 1930s, reaching 182,000 in 1938, while output in Germany expanded from 96,000 in 1929 to reach 275,000 by 1938. In the UK the peak year in the interwar period was 1937, when production was 390,000.

After the Second World War the car industry was one of the beneficiaries of the investment in wide strip mills. Renault, nationalized in 1945, dominated the domestic market in the 1950s with its Renault 4, which sold over over one million in that decade alone. Its rival, Citroën, which remained in private hands, did even better with its hugely popular 2CV (*deux chevaux*). Between 1965 and 1973, with car production growing by 10 per cent per year, France became the world's second largest exporter of cars. The years after the recession of 1974–75 were turbulent ones marked by horizontal concentration, industrial decentralization and increased professionalization as the industry tried to adapt, with the assistance of the state, to higher fuel prices and greater competition. Peugeot took over both SIMCA (a subsidiary of Chrysler), which disappeared, and Citroën, which remained as a trademark. It was mainly thanks to the unexpected success of the 205 model that Peugeot was able to recover the costs of its acquisitions. Renault, on the other hand, almost bankrupted itself by absorbing Berliet (the leading French truck and bus manufacturer). Whereas the car industry as a whole had employed 530,000 in 1973, employment had fallen to 380,000 by 1987. With investment subsidies from the state, the two remaining firms, Renault and Peugeot, built large plants outside Paris, mainly in Normandy and Brittany to reduce costs, and with reduced rates of VAT (from 33.3 per cent to 25 per cent) and import quotas placed on Japanese cars the industry recovered. By 1990 Renault was the largest industrial firm in France, employing 157,400 people. In 1992 it closed its factory in Boulogne-Billancourt, Paris, which had contracted from 30,000 employees in the 1960s to only 3,000 in 1992, and at the same time sold 25 per cent of the company to the Swedish firm Volvo. Two years later Renault was privatized, although the state retained a 15.65 per cent share. It went on to take a 36.8 per cent share of the struggling Japanese firm Nissan in 1999, increasing it to 44.4 per cent in 2002 after selling the machine tool division to the Italian firm Comau, affiliated to Fiat. When the new director, Carlos Ghosn, sold Renault's shares in lorry construction to Volvo, France lost control over the future of lorry construction as well as of machine tools.[63] At the same time the two firms moved much of their production outside France to lower waged countries. By 2018, although the French car industry was the second largest in Europe, France was a net importer of cars because two out of three cars sold by Renault on the French market were made outside France, while one out of two cars sold by Peugeot had also been made abroad.[64]

The car firms were not the only ones to move their production out of France. Over the ten years between 2006 and 2016 French foreign direct investment (FDI) nearly doubled, with most of it being invested in the eurozone and North America.[65] However, at the same time, FDI into France also expanded, with France still being seen as the most attractive country in Europe, well ahead of Germany, Italy and the UK. In spite of the perceived rigidity of the French labour market, discussed in Chapter 5, foreign investors in Airbus, EDF, Danone and Sanofi claimed to value fiscal stability above lower taxes.[66]

The 2008–09 financial crisis

Initially, when the crisis hit the US subprime market and spread rapidly to Europe it seemed as though the French economic model, based on high tax and redistribution policies to maintain domestic demand, relatively low exposure to international trade (in 2009 exports and imports together accounted for 23 per cent of GDP compared with 37 per cent for the EU 27), a relatively high savings ratio and a cautious investment strategy that favoured life insurance and savings plans, had paid off. When the American economy was plunged into recession the French economy managed to continue to grow, although only by 0.2 per cent. It then contracted in 2009 by 3.0 per cent, compared with 2.8 per cent in the United States and 4.4 per cent in the eurozone. The French economy then recovered, growing by 1.9 per cent in 2010 and 2.2 per cent in 2011. French banks suffered much less than banks in the UK or Germany and needed considerably less government support as a result. Their relative success was due to the fact that they had maintained a strong retail base in France and expanded it globally while developing a full range of investment banking activities. Although the state had liberalized and deregulated the banking sector from 1984 onwards, it had at the same time actively encouraged specific forms of financial innovation such as the trading of equity, interest rate and exchange rate derivatives rather than the securitization that had produced the subprime crisis in the United States and elsewhere. With the aim of making Paris the centre for trade in the ECU, the Chirac government had established the French futures market, the MATIF, in 1986. Ironically, it was the mutual banks that were worse hit since, having diversified into investment at least ten years after the other banks, they had then expanded too rapidly. The Crédit Agricole was particularly badly affected by the exposure of its investment-banking arm, Calyon, to the American subprime market.[67]

President Sarkozy's countercyclical package of public investment projects, which included four new high-speed rail lines, a new canal (the Seine–Nord Europe canal between Compiègne and Cambrai), the renovation of public buildings and investment in public enterprises, failed to stimulate private investment or domestic demand. By the end of 2009 unemployment was 9.5 per cent compared with 7.8 per cent in Germany. With public debt exceeding the limits allowed in the eurozone in 2010, Sarkozy announced a number of budget cuts, including changes in the means-tested benefits that targeted the poor, as well as tax increases. With the German economy growing at 3.6 per cent, Sarkozy lost the presidential election in May 2012 to the Socialist candidate François Hollande.

Hollande inherited an economy in which a further 500,000 jobs had been lost in industry since the financial crisis but, unlike the previous eight years, when more than one million new jobs had been created in the service sector, in the seven years after 2008 only 150,000 new jobs were created in services. Concern began to mount that after the decline of its industries France was starting to face the decline of its services.[68] Whereas France had been among the world's top exporters of services linked to construction, energy distribution and computing, with the service sector as a whole accounting for 85 per cent of growth, 77 per cent of employment and all the new jobs created, it was now losing ground. Exports from the big national champions, such as Vivendi, Accor, Carrefour, Veolia, GDF-Suez, EDF and SNCF, which had ranked third place in the world, were now slipping to fourth place and falling. Their turnover was almost half that of German firms and one quarter that of US firms. A critical question was whether it was more important to shore up services or try to reverse the decline in manufacturing. One problem was that 94 per cent of service sector firms employed fewer than ten people while serving a local market and making no positive contribution to exports. The fact that the French balance of trade was persistently in deficit, even though that deficit was slightly less than it had been, was seen by some as evidence that the sectoral distribution of labour had become too heavily weighted towards unmarketable services at the expense of manufacturing. As the growth of employment in the service sector declined, it was argued that services were in fact dependent on the manufacturing sector for their success.

It was observed that countries which had a trade surplus were those, such as Germany and Japan, which had preserved and developed their national productive base. Manufacturing, as a large consumer of marketable services and accounting for most exports and most private research and development (R&D), was now seen to be critical to the growth of the economy. Investment in machinery and equipment, including robots, at 28 per cent of total investment in manufacturing in France, was much lower than the 43 per cent in Germany and Italy. Insofar as machinery and equipment incorporated the latest technology, the low level of investment in new technology in France meant that it was missing out on productivity-enhancing investment. In comparison with its main competitors in the eurozone, total factor productivity had been falling in France since 2006. At the same time the investment in R&D in American, German and Italian firms was about twice as much as in French firms despite the generous support initiated by the de Villepin government to encourage firms to invest in R&D (the equivalent of a tax credit of 30 per cent of its cost up to €100 million), which had earned France the title of being a "tax paradise" for research. The lower investment in R&D contributed to a lower number of patents and a loss of market share in the most high-tech sectors. Similarly, in spite of a number of tax breaks given to firms and a reduction in the rate of corporation tax, France's trade balance remained in deficit.[69]

Nuclear energy

A further problem facing the Socialist government was that, after Japan's nuclear disaster at Fukushima in March 2011, several European governments, including most notably that of Germany, had decided to abandon nuclear power altogether. This put pressure on France and led to the first official questioning of its long-standing pro-nuclear position. The two Socialist candidates for the presidential nomination in the election of 2012,[70] Martine Aubry and François Hollande, were divided over whether to follow Germany's lead and abandon nuclear power production, or to reduce the nuclear share of France's energy consumption by one third to equate to 50 per cent by 2025. Whereas Aubry campaigned for the former, Hollande chose the latter option, promising to shut down the first generation of reactors, starting with the first one opened in 1977 in Fessenheim, Alsace. This promise was made in anticipation of the opening of a new European pressurized reactor at Flamanville in Normandy. The issue was complicated by the fact that, at a time of mounting international concern about global warming, France was one of the European Union's best performers in terms of greenhouse gas (GHG) emissions, mainly on account of its heavy dependence on low-carbon nuclear energy. By 2014 there were 58 nuclear reactors, mostly amortized, operating in France and offering some of the cheapest and the most decarbonized electricity in Europe. In 2015 per capita emissions of CO_2 in France were among the lowest in Europe: 5.1 tonnes compared with 6.2 in the UK, 9.6 in Germany and an average of 6.8 in the EU. The Belgians, Dutch, Italians and Spanish all had higher emissions than France, although they all paled in comparison with the United States, where the per capita emissions were 16.1 tonnes. On the other hand in sub-Saharan Africa they were 0.9 tonnes.

In November 2018 President Macron announced that France would close 14 of its 58 nuclear reactors by 2035 (ten years later than Hollande had promised), reducing its dependence on electricity from nuclear power from 70 per cent to 50 per cent. At the same time, the future of the Flamanville reactor was still in doubt. Started in 2007, it was to have been completed in 2012 at a cost of €3,300 million. But by 2018 with Flamanville still not completed, and with no likelihood that it would be before 2023 the cost had escalated to €12,400 million. Part of the delay was attributed to the loss of skills, the shortage of labour, particularly of welders, and the worsening conditions of work. The perceived danger was that if France were not careful it would lose the ability to construct nuclear reactors and to maintain those still in service, with China alone possessing the expertise.[71] In promising to shut down Fessenheim, the state was committed to indemnify EDF to the tune of €450 million, with the full dismantling estimated to take until about 2040.

CONCLUSION

Fourastié's description of the "30 glorious years" of high and unbroken growth rates after 1945 ascribed to that period a unity that disguised many differences between the Fourth Republic and the Gaullist years. Under the Fourth Republic a planned programme of investment, much of it state funded across all three sectors of the economy, was controlled in order to prevent inflation from squeezing consumption, in conditions of a labour shortage. In the 1960s as the postwar baby boom generation entered the labour market, investment in industry was prioritized over consumption, with state funding and control over that investment greatly reduced apart from in a few technologically advanced projects. Both rates of investment and growth of GDP were higher than under the Fourth Republic. Labour productivity rose over the entire period as sustained rates of investment encouraged hundreds of thousands of people to leave agriculture to work in the expanding industrial and service sectors and as the French economy was gradually opened up to competition within the European common market.

When the economic boom came to an end in 1975, rates of growth of GDP and investment slowed down. At a time when West Germany, Japan and the United States were adjusting to the changes in the international economy and increasing their investment in the sectors where global demand was expanding, such as electronics, information technology, data processing and medical imaging equipment, the French government invested in nuclear energy and transport while private investment declined. When the Socialist programme to expand both investment and consumption by nationalizing huge swathes of the economy and increasing social spending produced a large foreign trade deficit rather than a reduction in unemployment, it was social spending that was cut. Controls over capital movements were subsequently removed, making France the most attractive country for foreign investors in Europe.

With exports from the service sector beginning to overtake those of manufacturing, and with France second only to the US as an exporter of services in the 1980s, the government signed up to the Single European Act to liberalize trade in services. For the 14-year period after 1991 France enjoyed a trade surplus based on a slimmed down industrial sector and a greatly expanded service sector. But, as the liberalization of trade slowed down from 2013 onwards, France began to run a slight deficit in trade in services in addition to the trade deficit in goods. By 2018 it had fallen from second to fourth position in the world as an exporter of commercial services. It had also fallen from fourth to seventh position in the world as an exporter of goods, and unemployment had reached almost three million.

4

Regional inequality

In 1947 a young geographer in Jean Monnet's planning commission, Jean-François Gravier, published a best-selling book entitled *Paris et le désert français,* to highlight the economic disparities between the capital city and the rest of metropolitan France.[1] At that time income per capita in the Seine department of Paris was 80 per cent higher than the national average, while in the poorest parts of France – Brittany, Corsica, the south west and outside the cities in the southern Alps – the average per capita income was less than 75 per cent of the national average. Even worse was the fact that levels of inequality had been increasing rather than declining in the interwar period. After the war the consensus was that it was the central state, with its national plans to promote economic development, that was best placed to correct such disparities. However, disillusionment with the direction that national planning had taken under de Gaulle, illustrated by the sporadic outbursts of violence in the poorest regions, most notably Brittany and Corsica, by groups demanding some devolution of power or complete independence from France, led the Socialist party to consider the question of devolution.

The contraction of large parts of the manufacturing sector from the late 1970s onwards, which was as much a regional as a national economic problem, since most of the industries in question were located in the north and northeast of the country, added urgency to the debate. Under legislation passed in 1982 the new Socialist government promised to introduce local democracy by devolving power from the central state. The question was how much power and to which level of subnational government.

At that time there were 36,500 municipalities (communes) in France and 100 departments. Rather than merge the municipalities, as Denmark and Sweden opted to do, the Socialist government added a new layer of subnational government, that of directly elected regional councils. By 2015, regional inequalities in metropolitan France were judged to have reached their lowest level for 100 years. Average incomes in the Seine department were 35 per cent above the national average, falling to 27 per cent after income tax.[2] The nine richest departments had a per capita income more than 25.5 per cent higher than the national average, whereas after income tax the gap in incomes had fallen to 23.1 per cent.[3] By 2015, 30 years after the first direct elections to regional councils were held in France, there were no departments with an average per capita income below 75 per cent of the national average, while in some, particularly those along the Atlantic coast and in Brittany that had previously been among the poorest, per capita incomes had risen to reach the national average. In the north and vast areas of central and southern France and Corsica, average incomes remained below the national average but the gap had narrowed. Although the overseas territories and regions remained much poorer than metropolitan France, average living standards were well above those of neighbouring countries. Yet, in 2018 the questions of how much power and to which level of subnational government it should be given were still being debated in France. Far from ending the debate, the 1982 reforms were no more than a chapter in a long French story about the power of the central state. In this chapter we shall analyse it over the period 1945–2018.

THE ADMINISTRATIVE STRUCTURE
Deparaments in metropolitan France

Historically, France had been the archetype of a centralized and unitary state, dominated by its capital city, Paris.[4] At the time of the 1789 Revolution only 20 per cent of the population lived in towns, of which Paris was by far the largest.[5] It was the centre of wealth, culture, consumption and government. Its population of about 550,000 was larger than that of the six next biggest cities (Marseille, Lyon, Bordeaux, Rouen, Nantes, Lille) combined. There were no towns on the scale of those in England, such as Norwich, Manchester or Birmingham, at that time, while over ten million people lived in isolated farms or hamlets of fewer than 35 people. The way that the railways were built, imitating the road network that radiated from Paris rather than from Lyon as it had in Roman and feudal times, reinforced the centralized state control. When Paris was redesigned in the 1860s under the direction of the prefect of the Seine, Baron Haussmann, with new systems of sewers under the new grand boulevards, and electricity and telephone networks installed, Paris became the industrial centre of the country as well as the central seat of government, culture and education.

The revolutionary constituent assembly, based in Paris, had not tried to change the dominance of the capital city. But in abolishing the 32 provinces and replacing them with 83 departments, each roughly square in shape with borders drawn so that the main town was no more than one day's travel from anywhere in the department, it had tried to ensure some degree of territorial equality. It was Napoleon I who, in creating the position of the departmental prefect appointed by him and accountable to the government in Paris, ensured that the new political structure of the republic would be as centralized as the autocratic monarchy it replaced. This structure was to survive more or less intact until the creation of elected regional assemblies in 1982. By that date the number of departments in metropolitan France had risen to 96.

Departments and territories in overseas France

France also gained four overseas departments in 1946, when the overseas dependencies dating from the 1630s had chosen to become departments of France. These were Guadeloupe and its dependencies, Martinique, French Guiana and Réunion. At the same time, a number of overseas territories dating from the mid- to late nineteenth century opted for slightly more autonomy than the departments. These were French Polynesia, New Caledonia and its dependencies, the Wallis and Futuna Islands and French Antarctica (which was organized as an overseas territory in 1955). Together, the overseas departments and territories were called the Doms-Toms (Départements d'outre-mer, Territoires d'outre-mer). Another group of territories chose to have an even greater degree of autonomy. Known as collectivités territoriales, they were the eight islands of Saint-Pierre and Miquelon, the Comoros including Mayotte, French Somaliland and the New Hebrides. France lost three departments when Algeria became independent in 1962, and lost a number of territories that voted to become independent in the 1970s: the Comoros (apart from Mayotte), French Somaliland, which became Djibouti, and the New Hebrides, which became Vanuatu.[6]

Unlike the 14 British dependencies scattered across the globe, which are self-governing apart from in their foreign policy and defence, the French Doms-Toms are part of France and part of the European Union. French law applies, and they vote in French national and European elections. The exceptions are Saint-Pierre and Miquelon, Mayotte, New Caledonia, Wallis and Futuna and the two small dependencies of Guadeloupe (Saint-Barthélemy and Saint-Martin), all of which have their own customs, taxes and social security systems.[7] Among the many other differences between the French and British overseas territories are size, location and population. Altogether, the population of France overseas, at 2.5 million in 2018, was ten times that of the British territories. With a presence in each of the major oceans and seas these territories also give France an exclusive economic zone (EEZ) that is the largest in the world, slightly exceeding that of the United States but almost twice that of the United Kingdom.[8] French Guiana, the largest overseas territory of France (and of the EU), is one seventh the size of metropolitan France. Initially, it was probably best known for cayenne pepper, named after the capital. Today, however, French Guiana is more famous for the space station situated in Kourou from which the French Ariane rockets and the European space satellites have been launched (owing to its ideal location near the equator). With seven million hectares of largely uninhabited tropical forest, French Guiana is also one of the best functioning lungs of the planet. The economies of the French Doms-Toms (now officially called the Doms-Roms-Coms) are based primarily on tourism, although Guadeloupe, Martinique and Réunion export sugar and rum, Saint-Pierre and Miquelon export codfish, the Tuamotus in French Polynesia export pearls and New Caledonia exports nickel and cobalt used in alloys for aircraft engine parts and in lithium batteries for electric cars, while Mayotte exports the essential oil ylang ylang, an ingredient of perfume. Despite rising unemployment throughout the overseas regions, it is the continued allegiance of New Caledonia that is most in doubt. The favoured location for French nuclear testing when the Sahara Desert was no longer an option, it has long been divided over the advantages of remaining attached to a country on the other side of the world. In 1998 the French government agreed to allow it to hold up to three referendums on independence. In the first one, held 20 years later in 2018, 56 per cent of voters rejected independence. In the second referendum held on 4 October 2020 the majority voting against independence had fallen to 53 per cent.

The two small islands of Mayotte (Grande Terre and Petite Terre) became the fifth overseas department, and the 101st department overall, on 31 March 2011, having previously had a special "departmental collectivity" status since rejecting independence in 1994. With a per capita GDP almost half that of France's other overseas departments and four times lower than that of metropolitan France, in 2012 Mayotte was assigned an "ultra-peripheral region" of the EU by the European Council, which made it eligible for substantial structural funds.[9]

One reason why Mayotte, and indeed all the Doms-Roms-Coms, had chosen to remain part of France despite the huge gap in per capita incomes between them and the metropole was that they were increasingly much better off than neighbouring countries in spite of having expanding populations. In 2014 the per capita GDP of Mayotte, for example, was ten times higher than that of the Comoros and neighbouring Kenya, and 20 times higher than Mozambique or Tanzania.[10] (That may of course be due to the large number of French civil servants living there). Guaranteed a certain minimum level of funding, education and welfare benefits from mainland France, as well as the right to migrate there, they are much more dependent on metropolitan France than in 1945, when they had chosen to become departments. However, with unemployment increasing to much higher levels than in metropolitan France, and an increasing feeling of having been abandoned – a feeling that was exploited by the extreme right – solutions need to be found to their economic problems.[11]

Municipalities (communes)

In 1982, when the commitment to creating directly elected regional councils was made by a French government for the first time, most people in metropolitan France identified with the older structure of the commune. These ranged in size from Paris, which was both a commune and a department, to Rochefourchat in the region of Auvergne Rhône-Alpes (which by 2018 had a permanent population of one, albeit with a number of second home owners). About 15,000 communes had a population of under 300.[12] Each had an elected mayor who, unlike the prefect of the department, was traditionally from the area and remained in office throughout their career. As a result, unlike the prefect, who was moved from time to time to ensure that they did not prioritize the interests of the department over those of Paris and the central government, the mayor was seen to be in touch with local interests and concerns.

At home in their commune, historically, few people outside Brittany, Corsica, the Basque country and Alsace had any sense of belonging to a

Figure 4.1 French overseas departments and territories

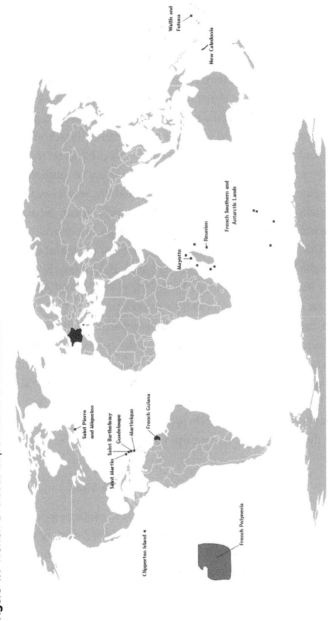

Source: by Hoshie, CC BY-SA 3.0, https://commons.wikimedia.org/w/index.php?curid=2342934.

region or demanding any devolution of political power to it. Even where regional groups did exist, such as the fascist one known as the "green shirts", founded in Brittany in the 1930s by Henri Dorgères, they wanted less rather than more government. Blaming politicians for the poverty experienced by peasants, they called for taxes and imports to be cut to safeguard what they considered to be the two constants in life: work and family. According to Dorgères and members of his peasant defence committees, France had no need for either the taxman or the school teacher.[13] This sense of rootedness in the soil, of family values based on restoring the authority of the father, defending the moral virtues of motherhood and encouraging unequal inheritance among children, was shared by many in the Vichy state. They too rejected the modern urban secular values of the republic, which were based on education, merit and rewarding labour. This went together with restoring much of the moral authority of the Catholic Church, which they felt had been undermined by the secular republic. But the law introduced by the Vichy state on 19 April 1941 to create new regional bodies owed little to such traditional values. Located between the central government and the department, the new regional bodies were designed to increase rather than reduce the control of the central state. At a time when communications were more difficult due to the disruption caused by the war, the purpose of the new regional bodies, headed by a regional prefect assisted by a police intendant and an economic intendant, was to maintain order and repress dissent.[14] It was not at all what the far-right regional groups had demanded in the 1930s.

REGIONAL PLANNING AFTER 1945

After the Second World War, the priority of the planners was to expand the national economy by investing mainly in industry, starting with heavy industry but very quickly including others. With much of the expansion taking place where industry was already located, in the north and east of the country as well as Paris and the Paris basin (the Île-de-France), this aggravated regional disparities. In 1950 the ministry for reconstruction and development had produced a detailed plan for managing rural develop-ment (the Plan national d'aménagement du territoire), but while a national fund had been set up to implement it, because it was not integrated into the national planning process the plan gathered dust on the shelves of the ministry in Paris. Some groups, most notably in Alsace and Brittany,[15] agi-tated for regional or regionalized economic planning, but the association of regionalism with Vichy undermined support for it elsewhere.

It was not until 1955, with the prospect of France becoming part of a common market in western Europe, a move that threatened to widen the territorial economic imbalance still further, that the first steps were taken to correct this inequality. The question of how best to do this was one that was to exercise politicians and officials for decades. In the first instance, under a decree law passed in June 1955, 21 new regions (Corsica was added in 1970) were envisaged, each to have a regional action programme drawn up by civil servants based in Paris. Apart from Brittany, Alsace and, later, Corsica, few of the regions were based on historical, cultural or ethnic identities.[16] Worse still, in order to avoid any hint of collusion or pressure from local interests, the civil servants were not allowed to visit the regions in question.[17] Seeing the futility of the exercise, they quickly abandoned it.[18] Nonetheless, the 1955 legislation laid down a marker, and in subsequent legislation in 1958, 1960, 1964 and 1972 the regions, or *circonscriptions d'action régionale* (areas for regional action) as they were known, were to become a necessary regional part of state-led economic and infrastructural planning.

In 1958 a regional committee was set up within the Commissariat général au plan to draw up separate economic and social development plans for each of the 21 regions. Until these had been completed, the third plan simply included in its single chapter on regions the issue of tackling the increasing concentration of economic activity in the Paris area.[19] The general objective was to reduce regional inequalities and maintain the via-bility of rural France. In 1963 a national administrative agency, DATAR (Délégation à l'aménagement du territoire et à l'action régionale), was set up, attached to the prime minister's office, to work in partnership with regional economic development commissions, CODER (Commissions de développement économique régional). This was the first time that regions were represented in a public body.[20] But, to reinforce central state control over regional planning, a regional prefect was appointed to supplement the work of the departmental prefect. Policies were determined by the central government and funds distributed downwards with little input from the regions.

One of the first tasks of DATAR was to devolve jobs from Paris and discourage the population drift from the provinces to the Paris area.[21] Between 1946 and 1954 net migration to the Paris region (the departments of Seine and Seine et l'Oise) had been 80,000 per year. It expanded to 90,000 per year between 1954 and 1962, but then fell to 60,000 per year between 1963 and 1968, after the creation of DATAR. With the average wage in Paris 50 per cent higher than in the provinces, the pull of the capital was difficult to resist. By the end of the 1960s, 21.5 per cent of those in employment lived in Paris, and the gap in average income per household between Paris and Provence Côte d'Azur (the second most wealthy region) was greater than between the latter and Limousin, the poorest region.[22] DATAR, through its control over a fund for regional policies, managed to influence the location of infrastructure investments and provide subsidies for firms locating in targeted areas, particularly in the west and south of France. The car firm Citroën, for example, was offered a subsidy to open a branch in Rennes in Brittany. In order to deter new investment and construction in Paris, special taxes were imposed on new office construction, while at the same time efforts were made to promote the development of infrastructure (in tourism, transport, telecommunications and education) in the targeted areas.

A combination of a general improvement in living standards and the extension of paid holidays from 15 days in 1936 to three weeks in 1956 and four weeks in May 1969 created an irreversible rise in the habit of going away for the summer holidays. Beginning in the early 1960s, over 20 million French people went on holiday in France, rising to 26 million in 1975 and 32 million in 1988: a trend that was not affected by the economic crisis in the 1970s and 1980s.[23] Together with an increasing number of foreign visitors, they made France the most important tourist destination in the world. In the early 1960s DATAR selected the poor area of Languedoc in the south of France as an ideal location for the creation of a number of new holiday towns along the coast. In 1975 the A9 motorway linking Orange and Narbonne was completed, followed by the opening of new air routes. The economic results were seen as impressive. In the 20 new coastal towns the objective of creating 328,000 beds and 65,000 jobs was exceeded, making tourism more successful than wine production in the area. But there were concerns when the number of second homes reached 80 per cent of the total, with accusations that the local economy was being sacrificed for the benefit of tourists.

Lessons were learned and the development of the coast of Aquitaine, in south-west France and its hinterland, was planned differently. In 1970 the Parc Naturel Régional des Landes de Gascogne was officially opened, and three years later a committee to preserve the environment of the Aquitaine coast was set up. Between 1970 and 1982 the number of beds created on this coast expanded from 310,000 to 515,000, but this time it was seen to be expansion on a human scale: *l'aménagement à visage humain*.

And with 45 per cent of French people spending their holidays by the sea compared with 16 per cent in the mountains, 23 per cent in the countryside, 8 per cent in towns, and 7 per cent touring around, by the mid-1970s, the development met demand.[24]

Private interests were quick to respond to the growing leisure market. As early as 1960, for example, a small hotel group, Accor, was established, which 60 years later had become the single largest hospitality company in Europe and the sixth largest worldwide. Modelled initially on the American motel, which combined standardized accommodation with car parking facilities, it was an entirely new concept in France at the time and one that lent itself to rapid growth. Accor went on to develop hotels catering to different budgets, opening the first Novotel outside Lille in 1967, the first Mercure in Sait-Witz in northern France and the first Ibis in Bordeaux in 1974. Six years later it bought the luxury chain Sofitel to add to its range. Over the same period the once exclusive winter sport of skiing was opened up to the French working class, with purpose-built Alpine resorts in Courcheval, La Plagne and Val Thorens being developed. In 1961, Baron Edmond de Rothschild spotted the opportunity to develop the small Belgian-owned Club Méditerranée (Club Med), which had been started in 1950 by Gérard Blitz, a yogi, as a small colony of tents on the island of Majorca, into a global holiday business. In 2013 it was bought by the Chinese conglomerate group, Fosun.

Another idea started under the fifth plan (1966–70) was to target a number of cities, or city-regions, to counterbalance the pull of the Paris region. Lyon-Saint-Etienne, Marseille, Lille-Roubaix-Tourcoing, Metz-Nancy, Bordeaux, Toulouse, Nantes-Saint Nazaire and Strasbourg were chosen partly because they were sufficiently far from Paris and partly because they were seen to have the potential for urban and industrial expansion or regeneration.[25] Incentives were given to firms to relocate in the hope that this would create growth poles to attract other firms. With the successful development of the aircraft industry in Toulouse, it was hoped, for example, to regenerate the surrounding area, particularly the former industrial towns of Decazeville, Pamiers, Tarbes, Auzat and Sabart, to enable it to match the industrial cluster around Lyon. Decazeville, 165 km northeast of Toulouse, was a town where coal had been mined since the fifteenth century and where one of the first coke-fired blast furnaces had opened in 1826. However, without local supplies of iron ore, skilled labour or good transport links it had been unable to compete domestically or internationally after 1860 and gone into a long period of decline.[26] Under the Monnet Plan (1947–52) the coal mines had been modernized but they remained uncompetitive. For this and many other reasons, including the fact that there were no other large cities in the region to match the cluster in the region of Rhône-Alpes, which included Lyon, Grenoble, Saint-Etienne, Valence, Annecy, Roanne and Chambéry, the strategy was not considered a success.

Another criticism levied against the government's entire regional policy was that it was too centralized. Since the regions themselves had no power, few people identified with them. When asked in 1965 to which region they belonged, 82 per cent of those sampled in Brittany said Brittany, but only 4 per cent of those in Midi-Pyrénées got the name of their region right.[27] Most people continued to identify most closely with their commune, but given that there were over 36,000 of these they were not considered a viable unit for regional policy.

Opposition to centralized power was one of the many grievances that sparked the protests in 1968. De Gaulle proposed a number of minor changes after 1968 in a hastily drawn up attempt to appease the growing demands for some devolution of power to the regions. These included giving control of public utilities, housing and urban development to the regions, and allowing them to borrow money as well as to enter into contracts and agreements with other regions. When de Gaulle put the reforms to the country in a referendum and offered to resign if they were rejected, with the opposition urging people to vote against the proposals and the popular former prime minister Georges Pompidou offering to stand as a presidential candidate if de Gaulle were to resign, the 80-year-old president stood little chance of winning. Predictably, the only areas that voted in favour of the reform were ten departments covering most of Brittany and part of Normandy, Corsica, the Basque country and Alsace. Following de Gaulle's resignation, President Pompidou went on to create councils in each of the regions in July 1972. However, they had limited powers and were still financially and administratively dependent on the central state and therefore legally and politically less important than the departments and municipalities. The only consultative powers they had were in relation to national planning. Regions were also created in the four overseas departments.[28] In 1976 the Île de France became a region, whereas previously it had been a district.

Unemployment as a regional problem

The rise of mass unemployment resulting from the economic crisis of the mid-1970s was more of a regional than a national problem in France, and it was this that undermined the credibility of national planning and brought regional reform firmly back onto the political agenda. The unemployment crisis hit different areas with varying levels of intensity. The worst affected was the northeast. Formerly one of the most industrialized and prosperous parts of France, by the 1970s its economy was still dominated by the traditional industries of textiles, mining (coal in Nord-Pas-de-Calais and iron in Lorraine), steel, machinery, automobiles and basic chemicals, although it did have some more recent industries such as household goods. Much of the employment was concentrated in large oligopolistic firms often controlled from outside the region. Levels of skills and education were low and lower than in the rest of France. A further problem was that there were no major towns. Between 1976 and 1986 more than 400,000 jobs were lost, representing almost 30 per cent of the initial industrial employment. In the Nord-Pas-de-Calais the fall in the numbers employed in industries other than coal, steel and textiles happened at a faster rate than in the economy as a whole (15.9 per cent compared with 12.5 per cent). Unlike elsewhere in France, the collapse of employment in industry was not offset by a boom in services in the private sector. Although about 250,000 service sector jobs were created, they were all in the public sector – in government, education and health – and funded out of taxation. One conclusion drawn was that the region lacked sufficient intellectual, entrepreneurial, financial or institutional resources to enable it to attract many new activities. Although more people left the area in search of employment than moved to it, the population growth was higher than the national average, resulting in more people looking for fewer jobs. Unemployment levels in the northeast were therefore higher than for the country as a whole, and those for the long-term unemployed were particularly high.

By contrast the south (Aquitaine, Midi-Pyrénées, Languedoc-Roussillon, Provence, Côte d'Azur and Corsica) was much less affected by the contraction of industry, mainly because there was much less of it to start with. Most of the industry in the south was in small or medium-sized firms making consumer goods: textiles, garments, shoes, wood, paper and food. Its share in value added or in total employment was much lower than the national average, reflecting the relative failure of the regional policy effort in the 1960s to promote industrialization in that part of the country. In 1982, levels of education, if not of skills, were high, with the share of people aged 15 or over holding a degree about 7.5 per cent, compared with 5.9 per cent for the northeast and 6.5 per cent for France as a whole (excluding the Paris region). Public education was provided free of charge and financed by central government. There was also a network of old well-functioning cities: Bordeaux, Toulouse, Montpellier, Marseille and Nice. Over the ten-year period 1976–86 only 70,000 jobs were lost in the south, representing 10 per cent of employment compared with 19 per cent for France as a whole and 29 per cent for the northeast. Employment in the consumer goods industry fell by 21 per cent, whereas it fell by only 5 per cent in equipment industry, largely due to the success of the aircraft industry (Airbus in Toulouse) and to all the related industries such as electronics, computers and other technology-intensive industries. While the entry of Spain and Portugal into the EC threated the agricultural sector in the south of France, it stimulated firms such as Alcatel, Ford, IBM, Matra, Motorola and Thomson, who were attracted to the region by the good climate and the educated labour force. The service sector also expanded, with many new jobs being created in finance and telecommunications, quite independently of industry. In fact, one of the problems was seen to be the contrast between the cities in the south and the surrounding hinterland.

The experience of Paris and the Île-de-France was different again. The area was highly urbanized, with its GDP in 1986 being 71 per cent higher than in the north, and 65 per cent higher than in the south. Its economy was highly diversified, continuing to dominate government, finance, education and research, and yet it had twice as many industrial jobs as in the south and 86 per cent of the number in the northeast. Where it lost industrial jobs (only 12 per cent between 1978 and 1984) this was intentional as part of a deliberate strategy. As a result, the income gap between Paris and the rest of France began to increase as the economy slowed down after 1974.

SOCIALIST REGIONAL REFORMS FROM 1982

It was in this context that the Socialist government elected in 1981 made decentralization and regionalism a central plank of its policy to democratize policy-making in France once again. Spearheaded by Gaston Defferre, the mayor of Marseille and minister of the interior and decentralization, the reforms officially aimed to give the regions the power and the financial autonomy to develop their own economic development plans, which would fit into, rather than be determined by, the national economic plan. Decentralization was to be an answer to the industrial decline and unemployment that afflicted certain parts of the country, while also responding to the demands for recognition of the distinct cultural and political differences felt in others. Central to the reform legislation passed in 1982 were direct elections to the 26 new regional councils, 21 in metropolitan France and 5 in the Doms-Toms, on which the new legitimacy of the region rested.

These regional elections were postponed until 1985, however, as the government sought to define its national economic policy. The official eighth plan, covering the period 1981–85, was shelved, to be replaced by a short interim one covering the two years 1982 and 1983. The decision taken in 1983 to abandon the reflationary policy of the first two years and cut back on public spending marked the end of any attempt to save the jobs in the traditional industries located in the north and northeast. When elections were finally held, it was the opposition parties on the right that won the majority of the seats in the new regional councils.

From 1984 onwards the interests of the financial services and of the small high-tech industries springing up in the south of France prevailed over those of the traditional industries in the north. Whereas the modernizing state of the 1950s had responded to a wide range of interests by channelling credit into productive investment, and in the 1960s the Gaullist state had supported large firms in order to build a powerful French industrial base, now in the 1980s the state was not only promoting small and medium-sized firms in industry but also, more importantly, promoting the service sector of the economy. The new direction of policy tied in with the enthusiasm for creating science parks that was spreading throughout the Western world at the time. Based on the idea that innovation stemmed from the cross-fertilization of ideas between research institutions and small, modern high-tech firms, it was argued that the regions were better placed than the central state to promote the essential networking between research and industry. The creation of the technology park at Sophia-Antipolis outside Nice, which was started in 1970 and completed in 1984, was ahead of its time in this respect. But it was the liberalization of trade in services as part of the Single European Act passed in 1986 (see Chapter 6) that created the framework for the new policy. Ironically, the completion of the single market in 1992, which included the removal of controls over capital movements within the new European Union, meant that neither the regions nor the central state could use many of the instruments, such as direct grants and subsidies, that had previously been crucial for promoting regional development. After 1992 firms were free to move out of France altogether if they did not like the terms being offered by the regions.

But, before the single market was completed, there was a brief transitional period between 1985 and 1992 that offered a window of opportunity for those regions that were politically united and had a clear objective to take advantage of their new powers. Brittany is one example of such a region. With the objective of building on the activities the central planners had started in 1961, when Rennes, the regional capital, had been chosen as a new base for the Citroën car firm, in 1985 the newly elected regional council managed to get state subsidies to attract the Peugeot car maker to create 14,000 additional jobs in the city. This was to make Rennes home to one of the biggest car plants in France for many years.

After 1992 and the completion of the single market, the regions had to rely much more on their own resources than on the central state to promote development. Although they were now free to adopt their own plans, having consulted with local authorities, they were not given any additional financial resources to accompany their new powers and responsibilities. They were not allowed to set up new taxes, since only the central government could do this according to the constitution. Facing considerable opposition to increasing taxes, the regions' budgets were generally too small to enable them to undertake any significant regional economic development programmes, had they even wanted to do so. In the view of one commentator, the system was clearly designed to control the financial autonomy of the region and the size of its budget.[29] As a result, in most regions priority was given to building secondary schools rather than intervening in the economy.[30]

In many ways the 1982 reforms increased the differences between strong and weak regions. Rhône-Alpes soon emerged as a strong region benefiting from having a high level of socio-economic development centred on the Rhône valley and the high-tech industrial complex around Grenoble. But weaker regions such as Languedoc-Roussillon and Corsica, which were very divided politically and culturally, proved unable to use their new powers to promote the regional economy. Since most people identified with the commune, with its mayor and town hall, where all the most important events in life were recorded, rather than with the region, the impact of the reforms was limited. For that same reason there was considerable resistance to all attempts to merge any of the 36,500 communes into larger units to improve the efficiency of their services. As an alternative, the government passed legislation in 1992 and 1999, accompanied by financial incentives, giving communes the right to join forces with others to form what were called "public intercommunal co-operation establishments" (EPCIs). But, instead of producing greater efficiency, the new legislation resulted in many cases in a duplication of services. To solve this problem, legislation setting out the division of power and responsibility between the three layers of subnational government was passed in 2003.[31] Regions were to take the lead in economic and employment issues, while departments would lead in health and social issues and communes would have responsibility for controlling building permits among other things.[32] Each of the three levels of subnational government still had the power to raise taxes but not to create new ones. They were obliged by law to fund all of their operating expenses out of their revenue and could borrow only to finance capital investment. The central state retained full responsibility for labour market and health policies, overseen at the local level by a regional prefect appointed by the state.[33]

Although France compared quite favourably with other OECD countries in terms of regional inequality in 2003 (the Gini index of inequality of GDP per capita between regions was lower in France at 0.12 than the average of 0.16 among the 26 OECD member states), it was felt that the increased competition stemming from globalization had called into question the very concept of local development.[34] The state could no longer give subsidies to prop up sectors or industries in decline. It could no longer dictate the location of industry, since firms could easily relocate. The evolution of policies in the European single market had reinforced this imperative leading to growing economic and political tension between rural and urban areas and between large metroplitan areas and regions. The financial crisis of 2008–09 made the problems much worse.

Whereas the effects of previous shocks in 1974, 1982 and 1992 had been lessened by targeted public spending, the crisis in public finance, known as the sovereign debt crisis, which followed the economic shock of 2008–09 meant that the state had to cut back rather than increase its public spending, according to the rules of the European Central Bank (see Chapter 6). On the eve of the 2008 financial crisis the total regional spending was about 20 per cent of total public expenditure. Of that spending, taxes covered about 50 per cent and transfers from central government about 35 per cent. These transfers were designed to reduce some of the differences in purchasing power (ratios of expenditure to revenue) between subnational governments. Following the crisis, and paying scant regard for the policy of decentralization, the state closed down hospitals, military barracks and law courts, thereby undermining the viability of many towns. It was said that the ministry of finance had become the sole arbiter of regional policy.

Impact of the financial crisis of 2008–09 on the regions

During the crisis, although 350,000 industrial jobs were lost, mostly in regions which were already in decline, household income continued to increase across all regions in metropolitan France. However, the incomes actually earned from productive work increased only in the Paris area and, to a lesser extent, in Rhône-Alpes and Provence-Alpes-Côte d'Azur. Elsewhere, it was due to public sector wages and social benefits that income levels held up. The six worst affected regions, where 30 per cent of the total jobs were lost even though they accounted for only 15 per cent of the population, were Haute-Normandie, Franche-Comté, Lorraine, Picardie, Campagne-Ardenne and Limousin. All apart from Limousin were the most industrialized parts of the country. While this had also been the case in 1982 and 1992, what was new in 2008 was that employment in the big cities, apart from Grenoble and Strasbourg, was maintained. Also spared the worst of the recession were the west and south of France, as was Corsica, where employment actually increased. But in the overseas regions of Guadeloupe, Martinique, Réunion and Guiana unemployment, which was already over 20 per cent in 2008, reached 24 per cent by 2014.

The crisis thus further fractured the national economy territorially and deepened the divisions between regions to reveal what were described as four different French economies.[35] The first was a dynamic productive economy concentrated in the biggest cities, where 36 per cent of the population lived and where the most competitive branches of the economy were located. The second was a non-productive yet dynamic economy situated to the west of a line drawn between Cherbourg in the north and Nice in the south, where 44 per cent of the population made a living from a combination of tourism, retirement pensions and public sector wages. The third was a struggling productive economy composed of depressed industrial areas mainly in the north of the country, where 8 per cent of the population seemed unable to reverse the area's long-term decline. Finally, there was a non-productive economy in the northeast, where industrial decline was so entrenched that the 12 per cent of the population who lived there existed entirely on social benefits.

It was not of course only in France that the future of regional policy was being questioned. At the height of the public debt crisis, with governments everywhere cutting their spending, Edward Glaeser, a professor of economics at Harvard University, published a book in 2011 entitled *Triumph of the City: How Our Greatest Invention Makes Us Richer, Smarter, Greener, Healthier and Happier*. To great critical acclaim Glaeser argued that regional policies had never worked and should be abandoned. Since it was large cities that had proved to be successful in attracting investment and expanding employment, Glaeser advocated a policy of investing in people rather than places and encouraging individuals to be free to live wherever they could find employment.

SOCIALIST REGIONAL REFORMS, 2014

In France, however, it was argued that in some respects regional policy had worked. It was thanks to the redistribution from wealthier to poorer that the most geographically peripheral regions in the west of France had enjoyed the greatest net creation of employment and the greatest reduction in poverty since the 1980s. The response of President Hollande's Socialist government to the problem of growing inequality in other parts of France, at a time when the deficit in public finance was also increasing, was to transform DATAR into the Commisariat général à l'égalité des territoires in 2013 and, the following year, to merge a number of regions, bringing the total in metropolitan France down from 22 to 13 while leaving the five overseas regions of Guadeloupe, Martinique, Réunion, French Guiana and Mayotte unchanged. The stated purpose of the reform was to align the size of the French regions more closely with those in other European member states, particularly Germany and Italy, by creating regions of about four million inhabitants, instead of two million. By ensuring that each region included a large city it was hoped to stimulate employment and thereby weaken the support for the Front National that was growing in many small towns and rural areas.[36] In the short term however the reform proposals provoked considerable opposition. In what proved to be highly charged negotiations, a new region in eastern France, called the Grand-Est, was to be an uncomfortable *ménage à trois* formed from Alsace, Lorraine and Champagne-Ardenne. This was resisted by Alsace,

which feared that Strasbourg would lose out to Metz and Nancy, but supported by Champagne, which had not wanted to merge with Picardy.
On the other hand there was no Grand-Ouest merger of Brittany, where
employment had been rising between 2000 and 2013 and which voted
for the left, with the Pays de la Loire to form an equally large region in
the west to rival the Île de France. Both Brittany and the Pays de la Loire
remained unattached, as did Corsica, the Île-de-France, the Centre-Val-
de-Loire and Provence-Alpes-Côte d'Azur. Apart from Corsica, which
had the status of a territory rather than a region, all were relatively prosperous and tended not to vote for the FN. Elsewhere, Aquitaine, Limousin and Poitou-Charentes, where support for the FN was growing, were
also obliged to agree to a *ménage à trois* known as Nouvelle-Aquitaine,
while the other regions of Burgundy and Franche-Comté, Upper and
Lower Normandy, and Auvergne and Rhône-Alpes were allowed to negotiate more traditional unions with one partner. This was also the case
for Languedoc-Roussillon and Midi-Pyrénées, which became Occitanie,
and Nord-Pas-de-Calais and Picardy, which became Hauts-de-France.
There was a 20 per cent economic gap between the poorest of the new
regions in metropolitan France, Hauts-de-France, and the second richest,
Auvergne-Rhône-Alpes. This was a smaller gap than elsewhere in the EU.
But the reform was not seen as a solution to the problem of the poorest regions with the highest unemployment. Of the merger of Nord-Pas-
de-Calais and Picardy it was said "deux fragilités ne peuvent donner une
force" (strength does not come from combining weaknesses).[37] Nor was it
seen to be an answer to the problem of the overwhelming power of Paris,
since no new region was created to be as rich as the Île-de-France,[38] which
had the highest GDP per capita and the lowest number of retired people.

But if the reforms had reduced the differences in GDP per capita
between the new larger regions, which all now included a successful city,
the greatest inequalities were found to exist at the level of the commune.
Since the communes were unable to raise much revenue from business
taxes and at the same time spent more to alleviate higher levels of poverty, increasing other taxes, such as those on property, was likely to cause

people to move out of the area, making the problems worse. It was now suggested that the policy of creating public sector jobs as a means of redistributing income from wealthier to poorer regions or within regions might have aggravated the inequality between households and neighbourhoods while reducing regional inequality. Since the public sector jobs created in poorer regions benefited mainly middle-class married women, thereby creating a second income and thus a great increase in household income, they accentuated the division between middle-class households and those most vulnerable to deindustrialization who could not, due to a lack of appropriate qualifications, take these jobs. As a result the income of those living in working-class neighbourhoods in poorer regions had fallen, dragging the area down. What was needed, it was claimed, was research into the impact on local neighbourhoods of public spending directed at reducing both interpersonal and regional inequality.[39]

With very low approval ratings, Hollande became the first head of state of the Fifth Republic not to seek re-election after his first term. On winning the second round run off against Marine Le Pen in the presidential elections in May 2017, President Macron called for some recentralization of power, arguing that if everything but the highest level of policy were decentralized, there would be nothing left for the centre to redistribute. But he and his party, La république en marche! (LREM), were accused of turning the clock back to before the 1982 reforms. On 26 September 2018 a new movement called Territoires Unis was formed in Marseille, bringing together the associations of French mayors, departments and regions to lobby for greater decentralization and accusing Macron of trying to play the regions off against each other in order to strengthen power at the centre. At the same time the FN was calling for even more centralization. Two months later the regional debate was given greater urgency when the introduction by President Macron's government of a new "green" tax on fuel to compensate for a reduction in corporation tax sparked months of protest across France. Led by the *gilets jaunes*, the protesters pitted rural France against the big cities, arguing that it was in the hinterland of cities and the small towns that the greatest inequality existed. Property prices in

Bordeaux, the city that emerged as one of the centres of the protests, had risen by 40 per cent over ten years, making it the second most expensive city in which to live in France.[40] The completion of the TGV line in July 2017, which reduced the train journey time from Paris to Bordeaux to two hours, had greatly accelerated the rise in property prices and rents in the city. For those who worked but could no longer afford to live there and were reliant on private cars, due to the years of underinvestment in local trains or buses, the introduction of the new tax was final proof that their interests were being ignored. Their protests were seen as part of the populist movement against globalization felt in many parts of Europe and the United States. They were part of the "revolt of the places that don't matter": part of the revolt against the big cities into which so much money and wealth had been pouring since the financial crisis.[41]

Table 4.1 Unemployment rates in the French overseas departments, 2003–14 (%)

	Total	Guadeloupe	Martinique	Guiana	Réunion
2003	24.6	22	17.2	20	30.6
2004	25.2	20.8	17.8	21.7	31.9
2005	23.5	21.7	15.2	20.8	29
2006	24.1	22.4	19.7	23.9	27.2
2007	21.5	20.6	17.9	18.4	24.4
2008	21.7	20	18.5	19	24.6
2009	23.1	20.7	19.2	17.9	27.3
2010	24.1	22.4	18.6	17.5	28.8
2011	24	20.9	18.2	18.4	29.3
2012	23.8	21.3	18.4	19.4	28.5
2013	24.9	23.5	19.6	21.8	28.7
2014	24.1	23.7	19.4	22.3	26.8

Source: INSEE, Marché du Travail. Séries longues, 2015.

Research, however, showed that the deepest poverty and the most entrenched segregation was in the big cities, among people without work, where inequality had increased considerably since the beginning of the millenium. The overall poverty rate within the richest region, the Île-de-France, was 15.9 per cent in 2015 compared with 12.3 per cent before the financial crisis.[42]

The rate was even worse in the overseas departments and territories, where their reclassification as regions had not reduced the growing inequality compared with metropolitan France. Unemployment rates of between 24 per cent and 32 per cent in Réunion over the period 2003–14 were higher than anywhere in the northeast of France.

CONCLUSION

The decision to create directly elected regional councils in France, with the opportunity and responsibility for drawing up programmes for the economic development of the region, was a tentative move away from the centralized policies and national planning that preceded their creation. Coinciding with the government's decision to promote the expansion of the service sector and of small high-tech industries, the regional reforms offered little hope for the declining regions in the north and northeast of France that had suffered from the greatest job losses in the traditional industries of textiles, coal, steel in the 1970s. The decision to complete the single market and thereby remove the instruments that the state had previously used to promote regional development, such as subsidies and public sector contracts, which now were known collectively as non-tariff barriers (NTBs) to trade, left the state with little option but to create public sector jobs in the poorest regions to reduce unemployment. The west and south west of the country, which had recorded the greatest levels of poverty in 1945, had become more prosperous and attractive places in which to work, visit or retire. At the same time, other parts of the south, particularly along the A9 motorway between Perpignan and Orange, contained great poverty. The Saint-Jacques district of Perpignan was singled out by INSEE in 2013 as being the poorest in France. In nearby Béziers the unemployment rate was 23.4 per cent in 2016.[43] Parts of the north, which had previously been among the richest and most industrialized in France, had become areas in which the majority of people relied either on public sector employment or social benefits. In the northeast most people relied entirely on social benefits. Decentralization had not led to the creation of new jobs to replace those lost in the 1970s and 1980s. To these problems was added a new one: that of growing interpersonal inequality, which was most marked in the wealthiest cities. The reclassification of the overseas departments and territories as regions did not change or improve their growing inequality compared with metropolitan France. Their unemployment rates were higher than anywhere in the northeast of France. The Covid-19 pandemic, known in France as the *crise sanitaire*, exposed the effects of years of austerity on public health provision across the country, although France still had three times as many hospital beds and twice as many beds in intensive care as the UK.[44] It also exposed the rising levels of interpersonal inequality, and it is to these that we now turn.

5

Interpersonal inequality

As we saw in Chapter 4, the greatest inequalities after the Second World War were between those living and working across a range of sectors and activities in Paris and those working in the rest of the country, in what Gravier referred to as the French "desert". Even in that desert there were distinctions within the agricultural sector between the large arable farms in the north and the Île-de-France, which employed paid labour, and the small family-run, mixed farms elsewhere. There were also distinctions between those working in industry, mainly in the north and northeast of the country, and those working in the service sector, spread across France. It was the rapid growth of the economy and the movement of millions of people out of low-productivity jobs into higher productivity ones that led to a rise in living standards and a reduction of the gap between Paris and the rest of the country. It was when growth rates slowed down after the mid-1970s and the tens of thousands made redundant in the traditional industries could not find alternative employment in the expanding service sector that inequality began to rise and mass unemployment became a structural problem. Although it was never as high as in the neighbouring countries of Italy and Spain, unemployment became a persistent problem for France, peaking at 10.8 per cent of the active labour force (2.8 million) in 1997, and reaching a new high of over 3 million people in 2015.[1] On the other hand, income inequality levels, although rising from the 1980s onwards, were also lower than in Spain and Italy, and were much lower than in the United States and the United Kingdom. In this chapter we shall analyse the record of the French government in addressing the main forms of interpersonal inequality over the period since the "30 glorious years" came to an end.

INCOME INEQUALITY

During the early 1980s, when many OECD countries were following the example of the United States and cutting taxes and public spending, the French Socialist government did the opposite. It increased income taxes on middle and high earners while introducing an entirely new tax on wealth to help fund its nationalization and expansionist public spending programme.[2] When the right-wing government under Jacques Chirac returned to power in 1986 with a commitment to reverse the national-ization programme implemented by the Socialists, it did not cut taxes.[3] Indeed, taxation as a proportion of GDP continued to grow in the decades that followed. Even after the financial crisis of 2008–09 and the ensuing sovereign debt crisis, which ushered in years of austerity throughout the developed world, France once again increased taxes and spending to mit-igate the impact of the crisis on those worst affected. As a result, whereas in much of the developed world the inequality in incomes and wealth that had fallen since the First World War began to rise again from the 1980s, in France the growth in inequality was much less marked.

The situation was particularly extreme in the United States between 1990 and 2018, where the poorest half of the population saw their share of national income fall by 25.6 per cent while that of the richest 10 per cent increased by 20.5 per cent. Taxes and social security contributions as a proportion of GDP fell from 29.1 per cent in 1974 to 24.3 per cent in 2018, while the proportion of GDP spent by America's federal, state and local authorities increased slightly from 33 per cent to 35 per cent over the same period. In France on the other hand, taxes and social security contributions as a proportion of GDP, rose from 35.5 per cent in 1974 to 48.4 per cent in 2018, the highest in the world,[4] while government spending rose from 39.7 per cent in 1974 to 57 per cent of GDP in 2018, also the highest in the world.[5] The stock of public capital in France expressed as a percentage of GDP, at 78 per cent, was second only to that of Japan at 120 per cent in 2015.[6] In sharp contrast to the United States, the share of national income held by the richest 10 per cent in France increased by 6 per cent, rising from 30 per cent to 32 per cent over the period 1990–2018, while the national income share of the poorest 50 per cent fell by 8 per cent, from 24 per cent of the total to 22 per cent.[7]

Figure 5.1 Inequality in disposable incomes in 2019 (as measured by the Gini coefficient)

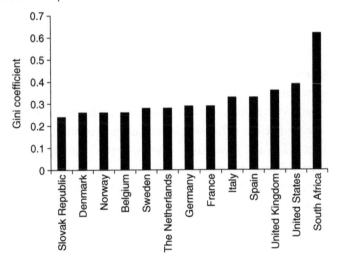

Source: OECD, "Income Inequality" (2020).

In 2018, the OECD judged France to be one of the most equal countries in the world in terms of income. Where disparities did exist they were, according to OECD, moderate and broadly stable over time, even among the wealthiest cohort. At the same time, it observed that the real disposable income of the poorest households had risen much faster than either the median or the top deciles since the beginning of the millenium. Housing conditions and work–life balance were also above the OECD average and monetary poverty was lower in comparison with other developed countries.

Based on the commonly used Gini scale of measurement, where a score of 0 equals full equality, and 1 complete inequality, France had a coefficient of 0.29 in 2019, similar to that of Germany, whereas the score for the United Kingdom was 0.36 and that for the United States 0.39.

WEALTH INEQUALITY

For French researchers at the forefront of investigations into the growth of inequality in the developed world, it was the growth of inequality in wealth in France since the 1980s, rather than in income, which they saw as the greater problem. What their research demonstrates is that the large number of people who were able to live off their wealth at the beginning of the twentieth century diminished as a result of the two world wars, while the redistributive fiscal policies put in place, particularly after the Second World War, reduced income inequality. With wartime destruction halving the proportion of household income derived from capital (from 20 per cent before the First World War to 10 per cent after the Second World War), the share of total income accounted for by the top decile fell from 45 per cent in 1900 to 30 per cent in 1945, while the share of the top 1 per cent fell by even more, from 20 per cent in 1910 to 7.5 per cent in 1945.

After the Second World War, the proportion of household income derived solely from labour grew, with the greatest increases occurring between 1950 and 1975. It was during the "30 glorious years" that the net annual wages of the average worker quadrupled and their working conditions improved considerably. Whereas in the mid-nineteenth century they worked a 64 hour week with no paid holidays and no form of social protection against life's many challenges, by the mid-1970s they worked a 40 hour week, with four weeks of paid holiday and contributed 9.7 per

Figure 5.2 Household income by source (%)

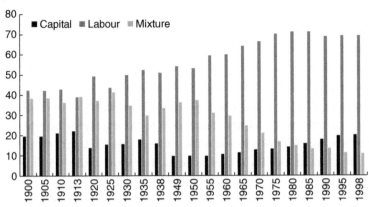

Source: Piketty, *Les Hauts revenus en France au XXe siècle.*

cent of their wages to their social insurance scheme, while their employer paid 37 per cent. Many of the improvements, such as two weeks' paid holidays and a 40-hour working week, were first introduced by the Popular Front government in 1936. In 1956 the Socialist government of Guy Mollet introduced a third week of paid holidays, with a fourth week added in 1968 and a fifth week in 1982. For many of those in work, France was "a super place to live – perhaps the best place in the world".[8]

In 1950 a guaranteed minimum wage was introduced for those working in sectors where they were unable to bargain collectively. This was then extended to agricultural workers, with both indexed to inflation. Under the terms of the Grenelle Agreements negotiated at the end of May 1968 and designed to restore social peace, the minimum wage (*salaire minimum interprofessionnel garanti* (SMIG)) was increased by 35 per cent, and average real wages by 10 per cent. As a result, the share of wages of the bottom 50 per cent in the national income not only rose, but rose faster than the economy as a whole during the inflationary years of the 1970s. However, the decision by President Mitterrand to bring this to an end as part of his fiscal U-turn in 1983, when he froze the minimum wage and ended the indexation of wages to prices, resulted in the share of national income held by the richest 10 per cent increasing, while that of the poorest fell and unemployment continued to grow. The introduction of a minimum subsistence allowance, Revenu minimum d'insertion (RMI), by the Socialist government in 1988 was designed to fight the growing spread of extreme poverty linked to long-term unemployment.[9] It was made available to those aged 25 and above (or aged 18–25 if they had at least one child) who had been unemployed for a long time, who had not contributed to the unemployment benefit scheme or were in low-income work. In some cases it meant that seeking work would entail a loss of benefits. For those under 25 or those who failed to find permanent employment, the result was dependence, extreme poverty and social exclusion. In 2008 the Sarkozy government changed the RMI to the Revenu de solidarité active (RSA), which allowed workers under a certain income to claim the benefit, but made it a condition for the unemployed that they took part in programmes aimed at their reintegration into the labour market and accepted any job that was offered. In 2012 the Hollande government made the RSA accessible to those aged between 18 and 25 years provided that they had worked for two years at least. In 2013 it introduced regulations to prevent interns being used instead of permanent workers, and increased the contributions to insurance funds for temporary work.[10]

At the other extreme, the wealth accumulating in the hands of the richest 1 per cent of people kept on growing from the 1980s onwards. While this has been difficult to quantify due to under-reporting, Piketty and his team of researchers have argued that it is the nature of the assets in a portfolio as much as their total monetary value that may have important implications for wealth inequality. Whereas the poorest 30 per cent held any savings in the form of bank deposits, and those in the middle of the distribution scale held their wealth in the form of housing, for those in the top 10 per cent and top 1 per cent, financial assets became the main form of wealth. Between 1984 and 2014 the proportion of financial assets held by the top 1 per cent doubled from 35 per cent to 70 per cent. The proportion of their income derived from labour fell by 38 per cent over the period 1970–2014, while that from capital increased by 59 per cent from 1984 to 2014. This led Piketty's team to conclude that the likelihood of top labour earners belonging to the top 1 per cent wealth group declined consistently from the 1970s. While the top 1 per cent of labour earners had a 29 per cent probability of belonging to the top 1 per cent wealth group in 1970, this probability had fallen to 17 per cent by 2012.[11] It was the growth of inequality in wealth which had reduced social mobility in France. With the removal of controls over capital movements following the collapse of the international monetary system of Bretton Woods and the introduction of the single market, the top 1 per cent were free to invest in economies outside France where rates of return were higher, at least in the short term.

THE STRUCTURE OF TAXATION

However, as we shall see, it was also the structure of taxation in France that contributed to the inequalities in income and wealth. It came as a shock for the French to read in *Le Monde* that although inequality in the United States was greater than in France, the American tax system was

Figure 5.3 Tax to GDP ratio, 2000–18

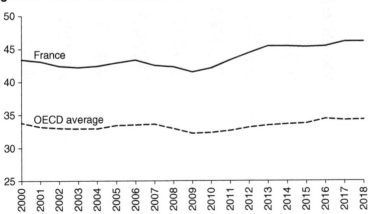

Source: OECD, "Revenue Statistics", 2019.

more effective in reducing it than their own one.[12] Calculations showed that, over the period 1990–2018, the pre-tax income of the richest 10 per cent of the population in France was on average 7.1 times higher than that of the poorest 50 per cent, whereas after tax it fell to 5.5 times. Redistribution had reduced inequality by 23 per cent. But, over the same period, the US tax system had been more redistributive. The pre-tax income of the richest 10 per cent of Americans was 15.1 times that of the poorest 50 per cent. After tax it had fallen to 9.9 times, which was the equivalent of a 34 per cent reduction. The French may have raised more in taxation than any other country in the world, but the way in which taxes were raised was in many respects regressive.

In every year since 2000 the tax burden in France (the ratio of taxes to GDP) has been considerably higher than the average for the OECD and, having fallen between 2006 and 2009, it has climbed since then. By 2018 it was higher than in Denmark and Sweden and considerably higher than in the United Kingdom.

Figure 5.4 Total receipts from taxes and social contributions, 2018 (% of GDP)

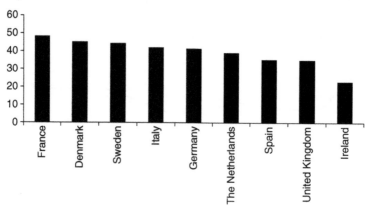

Source: Eurostat, main national aggregates.

Yet, of that revenue from taxes and social contributions, income taxes (the only taxes that are based on the ability to pay) have consistently accounted for a smaller proportion of total taxation in France than in most western European countries, and much less than in the United States. Social contributions account for more, although only part of those contributions are strictly classified as taxes. Taxes on goods and services account for less than the OECD average, although this is a recent phenomenon, while taxes on property account for more.

Since the mid-1960s the proportion of income taxes raised on a progressive basis has declined, while flat rate taxes on income (CSG) have risen (see below); taxes on corporations declined from a rate of 50 per cent between 1965 and 1985 to a rate of 33 per cent after 2006; employers' contributions to social security remained very stable, although from 1986 zero rates applied on the young, the contributions from employees increased slightly and after 1992 there was a decline in the proportion of taxes raised indirectly from goods and services.

Table 5.1 Structure of taxation in France (% of total taxation)

	1965	1992	1998	2018
Taxes on income				
of individuals	10.6	11.3	17.1	20.5
(of which CSG)	0	1.6	9.8	12.9
of corporations	5.3	2.2	3.1	4.5
Social security contributions	34.1	44	36	34.9
of employers	25.3	27.4	24.9	24.3
of employees	6.6	13.2	8.8	8.2
Taxes on goods and services	38.4	26.5	26.9	24.9

Source: OECD, "Revenue Statistics", 2019.

In 2018 taxes on individual incomes accounted for 20.6 per cent of total taxation in France compared with 40.7 per cent in the United States (27.2 per cent in both the UK and Germany) but, as we will see below when discussing social security contributions, since the 1990s a growing proportion of taxes on incomes have been levied on a flat rate rather than a progressive basis. We shall examine each of these in turn.

Table 5.2 Tax revenue of main headings (% of total tax revenue, 2017)

	Income & profits	Social security	Payroll	Property	Goods & services	Others	EU contrib.
France	23.6	36.4	3.4	9.5	24.5	2.5	0.2
USA	45.2	23	0	16	15.7	0	0
OECD ave.	34	26	1.1	5.8	32.4	0.4	0.4

Source: OECD, "Revenue Statistics", 2019.

Income taxes

To explain why income taxes should have contributed so much less in France than in other OECD countries we need to go back to 1914, when the legislation to introduce income taxation was finally passed by the French National Assembly after years of prevarication and opposition. Although the legislation introducing income tax was passed a few days before the outbreak of the First World War, it was not intended to cover the exceptional needs of the war. In fact, it was argued that the full cost of the war should not be borne by those who had to fight it but should be shared with those who profited from it either immediately or in the future, or indeed by those who had caused the war in the first place. Since these were questions to which there was no generally acceptable answer during the years of hostilities, the rates of income tax were initially set at such a low level that the war was mainly paid for by borrowing from the French population and from the Allies, as well as by printing money. It meant that the highly charged issues of assigning responsibilty for causing the war, the size of reparations to be demanded from Germany and the link between those reparations and the war debts owed to the US and the UK all became linked to the question of income tax in France. It was one reason why the yield from income tax was low. Another reason was the weight of the agricultural vote in the National Assembly, which ensured that French farmers, who on the eve of the First World War numbered about 40 per cent of the active population, were taxed on their estimated income (the forfait) rather than their actual one, which greatly underestimated their tax liability. A third reason was the opportunity for tax fraud among the self-employed, which subsequently, under the Nazi occupation, became almost a patriotic duty. As we have seen, the attempts to tackle fraud, which by 1952 was estimated to be about 20–25 per cent of total tax receipts, by imposing an extra tax (*taxe proportionnelle*) on the self-employed and sending out teams of tax inspectors to rural France to root out fraudsters, led to a national protest movement spearheaded by the shopkeeper Pierre Poujade. The *taxe proportionnelle* was abolished by de Gaulle in 1959. However, by far the most important reason for the low weight of income taxes in the French tax revenue was the introduction of the family quotient system in 1945. This was one of the first tax reforms passed by a legislature for which women had been allowed to vote for the first time. At that time the declining and ageing population was the issue of greatest national concern. The loss of life – 1.5 million young men killed in the First World War – as well the loss of potential life meant that the slow growth, if not the stagnation, of the French population had become a serious problem. In some years in the interwar period there were more deaths than births. The population was getting older, more concerned with stability than growth and in the public mind there was a direct link between the declining population in the 1930s and the defeat in 1940. Demographers and groups on the political right had for decades been warning about the decline of the population in France relative to other countries: the decline had started in the late eighteenth century when the birth rate had fallen in line with the fall in the death rate, whereas in the rest of Europe the birth rate did not adjust until almost a century later. The famous demographer Alfred Sauvy used the term "Malthusian" to link France's slow population growth to an economic mentality that was afraid of change and preferred stagnation to growth.[13]

But, as we saw in Chapter 1, it was the wealthiest groups in French society that had reduced their birth rate first, and for entirely rational reasons, in the nineteenth century. Similarly, after 1945, it was not de Gaulle's exhortations on French women "to produce twelve million beautiful babies" to restore the greatness of France that led to a sustained increase in the birth rate but the fiscal legislation passed in December 1945.[14] Under the new family quotient system of tax splitting, introduced as part of that legislation, the tax system was changed to reward wealthy families disproportionately if they produced more children. One consequence of the family quotient system was that receipts from income taxes were lower than in other countries. The main objective, though, was achieved insofar as the French population started to grow again, increasing by about 12 million between 1946 and 1974. While there was a marked rise in the birth rate across the developed world in the years after the Second World War, what was significant was that the French population grew faster than elsewhere, and continued to grow faster as it slowed down elsewhere after 1964. Even after the end of the French baby boom, the French population increased at an annual rate of 0.52 per cent until 2019, compared with 0.11 per cent in Germany, 0.21 per cent in Italy and 0.38 per cent in the UK.[15]

Wealth tax

In 1982 the Socialist government aimed to improve the progressivity of the tax system by placing a limit on the tax reductions due to family size. It also introduced a new wealth tax imposed on all financial assets including housing, with a top rate of between 1.5 per cent and 1.8 per cent. Although repealed in 1986 by the Chirac government, the wealth tax was reimposed in 1988 when, following Mitterrand's re-election as president, a Socialist government was also elected (see Appendix). At its peak it raised about 1 per cent of total tax revenue. When the Socialist government under President Hollande introduced an additional levy of 75 per cent on incomes of more than €1 million in 2012, at least 10,000 wealthy people moved their country of residence to avoid paying the tax. It was scrapped four years later. In September 2018 Emmanuel Macron replaced the wealth tax with a property tax, which he hoped would encourage investment in productive activity in France rather than in property.

Social security contributions

The French welfare state was initially set up as a collection of insurance-based schemes funded from contributions at the workplace rather than a single universal system funded mainly out of taxation and to a lesser extent national insurance contributions, as in the UK. The benefits that employees could expect in France varied according to their contributions and type of work. Initially, the scheme covered sickness, accidents at work and retirement pensions. It was not until 1959 that unemployment was added – a reflection of the labour shortage in France after the Second World War when the system was put in place. Employers were expected to contribute much more than employees in a system that was managed by the social partners, including the main trade unions, the CGT and CFDT, even though they represented a minority of workers. Over the postwar period the number of risks covered by the schemes grew, as did the cost of the entire system, due to the ageing of the population, the rise in the unemployment rate, the growth of medical costs and the growing numbers and needs of the poor.

In 1986 the incoming Chirac government's remedy for the growing levels of unemployment, particularly among the young, was to waive the contributions to social security costs paid by employers on every young person they recruited. The measure had little impact on youth unemployment, but it left a hole in the social security budget that had to be filled by other means. In 1991 the government introduced an entirely new tax, the Contribution Sociale Généralisée (CSG), payable by all individuals living in France who benefited from the compulsory health insurance. It was universal but, unlike income tax, it was a flat rate contribution. Initially set at a rate of 1.1 per cent, over the years it grew to become one of the largest contributors to the French Treasury, bringing in more than income tax. In its first year (in 1992), the revenue from the CSG was 17 per cent of that raised from income tax. In 2010 the CSG brought in €23,000 million,[16] and by 2018 it was raising almost twice as much as the income tax. Because it was a proportional rather than progressive tax and was deductible from income tax liability, it added to the regressive nature of the tax system.

Table 5.3 Revenue from income tax, 1992–2018 (in thousands of euros)

	1992	1997	1998	2018
Individual income tax	45,018	40,432	42,673	77,572
CSG	7,617	28,854	58,072	140,391

Source: OECD, "Revenue Statistics", 2019.

Table 5.4 Funding of social security (% of total)

	1978	1991	2007	2014
Contributions	97	95	72	63.5
Taxes	3	5	28	36.5
of which CSG	0	2	19	16.1

Source: INSEE, Les comptes nationaux.

Indirect taxes, including VAT

We have seen that France was the first country to replace the cumulative tax on production, with a tax on value added in 1954. Revenue from VAT expanded as the economy grew, particularly as it was applied to services as well as production. For many years it was the highest yielding tax in France. However, since it was regressive and not based on people's ability to pay, as poverty grew in the 1990s, in the interests of equity an increasing number of exemptions or reduced rates were applied to basic necessities. It was calculated that in 2014, had reduced rates not been applied, the revenue would have risen by over 10 per cent.[17] By 2017 VAT accounted for only 15.3 per cent of all tax revenue, one of the lowest in the EU. As a consequence of the low yield from VAT and from taxes on income, taxes on labour, particularly the social security contributions of employers, were among the highest in the EU, as were levels of corporation tax. Responding to the argument that the high level of taxes on companies was an obstacle to private investment and growth, Macron chose to increase the rate of the flat CSG tax rather than increase the progressive rates of income tax.

LABOUR MARKET

One of the most common explanations for the persistently high levels of unemployment in France, frequently cited before the financial crisis of 2008–09, was the rigidity of the labour market. This, it was claimed, was due to high standards of employment protection legislation and the high costs to the employer of social security payments. Much of this legislation dated back to the Grenelle Agreements of 1968 that introduced further restrictions on redundancies and dismissals as well as allowing a greater role for workers' representatives in companies employing more than 50 people. The result, it was asserted, was that French firms chose to relocate to countries with lower or more flexible standards and capital was invested outside France where rates of return were higher. According to the OECD "the strong protection accorded by open-ended contracts hinders labour mobility".[18] Only by deregulating the labour market would unemployment be reduced.

It was frequently argued that France should follow the example of Germany's labour market reforms, introduced by the Social Democratic government led by Gerhard Schröder in coalition with the Greens in 2003–05. Under what was known as the Hartz reforms, named after Volkswagen's director of human resources, Peter Hartz, the package of measures was designed to reduce unemployment in Germany. Standing at 13.4 per cent in 2002, the reforms aimed to integrate two million of the unemployed into the labour market. The central element was the encouragement given to employers to hire workers on part-time, fixed-term contracts with higher thresholds for taxes and social insurance payments and less worker protection. Small and medium-sized firms were offered loans of up to €100,000 if they hired a previously unemployed person. By 2012 Germany's unemployment rate had fallen to 5.5 per cent, although how much was due to the controversial reforms remained in dispute.[19]

Research on France showed that the civilian employment rate (as opposed to the unemployment rate) as a share of the active population fell between the mid-1950s and mid-1980s only to rise again thereafter, so that by 2010 it was almost as high as it had been in the mid-1950s. The conclusion was that higher unemployment was driven more by an increase in the labour supply than by an increased reluctance of employers to hire workers on contracts that were too rigid.[20] The increase in the labour supply was mainly due to the return of women to the labour market and the effects of the higher birth rate after the war. Where unemployment had the greatest impact on income inequality was in the income gap between the increasing number of two-income households and the single-person household without any form of employment.

The rise of mass unemployment from the mid-1970s represented a fall in male employment coinciding with a return of female employment to the level last seen in 1906. At the beginning of the twentieth century the overall female activity rate (the numbers in work as a proportion of the population of working age) in France (46.7 per cent) was higher than in Germany or Great Britain and much higher than in the United States.[21] It was high in France because of the large size of the textile and clothing sector in relation to industry as a whole, and the very high dependence of these industries on women employed in domestic piecework. In 1906 female labour accounted for 34 per cent of the total industrial workforce. However, as the textile industry declined relative to mechanical engineering this fell to 28 per cent in 1931 and 23 per cent in 1962. The growing proportion of women in the service sector between the First World War and the mid-1970s did not wholly offset the fall in female employment in agriculture and industry. But in the late 1960s female employment began to rise as a result of changes in legislation that encouraged many middle-class women to look for work. One change resulted from the Raynaud Report of 1965, which, in making the separation of goods and property the norm, enabled married women to open a bank account for the first time without getting the permission of their husband. The second change came two years later when the Neuwirth Law overturned the legislation of 1920 under which all forms of contraception, and all information relating to it, had been banned. Even though it was not applied until 1971, the Neuwirth Law brought France more into line with northern European standards and practices.[22]

At the onset of the recession in 1974, the activity rate was, at 65.1 per cent, higher than it had been at any time since the First World War. Between 1974 and 1980, while the employment rate for men declined from 82.1 per cent to 79.5 per cent, that for women increased from 48 per cent to 52 per cent. As Figure 5.5 shows, these trends were to continue, as male employment in manufacturing fell and female employment in services rose. Between 1982 and 2006, 84 per cent of the 3.4 million new jobs created were taken by women compared with 0.6 million new jobs for men. Most of this took place in the period 1982–99. However, between 1999 and 2006 this began to change, as 38 per cent of the new jobs created were taken by men.[23]

Figure 5.5 Male and female employment rates, 1872–2012 (% of working age)

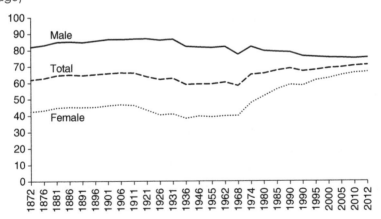

Source: Wieviorka, *La France en Chiffres*, 171.

The expansion in the number of working women led to a continuous decline in gender inequality in income. Whereas in 1970 men aged between 30 and 55 earned 3.5 to 4 times as much as women of a similar age, by 2012 this had fallen to 1.25 times. However, by 2012 men aged between 55 and 65 earned 1.64 times as much as women of a similar age, with the final salary having implications on respective pensions income.[24] And, as in other countries, French women did not access higher paying jobs.

Figure 5.6 Female as a proportion of male remuneration, 1951–2005 (%)

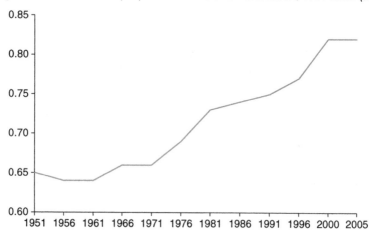

Source: Wieviorka, *La France en Chiffres*, 190.

Effect of the 2008–09 crisis on employment

By 2007 more than half (56 per cent) of the jobs in the private sector were held by men, but men suffered almost all (92 per cent) of the job losses in the two years between December 2007 and December 2009. These amounted to 350,000 in comparison with 30,000 female job losses. The sectors that were least affected by the crisis were those in which employment was predominantly female in 2007. These included health and social services (94 per cent), real estate management (69 per cent), administration (87 per cent), management consultancy (55 per cent), insurance (67 per cent) and accountancy (69 per cent). However, although female employment suffered less in the immediate aftermath of the crisis, by 2015 France had the lowest employment rate for women among developed countries. At just over 60 per cent it compared unfavourably with 70 per cent in Denmark and Germany. Thirty-three per cent of the female labour force worked part-time, compared with 7 per cent of men, accounting for 80 per cent of all part-time workers.[25] Since single women without children and mothers with one child tended to have the same working patterns as men in similar age groups, this suggested it was family size and the cost of childcare relative to female income that largely determined labour market participation. The experience of women in the labour market challenged the argument that it was the high cost of employing labour and the inflexibility of the labour market legislation that explained the persistently high rate of unemployment in France.

OTHER FORMS OF INEQUALITY

Due to the growing pressure from some economists for a reform of national accounting, the OECD began to call on governments to measure widening inequality not only in terms of incomes and wealth but also in terms of differences in health, education and skills and in the ability to make the transition between school and employment.[26] Where the OECD judged France to be weakest was in levels of social and generational mobility as well as in access to housing and healthcare. In France, as in Germany, it took six generations for children in the bottom 10 per cent to reach the mean income of society, in comparison with two generations in Denmark. The OECD country with the worst intergenerational mobility was Hungary, where it took seven generations for those at the bottom to reach the mean income. In the UK it took five generations.[27] Despite the relatively low poverty rate in France, the difficulties facing low skilled workers and new entrants to the labour market accumulated over time and were reproduced across generations. In France there was a particularly strong link between family background and school results.[28]

There was also a strong link between school results and unemployment. On the eve of the financial crisis, when unemployment stood at just over two million (7.4 per cent of the active population), the hardest hit were the unskilled (15 per cent). When unemployment peaked at over three million in 2015 (10.4 per cent) the hardest hit once again were the unskilled (20.6 per cent). This was higher than the proportion of immigrants, of whom 18.4 per cent were unemployed.[29] And there was a close connection between unemployment and intermittent career paths and poverty, defined as having a disposable income (after social transfers) of less than 60 per cent of the national median.[30] Although the risk of poverty and social exclusion was lower in France than the EU average in 2017, and had fallen since the peak in 2012 (lower than in Germany or the UK but higher than in Finland, Slovakia or the Czech Republic), in 2017 there were almost 9 million people living below the poverty line (down from 11.8 million in 2012), subsisting on less than €1,026 per month and often on much less.[31] Of those, single women with or without children, the elderly and foreigners without legal status (and therefore denied the right to work or benefit from welfare) were the most vulnerable. Of the unemployed, two thirds lived on the RSA, the basic form of job-seeker's allowance, which gave them an average monthly income of €500.[32]

Education and skills

The OECD identified the French educational system as one of the main reasons for the lack of social and economic mobility in France and thereby for perpetuating inequality. This was based to some extent on the results of the programme for international student assessment (PISA), which had surveyed the achievements of 15-year olds across 79 countries every three years since 2000. According to the conclusions of its 2018 inquiry, France was the country where the socio-economic background had the greatest bearing on a student's performance at school and where poorly performing students were the most likely to attend the same poorly performing school.[33] If there was one area in promoting equality that France had prided itself in since the late nineteenth century, it was in education. Under the Third Republic, the numbers attending elementary school had expanded rapidly. With the objective of instilling the values of the secular republic in a new generation of school children, the percentage enrolled in elementary school had risen from 57 in 1870 to 86 in 1900, while in Germany it had risen from 67 to 73, and in England and Wales from 49 to 74 over the same period. The same progress was not achieved in secondary education though, with no expansion in the number of boys attending lycées or colleges between 1880 and 1930. However, under the Popular Front government of 1936 the school leaving age was raised to 14 and it was raised again to 16 in 1959. During the 30 postwar years the numbers attending secondary school expanded from 740,000 in 1946 to 3,982,300 in 1975, with only 30 per cent of this due to the rise in the birth rate. The rest was due to the belief that education led to social advancement. Public spending on education, including university level, expanded from 7 per cent of the budget in 1950 to 17 per cent by 1967. The numbers attending university went up from 129,000 in 1946 to reach 232,600 in 1961, 697,800 in 1971 and 806,300 in 1975.[34] In 1963 secondary school education was reformed, with a single college for all 11–16-year olds, followed by a lycée for those who hoped to continue their studies and pass the leaving exam, the baccalauréat (the "bac"), which was the entrance to university.

It came as a shock when in 1964 Bourdieu and Passeron published a ground-breaking book, Les Héritiers, which challenged the assumption that the expansion of secondary school places after the Second World War had democratized French education and expanded opportunities for the less advantaged in society.[35] Their stark conclusion that "the son of a senior executive was 80 times more likely to go to university than the son of an industrial worker" increased the pressure for further educational reforms. By 1985 the target was set to move from 30 per cent to 80 per cent of final year school children achieving the level of the bac by 2000. Although the target was not reached, by 2006 more than 60 per cent of school leavers had attained the bac and were entitled to go to university, where the tuition fees were negligible. The non-selective nature of France's university courses was judged to have been one of the most important elements of social mobility in the country. Whereas only 7 per cent of men and 4 per cent of women born between 1918 and 1929 had gone to university, of those born between 1980 and 1984 the corresponding proportions were 40 per cent and 51 per cent.

However, entry to the most prestigious *grandes écoles* (set up after the Revolution to be based on merit at a time when universities were tied to the religious authorities and the aristocracy) had become highly selective. Research found that after 2003 most of the French economic, political and academic elite were among the 5 per cent who had successfully completed the preparatory two-year programme required for entry. Young people from the higher social classes remained five times more likely than their working-class peers to graduate from a *grande école*, and they were much more likely to benefit from their qualifications on the labour market than equally able working class or female students. There was in fact greater social mobility among graduates from a three-year university degree programme than from a *grande école*, leading to the conclusion that "educational merit remains better rewarded on the labour market among the better off."[36]

Because the large numbers of young people studying in France or abroad (in 1975 about 14,000 went abroad, whereas in 2015 the numbers studying or in their first job abroad was about 102,000) were excluded from the 15–24 age cohort when calculating youth unemployment, that rate was artificially high. However, even the more accurate unemployment ratio was higher in France than the average for the EU, and significantly higher than in Germany in 2018.

And, in spite of the increasing numbers of young people graduating with a degree, there was a growing mismatch between their qualifications and the skills required by employers. Some employers complained of a shortage of skills in engineering, particularly in automation and industrial robotics, and of a shortage of housing and other infrastructure necessary to attract skilled workers from elsewhere. Macron had prioritized the overhaul of professional training to stimulate growth and bring down the unemployment rate citing the Nordic model of life-long learning as a possible one to follow.[37] The fact that there were between 200,000 and 330,000 unfilled vacancies in 2018, when the youth unemployment rate was 20.7 per cent (see Table 5.5) was seen as a reflection by some that welfare benefits were too generous, although a more plausible explanation was that there had been too little investment in suitable training and equipment.

Table 5.5 Youth unemployment rates and ratios, 2008 and 2018

	Rate (%)		Ratio	
	2008	**2018**	**2008**	**2018**
France	19	20.7	7.1	7.6
Germany	10.4	6.2	5.5	3.1
Denmark	8	9.3	5.8	5.9
Spain	24.5	34.3	11.7	11.3
Italy	21.2	32.2	6.5	8.4
Netherlands	8.6	7.2	6	4.9
Sweden	20.2	16.8	10.7	9.1
UK	15	11.3	9.2	6.4
EU-28	15.9	15.2	7	6.3

Source: Eurostat.

Immigration

Studies found that it was immigrants and children of immigrants from outside the EU who were much less likely to be in full-time employment than the rest of the population. Those who felt most discriminated against were immigrants and children of immigrants from North and sub-Saharan Africa. They also had the greatest difficulty in making the transition from study to the labour market. Descendants of Turkish immigrants were the most able to rely on family networks to find employment.[38]

The composition of the immigrant population had changed markedly since 1975. In that year immigrants from Italy, Spain and Portugal made up 49 per cent of the total, whereas by 2018 they were no more than 18 per cent. The proportion of other Europeans remained stable at 15 per cent over the same period. At the same time the proportion of immigrants from North Africa increased from 26 per cent to 30 per cent of the total immigrants; of those from sub-Saharan Africa (mostly Mali, Cameroon, Ivory Coast and Madagascar), the proportion rose from 2 per cent to 15 per cent, while those from Asia rose from 4 per cent to 14 per cent, with most of the increase accounted for by China.

Figure 5.7 Composition of the immigrant population, 2018 (%)

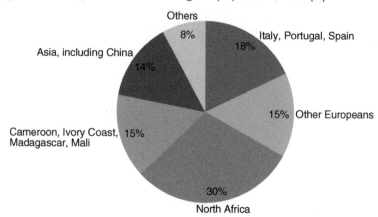

Source: INSEE, Tableaux de l'économie française, 2019.

While most (56 per cent) of the immigrants after the Second World War had been single men without any qualifications responding to the need for manual labour, after 1975 more women arrived and by 2018 women represented 52 per cent of the immigrant population, and African women 49 per cent of the entire immigrant population. Immigrants were also becoming more skilled, with 28 per cent arriving in 2018 with qualifications, compared with just 3 per cent in 1975. As a proportion of both the total population and the active population, the number of immigrants in France was much lower than in neighbouring countries. In 2016 immigrants made up 6.6 per cent of the total population compared with 10.5 per cent in Germany, 8.6 per cent in the UK and 8.3 per cent in

Italy. As a proportion of the active economic population they were 6.2 per cent in France, 11.4 per cent in Germany, 11.3 per cent in the UK and 11.1 per cent in Italy.[39]

As a result of the changing character of immigration, in comparison with the first wave of immigrants after 1945, who were unqualified male workers, their children and subsequent immigrants tended to be a much more heterogeneous group. How they fared in the labour market depended to some extent on their country of origin and level of skills. Surveys covering the period 2013–17 found little discrimination in terms of wages, with children of immigrants having a higher socio-economic status than their fathers, which was also true for the rest of the population.[40] While second generation male immigrants were more likely to be manual labourers (*"ouvrier"*) than the rest of the population (48 per cent compared with 36 per cent) this varied according to the country of origin: in the case of Portugal it was 63 per cent, Turkey 59 per cent, Morocco and Tunisia 53 per cent, Algeria 49 per cent and Spain and Italy 36 per cent.

Second-generation female immigrants were no more likely to be employees than the rest of the population (50 per cent compared with 49 per cent) but they were more likely to be unqualified employees (37 per cent as opposed to 23 per cent). Those most likely to be employees were from sub-Saharan Africa (67 per cent) and North Africa (60 per cent). On the other hand, female immigrants from South East Asia were almost as likely to be manual workers (29 per cent) as employees (34 per cent) and those of Turkish origin, when they worked, were much more likely to be manual workers (42 per cent).

At the same time a non-negligible proportion of second-generation immigrants were managers ("cadres"): 13 per cent of male and 12 per cent of female immigrants compared with 17 per cent of men and 13 per cent of women in the rest of the population. Those who were the most likely to become a manager were the sons of immigrants from South East Asia (34 per cent), and the least likely from Portugal (8–9 per cent).

Many of the sons of immigrants were also employed as manual workers, in a smaller proportion than their fathers, but more than in the rest of the population (41 per cent compared with 36 per cent for the majority population). Those most likely to be manual workers were the sons of Turkish immigrants (62 per cent), followed by Algerian (47 per cent), Portuguese (46 per cent), Moroccan and Tunisian (40 per cent). In general, the daughters of immigrants were more likely to be employed than their mothers, although the proportions varied by country of origin and religion. Of those from Turkey, female employment rose from first to second generation (from 25 to 44 per cent), with increases for those from North Africa from 35 to 60 per cent and from Asia from 46 to 74 per cent. A low rate of participation in the labour market was found to be particularly widespread among women from Muslim countries.[41] There was a higher proportion of skilled workers among second-generation women from all origin groups apart from Turkey, with Asian women being the most likely to be in skilled jobs. This reflected the rate of higher education among almost all the second-generation groups with the rate among Asian women exceeding that of the majority population.

The sector where most immigrants, the children of immigrants and the rest of the population was employed was that of services. The crisis of 2007–09 increased the gap between those households where a single male breadwinner became unemployed, and the two-income households that kept their jobs. With many immigrants working in service sector jobs in the bigger cities and holding onto their jobs, the racist message of the Rassemblement National, which linked unemployment with immigration, resonated with many French people outside the big cities. However, immigrants and natives of "Doms" and their children who lived in the Paris area were most likely to live in parts badly served by public transport, necessitating longer commutes to work. Outside of the Paris area, those who took the longest were those from sub-Saharan Africa and South East Asia, because they were less likely to own a car (60 per cent and 69 per cent compared with 93 per cent of the rest of the population).

They were also least likely to work in the public sector, since 59 per cent of immigrants did not have French nationality. However, despite a high proportion (82 per cent) of South East Asians becoming naturalized, only 11 per cent worked in the public sector. Lack of qualifications, inadequate knowledge of the French language and inability to pass competitive examinations were the most frequently cited reasons.[42]

CONCLUSION

In the 30 years after the Second World War, income inequality fell in France as high growth rates in the economy enabled millions of people to move out of low-productivity jobs, particularly in agriculture, into higher ones in industry and services. The destruction of much wealth in two world wars and the Great Depression of the 1930s meant that a much higher proportion of the population relied on income from labour alone than had been the case at the end of the nineteenth century. As growth slowed down after the first recession of 1974–75, and high levels of unemployment became endemic, taxes were raised to redistribute income to those being left behind. But the way that taxes were raised became increasingly regressive. Taxes on income, the only tax based on ability to pay, accounted for less and less of the total revenue raised from taxation. At the same time, levels of accumulated wealth increased, meaning that the income of an increasing proportion of people was derived from a combination of earned income and income from capital. It became increasingly difficult for those dependent on earned income alone to climb the social ladder.

As more married women entered the labour market from the early 1970s, many taking jobs in the expanding public sector, the gap between two-income households and the unemployed grew. Immigrants were much less likely to take public sector jobs, but the likelihood of second-generation immigrants taking the same job as their fathers (most first-generation mothers did not work outside the home) was greater than for others. While a high proportion of young people had tertiary level education, many were not equipped with the skills necessary for the labour market. Employment rates, particularly for the young, the low-skilled and older workers were low. Despite the high rates of taxes and transfers, weak social mobility tends to perpetuate economic situations between one generation and the next.[43]

By increasing the rate of the flat tax, the CSG and reducing benefits including housing subsidies, the reforms of 2018 threatened to increase inequality, while the abolition of the wealth tax carried no guarantee that the savings made would be invested in the French economy rather than abroad.

6

The French economy and European integration

Although France was one of the founding members of the European Economic Community, the potential benefits of membership of an integrated European economy divided opinion from the outset. On two occasions, in 1992 and 2005, the French public was consulted directly in a referendum on proposals to deepen integration through treaty changes.[1] The first referendum was held on 20 September 1992 on the question of completing the single market and preparing for monetary union (EMU) under the Treaty of Maastricht. On that occasion, on a large turnout of 69.7 per cent, a narrow majority (51 per cent) voted in favour. The second referendum, on the question of ratification of a constitution for the European Union (EU), was held on 29 May 2005. On a similarly large turnout of 69.4 per cent, 54.7 per cent voted against. All other treaties starting with the Treaty of Paris setting up the European Coal and Steel Community (ECSC) signed on 18 April 1951 were approved by a majority in Parliament.

Attempts by historians to separate the effects of European integration from all the other factors influencing the performance of the economies of member states since 1951, and to quantify them, have proved to be very difficult indeed.[2] While it is not possible in a short chapter to analyse the full range of issues that membership of the EEC/EU has involved for the French economy, the aim of this chapter is to summarize some of the most significant ones. These are: the European Coal and Steel Community (ECSC); the European Economic Community (EEC) and its common agricultural policy (CAP); the European Single Market; and the Economic and Monetary Union (EMU).

THE EUROPEAN COAL AND STEEL COMMUNITY

The proposal in May 1950 to place the coal and steel industries of France and the Federal Republic of Germany under the supervision and control of a common High Authority was a French initiative designed to achieve two main objectives. The first was to maintain the consensus within France that the Monnet Plan had achieved, while the second was to build a positive relationship with the new Federal Republic of Germany. More specifically, the proposal was designed to ensure that the Monnet Plan's objective of increasing the production and productivity of the French steel industry and thereby all the major steel-consuming industries in France could be achieved when Allied controls over German steel production were removed. One of the many factors seen to have undermined the size and competitiveness of the French steel industry relative to that in Germany was French dependence on Germany for much of its coal and coke supplies.[3] The French coal industry was small in comparison with that of Germany and Britain (its coal reserves were one-hundredth of those in the United Kingdom), and its output of coking coal, necessary for steel making, was particularly inadequate. Because many German steel firms owned their own coal mines through a process of vertical integration, they were able to pay less for raw materials than they charged on the export market. At the insistence of the French government the International Authority for the Ruhr (IAR) had been set up to manage the allocation and price of the scarce quantities of coal available between users in the western occupation zones of Germany and neighbouring countries in return for the French government removing its opposition to the western zones of Germany receiving Marshall aid, but this was only ever to be a temporary measure.[4] Monnet's answer to the imminent dissolution of the IAR, following the creation of the Federal Republic of Germany in 1949, was to replace the IAR with a new authority overseeing not only the Ruhr coalmines but also the coal and steel industries in France and West Germany. The ECSC was to be the first form of supranational governance in postwar Europe, designed to create, over a five-year period, a level playing field in the production and trade in coal and steel between France and West Germany and any other country in western Europe that was prepared to join on the terms laid down by the French.

However, following the conference in Paris in 1950 at which Monnet's proposal was presented, governments of the European countries that signed up to the plan (West Germany, Belgium, the Netherlands, Luxembourg and Italy, as well as France) quickly moved to ensure that they retained control over the subsidies and prices that they applied to coal, while agreeing to harmonize rather than eliminate the tariffs on steel.[5] Crucially, though, the negotiations leading to the ratification of the ECSC were not derailed when, following the outbreak of the Korean War on 25 June 1950, the United States called for West Germany to be admitted into NATO, its steel production increased and Allied plans for the deconcentration of its steel industry had to be abandoned. Monnet's proposed defence plan, announced by Prime Minister René Pleven in October 1950, for West Germany to be admitted into a European Defence Community (EDC) instead of NATO provided sufficient time for the Treaty of Paris setting up the ECSC to be signed and ratified in 1951 and the Monnet Plan for the economy to be completed before the French national assembly had a chance to abort the defence plan. Even with the expansion of the West German steel industry, the Monnet Plan's target of producing 15 million tonnes of steel in France, compared with an interwar peak of 9.7 million tonnes, was reached, although in 1959, rather than 1955, as planned. In 1959, the production of steel in West Germany was 29.4 million tonnes. At the same time, much of French industry was able to benefit from the removal of controls over West German industry and, in particular, over the production of machine tools, with imports of German machine tools contributing to the continued modernization of the French economy throughout the 1950s.

As far as French coal supplies were concerned, even with the ECSC it was expected that the postwar shortage of coal in France and western Europe would continue for many years. To address this problem, the French government imported coal from the United States and Poland, substituted imported oil for coal and embarked on a programme of producing nuclear energy. Since its creation in 1945 the French Commissariat à l'Énergie Atomique (CEA) had been researching the production of nuclear energy based on the natural uranium–graphite–gas method. However, as EDF found when it started to build a reactor using this method in 1952, the technical and financial costs were considerable.[6] One member of the CEA, the engineer Louis Armand, spotted an opportunity to reduce those costs by drawing West Germany into the programme in 1955. Following the defeat of the EDC proposal by the Gaullists and Communists in the French national assembly in 1954, West Germany had become a member of NATO and of the Western European Union (WEU). Under pressure from the WEU it had taken the decision not to develop its own nuclear weapons but begun to develop a civil nuclear energy programme instead. Arnaud convinced Monnet (now president of the High Authority of the ECSC) of the financial and technological advantages that cooperation with the German civil nuclear programme could offer to the development of nuclear energy in France. To those advantages Monnet added that it could give the French and possibly the Americans an opportunity to keep an eye on, if not control, German nuclear developments.[7] Monnet lost little time and resigned from his post in the ECSC to promote the idea of creating a European Atomic Energy Community (Euratom) to sit alongside the ECSC.

THE EUROPEAN ECONOMIC COMMUNITY

If the proposals to set up the European Coal and Steel Community and the European Atomic Energy Community were French ideas designed to meet very specific needs in the French economy, the proposal made in 1955 to extend the trade liberalization of coal and steel to cover all sectors of the economy in a European common market was not a French but a Dutch idea. As a small, trade-dependent economy, the Netherlands had, since the end of the Second World War, been anxious to find a way to persuade the larger, more protectionist countries in the ECSC, such as France and Italy, to reduce their tariffs.[8] The liberalization of intra-European trade within OEEC, which was one of the conditions attached by the United States to Marshall aid, had been deliberately interpreted by the French and British governments to mean reducing quantitative restrictions on trade while they maintained high tariffs. Many in France feared that much of French industry would not survive if exposed to competition, particularly from West Germany, in a European common market. At an official level the idea of participating in a European common market was opposed by the French Foreign Ministry (the Quai d'Orsay) and by the organization of French employers, the Confédération Nationale du Patronat Français (CNPF).[9] Jean Monnet, for his part, argued that the integration of nuclear energy was a more viable option. But, if France wanted to win support from the other members of the ECSC for the integration of nuclear energy, it needed at the very least to participate in the discussions about setting up a common market. If many in France were opposed to joining a common market, others, particularly in the Socialist party elected to government in January 1956, were in favour of gradually exposing French industry to competition as a way of continuing the economic modernization begun under the first and second plans, and pointed to the fact that the structure of the economy and of foreign trade was changing, with heavy industry gradually contributing a larger share of total output and exports, while lighter industries such as textiles were contracting. As a share of total French exports, textiles and clothing, for example, had fallen from 40 per cent in 1929 to 17.4 per cent in 1955.

It was not simply the structure of trade that was changing, but also the destination. The French colonies and Algeria, which together with metropolitan France formed the common currency area of the Franc Zone, had long offered a protected market for French exports, particularly in the 1930s, when the franc was overvalued. After the Second World War, trade with the Franc Zone intensified since imports, particularly of foodstuffs, represented a saving on dollars. Imports from the Franc Zone more than doubled between 1948 and 1955 such that by 1955 the Franc Zone accounted for almost one quarter of all imports into metropolitan France, while exports almost tripled, reaching 32 per cent of total exports by 1955, giving France a trade surplus with the Franc Zone. However, over the same period, imports from the ECSC countries had also increased such that they accounted for about the same proportion of trade as the Franc Zone by 1955. Over the period 1948–55 imports from the ECSC countries had increased by 3.7 times, reaching 20 per cent of all imports by 1955, while exports had shot up 5.4 times to reach 24 per cent in 1955. Exports to West Germany increased 7.6 times, far faster than to Algeria, which nonetheless remained the single largest export market. What was significant was that trade with western Europe was increasingly in the products in which world production and demand were expanding most rapidly, particularly in machinery and transport, while exports to the Franc Zone included a higher proportion of goods such as textiles and clothing for which demand was rising less rapidly.[10]

If the French government feared that many industrial sectors would not be able to compete if exposed to competition within a small European customs union of six ECSC countries, it knew that they were very much less likely to survive in an increasingly open international economy dominated by the United States. A possible alternative to the two was the option, proposed by Prime Minister Guy Mollet to the British government in September 1956, of uniting the sterling and franc monetary areas to form an economic union with a large preferential trading bloc to rival that of the United States. Proposed at the height of the Suez crisis, it was rejected by the British Cabinet after several days of debate. Ultimately, the British argument was that forming an economic union with a protectionist country like France would give unwelcome encouragement to uncompetitive sectors of the British economy to demand continued protection.[11]

Following the rejection of its proposal by the British government, the French concluded that the benefits of locking West Germany into an institutionalized trading system in western Europe, rather than leaving it free to liberalize its trade with the rest of the world, as Ludwig Erhard, the German minister for the economy, wanted would outweigh the risks to some sectors of the French economy, provided that a number of preconditions were met. These included the harmonization of wages, hours of work and social security benefits, the adoption of the Geneva convention on equal pay legislation, a longer transition period than the five years agreed in the Treaty of Paris for coal and steel to give less competitive industries time to adjust, the continued protection of agriculture and the association of the French colonies and former colonies in a preferential trading arrangement with the European common market.[12] Compliance with the provisions of the treaty rules would be monitored by a supranational commission, which would also have responsibility for negotiating commercial policy on behalf of the member states. The Treaty of Rome setting up the EEC was signed on 25 March 1957. Although the Treaty setting up Euratom was signed at the same time, it did not lead to greater cooperation in the development of nuclear power, since no government was prepared to give up control over such a sensitive sector. Relations between the French government and Euratom remained tense for this very reason.

The Impact of the EEC on French Trade

When France signed the Treaty of Rome in 1957, along with Italy, it still had the most protected market of the ECSC members for many categories of goods. At that time the average French tariff was 17 per cent, compared with an average German tariff of 6.4 per cent and Benelux tariffs of 9.7 per cent, but these averages hid a huge range of tariff protection.[13] Of even greater importance than tariffs were the quantitative restrictions placed on non-government trade that France had made little progress in removing according to the schedule agreed within OEEC. While these restrictions were in place there were significant changes, as we have seen, in the destination and composition of trade. Some of these trends continued in the 1960s as France participated in the trade liberalization measures of the EEC, with exports to the common market increasing as protection was reduced. Quantitative restrictions had been removed by the end of 1961, and intra-EEC tariffs were removed in stages, with the only tariffs remaining in 1968 being on agricultural products. Between 1960 and 1970 French imports from the EEC as a proportion of total imports had grown from 30 to 49 per cent, while exports had risen from 30 to 50 per cent of the total.

Table 6.1 French trade by geographical area, 1952–70 (% of total)

	1952	1960	1970
Exports to:			
Franc Zone	42	30	10
Other developing countries	15	10	13
EEC	16	30	50
Socialist countries	1	3	4
Other industrialized countries	26	27	23
Imports from:			
Franc Zone	23	23	9
Other developing countries	28	17	14
EEC	15	30	49
Socialist countries	1	2	2
Other industrialized countries	33	28	26

Source: INSEE, Fresque historique du système productif, 210.

The common external tariff on trade with the rest of the world was the average of the existing tariffs of the member states. For many products this was higher than the existing French tariffs. As a result of these new tariffs French trade shifted away from the United States and the Franc Zone to concentrate much more on the EEC. Imports from the Franc Zone fell from 23 per cent in 1960 to 9 per cent in 1970, while exports to the Franc Zone declined from 30 per cent in 1960 to 10 per cent in 1970.

Trade agreements with former colonies

As a precondition for signing the Treaty of Rome the French government had insisted that the EEC should fund part of the development costs of all the colonies and former colonies of the member states from its common budget. The first such agreement governing the terms of investment and trade covered the turbulent period 1958–63, when almost all of the colonies of France and Belgium in Africa became independent. At the request of 18 of the newly independent states in Africa, the European Commission replaced the first agreement with another one, signed with those 18 African states in Yaoundé, Cameroon, to cover the period 1964–69. This first Yaoundé Convention was followed by a second one covering the period 1971–75, and then by a further four conventions signed in Lomé, Togo. These four conventions, spanning the period 1975–2000, included many more countries, following the accession of the UK to the EEC. The most recent agreement, signed in Cotonou, Benin, was between the EU and 78 states in the African, Caribbean and Pacific (ACP) group in June 2000 for a 20-year period. When it was signed, exports to the ACP countries had been declining. Whereas in the 1980s they had accounted for 2.9 per cent of the total exports of the EU member states and 3.1 per cent of their imports, by 2000 the equivalent figures were 1.53 per cent of exports and 1.71 per cent of imports.[14] As the agreement came to an end in 2020, exports and imports of the EU to the ACP countries had risen to about 5 per cent. The trade agreements have become a model for the preferential agreements the EU has signed with countries across the world and that have proved to be more stable and effective in increasing trade than the tariff reductions based on the most favoured nation clause negotiated within the framework of GATT and, subsequently, the WTO.

The Common Agricultural Policy

It was not until after the EEC had been set up that the form agricultural protection would take was agreed. At the beginning of the 1960s it was only in certain products, mainly wheat, that France had a surplus: overall it had a trade deficit in food and agricultural products. While French agriculture was most interested in securing guaranteed markets in the EEC for any surpluses it might produce in the future, it was the Dutch who insisted that protection of European agriculture should be based on common prices as well as guaranteed markets. After much negotiation, the common prices that were agreed were generally higher than the prices in France for all agricultural products apart from sugar, due to the higher productivity of French agriculture. This represented a significant change in comparison with the performance of French agriculture in the nineteenth century and interwar period, when its productivity levels had been below much of Europe. As a result of the guaranteed prices and markets, France, which had the largest area of cultivable land in the EEC, was the largest beneficiary of the CAP. But equally, because of the CAP, there was a much faster increase in the output and exports of French cereals after 1964 than of the animal farming sector.[15] Production of cereals increased by 7 per cent per year between 1959 and 1972 as compared with about 3 per cent for the whole of the agricultural sector.[16] Unlike the manufacturing sector, where the removal of tariffs within the EEC is considered to have created trade and enhanced welfare rather than diverted it from the rest of the world, the CAP led to an increase in intra-European trade in agriculture at the expense of trade with other countries. The former French colonies lost out, with wine exports from Algeria (not considered a former colony by France) being a major casualty. With agricultural exports from metropolitan France increasing much more quickly than imports, in 1975 the French balance of trade in agriculture had recorded a surplus for the first time. Between 1968 and 1979 the real increase in net farm income per person in France was higher than anywhere else in the EEC. The ones who benefited most were the large grain and sugar beet farmers in the Île-de-France, whereas the two-thirds of French farmers whose incomes were less than 80 per cent of the non-agricultural incomes in their region fell behind.

After 1985 surpluses became more stable, with food and agricultural products now accounting for between 15 and 20 per cent of all French exports. Two thirds of those exports went to the markets of the EEC/ EU, with France by far the largest exporter of cereals and oil-producing plants. It was also an important supplier of drinks, sugar and milk products. But whereas it had been the second largest exporter of meat and charcuterie in 1962, by 1972 it had fallen to seventeenth place.[17] Since demand for meat and charcuterie was greater than for cereals as incomes increased, this indicated that the structure of French agriculture was not adapting to changes in the market. But, because it was such a large beneficiary of the CAP, the French government staunchly defended the policy, even when mounting surpluses, particularly of wine, milk, and butter, provoked hostile reactions within the rest of the EEC and GATT during the 1970s.

The French government was particularly opposed to the inclusion of agriculture in the trade negotiations of GATT, but having successfully resisted it during the Tokyo Round (1973–79) it finally conceded to its inclusion during the Uruguay Round (1986–94). Under what became known as the MacSharry reforms in 1992, it was agreed by the EU that the price guarantees of the CAP would be replaced by a new form of direct income support to farmers, while the price of wheat and other cereals was cut by 29 per cent.[18] The change led to a major restructuring of French farms. Over the period 1988–2000 the proportion of large, mainly arable farms of over 50 hectares almost doubled, rising from 16.9 per cent of the total to 30.2 per cent. This was at the expense of medium-sized farms of between 10 and 50 hectares, which declined from 44.75 per cent to 31.48 per cent of the total. The small family farm of less than ten hectares was unchanged.[19] Annual output of wheat in France, which had risen from 7.7 million tonnes in 1950 to reach 31.4 million tonnes by 1990, continued to rise, reaching 35.7 million tonnes by 2000.[20]

Even when the system of guaranteed prices was replaced by single payments to farmers as part of the MacSharry reforms, France continued to be the largest beneficiary of the CAP. Once again it was the large arable farmers of the north and the Paris basin who benefited much more than the subsistence farmers of the south, for whom the high price of fodder and the cost of investing in machinery, which was scarcely profitable on small plots of land, led to debt and impoverishment. The rural exodus continued. As the EEC expanded in the 1980s, French agriculture faced increased competition in fruit, vegetables and wine from Spain, Portugal and Greece. And it suffered further when the Central and Eastern European countries began to join the EU in 2004, and the CAP, which until then had taken the lion's share of the budget, was reduced to enable structural funds to be spent on the new member states.

THE SINGLE MARKET

By the 1980s, when France had finally managed to produce stable surpluses in its agricultural trade, it was beginning to produce surpluses in services as well. It was a sector that was still highly protected within the EC, and in the international economy, partly because many services were not traded and partly because much of the protection took place behind, rather than at, the borders. Although many of these non-tariff barriers (NTBs) as they were called, which included taxes, technical standards, state subsidies and calls for tender, were well-established instruments of regional, industrial and social policy, they were now seen as hindering recovery and growth on both a European and a global level. Under the impetus of the British government led by Margaret Thatcher, and with the enthusiastic support of the new president of the European Commission, Jacques Delors, a programme to eliminate NTBs, as well as all impediments to the free movement of goods, capital, people and services (the "four freedoms") was agreed. The Single European Act, introducing the single market, was signed by the Chirac government in France and ratified in 1987, to come into force in December 1992. Thus, whereas member states had been allowed ten years to remove tariff barriers, they now had only five years to remove non-tariff ones. Although Delors had hoped to balance the new economic freedoms with European-wide funds to redistribute some of the gains made to those who lost out, the cohesion funds that were agreed were to help disadvantaged regions not households, and were but "the crumbs of solidarity".[21]

Studies by the European Commission identified the 40 industrial sectors most at risk in each country from exposure to full competition. In France, as in the UK, Belgium and Spain, employment was distributed quite evenly between high- and low-performing sectors, whereas in West Germany and Italy there was a concentration of employment in high-performance sectors. In France the sectors credited with good performances according to the indices selected represented 29.6 per cent of industrial employment, compared with the 16 per cent for those with poor performance records. However, as much as 9.3 per cent of French industrial employment was in sectors with extremely poor performance records, such as machinery, shoes and clothing. On the other hand 12.8 per cent of industrial employment was in sectors with high performance such as drinks, aeronautics and railway equipment.[22] Companies in the French pharmaceutical industry were judged not to be sufficiently large or exposed to enough international competition to justify high levels of research and development. In 1988 a report initiated by the European Commission calculated that, were the single market to be implemented in full, it would lead to an increase in output of between 2.5 and 6.5 per cent of GDP over a ten-year period.[23]

In anticipation of the completion of the single market, French exports to the EEC expanded from 49 per cent of the total in 1980 to 63 per cent in 1992.[24] Coinciding with the relaxation of controls over capital movements, the impact on foreign direct investment (FDI) was even more dramatic. Whereas over the period 1980–85 about 25 per cent of French FDI was directed to the EEC, it had risen to 68 per cent by 1991. In 1992 as much as 80 per cent of all new FDI went to the EEC.[25]

After the introduction of the single market in 1992, the rate of expansion of all trade with the EU slowed down, but by 1999 it was still overwhelmingly the largest market for French exports, taking 64.2 per cent of the total. However, if the French and other governments had hoped that the single market would contribute to a growth in trade in services, they were to be disappointed. In a study carried out by the European Commission in 2007 the conclusion reached was that cross-border trade in services had scarcely increased, due to the persistence of domestic barriers to such trade.[26] Following the financial crisis of 2008–09, the Commission admitted that the single market was less popular than ever, at a time when Europe needed it more than ever. The recommendations of a report commissioned from the Italian economist Mario Monti in 2010 stressed the importance of reaching a consensus on reforming the single market to ensure that most members of society would view it as being beneficial to their interests.[27]

A subsequent study published in 2019, which looked at the impact on regions of the single market, concluded that those which benefited most were those closest to the centre and consequently with greater access to the market, as well as those with a robust manufacturing or service sector. As far as France was concerned, the single market had reinforced the east–west division, with per capita gains greater in the east, in the new Champagne-Ardenne-Alsace region that was close to Germany, than in the west. Western regions such as Poitou-Charentes-Limousin and Basse-Normandie were all in the lowest quintile of gains. Paris and the Île-de-France benefited greatly due to being a multinational hub within a centralized economy, the study concluded.[28]

THE SINGLE CURRENCY

Whether by design or political accident, the introduction of the single market in 1993 coincided with a renewed commitment to create a single currency in the European Community.[29] Under the Treaty on European Union, signed at Maastricht on 7 February 1992, member states committed themselves to achieving an economic and monetary union, including a single currency administered by a single independent central bank. This was to be achieved in three specific stages. The third stage, which was to start no later than 1 January 1999, committed those countries that had fulfilled four agreed criteria to proceed to the adoption of a single currency.[30] These criteria were based on monetary convergence indicators such as exchange rate stability, levels of public debt and deficits, and rates of inflation, rather than convergence indicators based on economic policy coordination.[31] By accepting these, European member states were, it would seem, following the preferences of the French rather than the German government, but it was a price that the united Germany was willing to pay.[32]

It is plausibly claimed that in the twentieth century France was probably the strongest campaigner for an international monetary system that would deliver stable exchange rates through a process agreed among equals.[33] The first example and the model of what it envisaged was the Tripartite Agreement of 1936 reached between the governments of France, the United States and the United Kingdom. Under this agreement, rather than deciding the exchange value of the currency unilaterally, as had happened when both sterling and the dollar had been devalued in 1931 and 1933, respectively, the exchange value of the franc was determined by all three governments together.

However, between 1941 and 1944, when the terms of the postwar international monetary system culminating in the Bretton Woods agreement of 1944 were being debated, there was little doubt that the United States was the hegemonic power and the dollar would be the hegemonic reserve currency. A counterproposal drawn up by two French financial experts, Hervé Alphand and André Istel, which envisaged not the dollar but a basket of currencies and key raw materials held as reserves, merited no more than a footnote in the Bretton Woods Agreement.[34] De Gaulle's attempts to undermine the hegemonic role of the dollar, after the European currencies had become convertible into gold and dollars in 1958, eventually brought down the entire Bretton Woods international monetary system, and with it the Werner Plan agreed by European Community heads of state at their summit meeting in The Hague in 1969 to form a stable union of their currencies in an increasingly unstable world.[35]

In the subsequent arrangement, known as the "snake", in which European governments agreed to hold the fluctuations of their currencies within an agreed band, it soon became clear that the German Deutsche Mark had become the hegemonic currency in Europe. This meant in practice that the burden of adjustment fell on countries that were running deficits, such as France, to deflate domestic demand in order to correct their deficits. Countries that were running surpluses, such as West Germany, did not need to take any symmetrical action to expand domestic demand. Rather than comply, France left the snake several times. When invited by the West German Chancellor, Helmut Schmidt, to bilateral discussions to reform the operation of the snake in 1978, Giscard d'Estaing felt that in those negotiations he had won the case for both surplus and deficit countries to adjust their domestic policy in the event of currency imbalances. However, no sooner had the newly negotiated European Monetary System (EMS) been set up than the independent Bundesbank rejected the obligation to intervene in favour of weak currencies in the interest of stabilizing exchange rates. Nonetheless, in March 1979 all the EC member states except the UK agreed to participate in the new EMS, whose centrepiece was an exchange rate mechanism designed to keep the fluctuations between currencies to a maximum of 2.25 per cent on either side of a par value expressed in terms of the average of the EC currencies. Italy was given a margin for the lira of 6 per cent.

Between 1981 and 1983 the French franc was devalued three times (3 per cent, 5.75 per cent and 2.5 per cent). This was the result of the Socialist government's priority of reducing unemployment by expanding the French economy following the second large increase in the price of oil in 1979 while other members of the EMS reduced domestic demand. After the third devaluation of the franc, the French government decided to pursue a less expansionist policy that would be more in line with that of other members, particularly West Germany.

This famous policy U-turn of 1983 by Mitterrand produced greater stability in the French exchange rate, with one revaluation of 2 per cent in July 1985 and one devaluation of 3 per cent in August 1986. It has been suggested that the determination of French governments in the 1980s to maintain what was an over-valued exchange rate ("franc fort") may have contributed to the high levels of unemployment experienced in that decade.[36] What is clear is that, after the ratification of the Treaty of Maastricht, the determination of French governments in the 1990s to prepare the French economy for participation in the common currency of the euro, according to the convergence criteria, by cutting public expenditure and increasing the already high levels of unemployment provoked years of social unrest.[37] When the Socialist government elected in May 1997 to cohabit with President Chirac attempted to find a way to enable policies designed to promote growth and reduce unemployment to be pursued once the common currency was in operation it failed. The Stability and Growth Pact adopted in July 1997 may have included the word "growth", but financial stability remained the priority. Subsequent labour market reforms, named after the Socialist labour minister Martine Aubry, that were designed to reduce unemployment through a range of measures that included cutting the working week to 35 hours and limiting access to benefits to those unemployed who signed up to personalized job search programmes, failed to work as intended, costing the Socialist party two elections and ten years in opposition.[38]

While domestic unemployment continued to rise following the introduction of the euro in 2002, the flows of FDI from France also increased, with the stock almost doubling between 2006 and 2016. Rising from €625 billion in 2006 to reach €1.2 trillion in 2016, almost all the FDI from France went to the eurozone and the United States. However, over the same period FDI into France also expanded, but by very much less than the investment leaving the country; the total in 2016 was €661.8 billion.[39] Despite its high taxes and less flexible labour laws, in 2019 France was in fact the most attractive country for FDI in Europe. It was well ahead of Germany and Italy and of the UK after Brexit, and with firms such as Airbus, EDF, Danone and Sanofi being among the main recipients, investors claimed to prefer stable rather than low rates of taxation.[40]

While the goal of financial stability was severely challenged in the European sovereign debt crisis, and, following the financial crisis of 2008–09, eluded Greece in particular, it did not lead to any relaxation of the rules. Quite the contrary. Whereas the rules had been softened in 2005 following the refusal of the EU Council to impose fines on France and Germany for having exceeded the permitted deficits in 2003, they were to be enforced more vigorously after 2010.[41] If, under the 2005 reforms, it was stated that countries with low debts or those trying to implement costly structural programmes could deviate from the strict financial rules, under the European Stability Mechanism (ESM) signed by all 17 euro-zone members in February 2012 to provide extra liquidity to those governments most in need, Germany was able to set limits to the lending capacity of the funds.[42] Under the new "fiscal compact" the balanced budget rule was to be incorporated into the legal systems of member states at the constitutional or equivalent level. Years of austerity followed, with levels of inequality within and between member states rising. It was only in the face of the Covid-19 pandemic, which affected all the member states although in varying degrees of intensity, that the budgetary discipline rules were suspended for the first time.

THE FRANC ZONE

It is often overlooked that France participated in the international monetary system and then in the European Monetary Union as head of a currency area, known as the Franc Zone. Formally created in 1939 when the French government had introduced foreign exchange controls, the Franc Zone is composed of 14 Central and West African states, plus Comoros, all of which had formed part of the French empire. Apart from Comoros, which became independent in 1975, and Djioubti, which became independent in 1977, these states all gained independence between 1958 and 1962.[43] As a monetary area the Franc Zone had, however, existed in a loose form since the nineteenth century, when the currencies of the various African territories had been pegged to the metropolitan franc. The area gained greater cohesion towards the end of the Second World War, when the component currencies became convertible into each other, and shared common rules when dealing with third countries. On 26 December 1945, when the French government registered a par value for the franc with the IMF, it also created two linked currencies: the CFA franc (for French colonies in Africa) and the CFP franc (for French colonies in the Pacific). The term "empire" was replaced by that of "union" in the constitution of the Fourth Republic to signify the intention of replacing the former imperial relationship with that of an association.[44] However, since both the CFA and the CFP francs were higher in value than the metropolitan franc, the continued imbalance in the relationship was clear. The empire was to continue to offer a protected market for French exports, particularly of textiles and foodstuffs, while earning foreign exchange for the Franc Zone as a whole through its exports of raw materials and foodstuffs to the rest of the world.[45] Following the nationalization of the Bank of France in December 1945, responsibility for issuing banknotes was gradually transferred from private banks to public institutions throughout the Franc Zone. This transformed it into a highly centralized area characterized by common foreign exchange controls, the pooling of foreign exchange reserves and the free convertibility of the currencies in the area on a fixed peg basis. The Banque de l'Algérie was nationalized in May 1946, and the Banque de Madagascar et des Comores became a semi-public institution in 1950.

Five years later, issuing banks were set up in French West Africa, Togo, French Equatorial Africa and Cameroon. While some countries did leave the zone when they became independent, the zone as a whole did not break up.[46] France, however, did recognize the right of the newly independent sub-Saharan African countries to have their own issuing bank. In West Africa six newly independent countries formed the Central Bank of West African States (BCEOA) in April 1959 to manage their common currency, the CFA franc, which in an attempt to shake off the colonial past now stood for Financial Community of Africa.[47] In central

Africa five states formed the Central Bank of Equatorial African States and Cameroon (BCEAEC) to manage their CFA franc, which had the same parity with the metropolitan franc as the West African currency.[48]

Figure 6.1 The Franc Zone (the Comoros archipelago, not shown, is also a member of the Franc Zone but not of the CFA monetary unions)

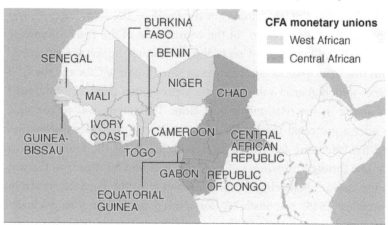

From 1965 onwards the ministers of finance and central bank governors of the Franc Zone met twice every year just before the meetings of the IMF and the World Bank. After France lifted its foreign exchange controls in 1967 the Franc Zone became limited to countries that had signed monetary cooperation agreements with France and that held an account at the French Treasury. The first agreement was signed between France and the central African bank in November 1972. One year later, on 14 November 1973, the West African states formed a monetary union, which then signed a cooperation agreement with France the following month. For its part, the French Treasury provided unlimited convertibility guarantees in return for the African banks depositing a proportion of their foreign exchange reserves (between 50 per cent and 65 per cent) with the French Treasury and allowing free capital flows throughout the area. The parity of the Comorian franc was the same as the CFA franc from the time the Comoros Islands became independent in 1975 until 1994, when it was devalued by 33 per cent.

In 1975 an economic community of 15 West African states, ECOWAS (CÉDÉAO in French), was formed, composed of the eight members of the West African Economic and Monetary Union[49] together with seven countries outside it: Nigeria, Ghana, Guinea, Liberia, Sierra Leone, The Gambia and Cape Verde. Its stated long-term goal was to form a monetary union to accompany a process of integration that included greater regional trade overseen by common institutions.[50]

When the metropolitan franc was replaced by the euro on 1 January 1999, the euro became the anchor for the CFA franc and the Comorian franc, but the mechanisms for monetary cooperation in the Franc Zone were to carry on as before and the European Central Bank did not assume any obligations to support the CFA franc.[51] It was not the replacement of the French franc by the euro that threatened the stability of the Franc Zone but the announcement on 20 April 2000 by the leaders of six West African states, led by the first democratically elected head of state in Nigeria since the 1993 military coup, of their intention to introduce a single currency into the monetary union of the non-CFA franc countries by January 2003. This was to be the first step they claimed towards a wider monetary union including all the ECOWAS countries in 2004.[52]

A West African monetary union with its own common currency posed a potential challenge to the euro-backed CFA franc and raised questions about who actually benefited from the Franc Zone. Many in West Africa claimed that the overvalued exchange rate of the CFA franc, far from attracting foreign investors to develop the productive capacity of the region, had in fact served as an import subsidy for French exporters while damaging local producers. The CFA franc was, in their view, no more than a new form of servitude under a different name. As evidence they cited the fact that, although France provided development assistance (it provided over one quarter of the assistance to the Franc Zone between 1990 and 2008) and although the CFA franc delivered low inflation, growth was no better than in other sub-Saharan countries and inter-regional trade remained low. At the same time trade between France and the rest of the Franc Zone had increased. As part of the terms of their independence the sub-Saharan governments had signed two types of secret cooperation agreements with France. The first one offered France privileged access to its former colonies' raw materials, while the second one, demanded by the African presidents themselves, concerned the guaranteed military protection of their new regimes by the French state. French aid was held to have guaranteed a virtual monopoly for French firms conducting infrastructure projects in Africa, leading to a sort of neo-colonial society emerging in the capitals of the former empire. In the first ten years after the independence of the Côte d'Ivoire, for example, the number of French people living there had risen from 10,000 to 50,000.[53]

However great the resentment towards France and the CFA franc, the new rival currency that was to have been launched in 2004 did not appear. Finally, in June 2019 the leaders of ECOWAS announced that the new currency, to be named the "eco", would be introduced the following year. In response President Macron, while on a visit to Abidjan in the Côte d'Ivoire in December 2019, let it be known that the West African Central Bank would no longer be obliged to deposit half of its reserves in a special account at the French Treasury on which the French paid 0.75 per cent interest.[54] The CFA franc, he declared, was finished, soon to be replaced by the eco.[55] No mention was made of the fact that the central African bank would still hold the CFA franc. At the same time, what benefit the French Treasury has derived from holding part of the reserves of the two African central banks is not clear. According to the French Ministère de l'Europe et des Affaires Étrangères, France does not use the African currency reserves deposited with the French Treasury to finance its external debt.[56]

CONCLUSION

Since the first proposal made in 1950 to integrate two sectors of the French economy into a wider European economy, the degree of integration has expanded to such an extent that in 2018 almost 70 per cent of French imports and nearly 60 per cent of its exports were with the EU.[57] In 2016 almost 70 per cent of all FDI from France went to the eurozone. However, while it is straightforward to measure trade and investment flows it is much harder to analyse the extent to which the original objectives underlying the historic proposal of 1950 have been achieved. As we have seen, those objectives were to preserve the domestic consensus underpinning the Monnet Plan's ambition to restructure the French economy so that it resembled more closely that of other developed economies, and thereby delivered higher living standards, while establishing a positive relationship with the new Federal Republic of Germany. The ECSC contributed to the achievement of both objectives. It facilitated the gradual transformation of the French economy from one dominated by agriculture and light industry to one in which heavy industry contributed a larger share of value added. At the same time it enabled controls over the expansion of German industry to be removed, which in turn benefited the French economy.

The EEC was to deliver similar objectives over a longer period of time. The shift in trade from the protected markets of the French Union to the increasingly open and rapidly growing ones of western Europe contributed to improvements in living standards in France. The benefits to the agricultural sector were less evenly distributed, however, since it was the large cereal and sugar beet producers in the centre and north of France that benefited disproportionately from the CAP.

The single market and the single currency proved to be more successful in delivering the second of the original two objectives insofar as they provided a framework into which the French could accept a unified Germany after 1989. But, in focusing on the potential benefits to some sections of the service sector and to private French investors, the single market did little to address the problems facing much of the manufacturing sector and the regions in France wholly dependent on it. These problems were exacerbated by the rules governing the single currency, even if those rules were relaxed somewhat in their application, before being tightened in the aftermath of the sovereign debt crisis. However, the defeat of the RN candidate Martine Le Pen to the determinately pro-European candidate Emmanuel Macron in the second round of the presidential elections of 2017 led to a softening of the party's policy towards the EU. Rather than follow the British example and leave the Union, the party advocated a return to the Gaullist policy of a Europe of nation-states ("*l'Europe des patries*") that would pursue a protectionist policy in terms of trade. As the 2022 presidential elections appeared on the horizon, early opinion polls suggested that the second round would be a repetition of 2017 between Macron and Le Pen, with the result too close to call.[58]

7

Conclusion

The long and acrimonious Brexit negotiations between the British government and the European Commission representing the 27 member states of the EU succeeded in uniting all the main political parties in France in opposing a similar French exit from the EU.[1] If this seemed to be a ringing endorsement of President Macron's unwavering support for the Union, the Front National, renamed the Rassemblement National in June 2018 by its leader Marine Le Pen,[2] made clear that its change of policy towards membership of the EU was conditional on the latter adopting a protectionist policy in its trade with the rest of the world, and ending the free movement of labour within the European Single Market. With protectionism on the rise across the world, Le Pen's policy was increasingly popular in France, where a growing number of voters were happy to blame the persistently high unemployment and rise in poverty and inequality on immigrants and imports.

As the Covid-19 pandemic began to spread across the world it revealed and widened inequalities both within and between countries. Not only did it expose differences in income and living and working conditions but it deepened the division between the digital and the non-digital economy, thereby revealing the extent of European dependence on the US technology giants that had been its main beneficiaries. There was no European equivalent of Google, Apple, Facebook or Amazon.[3] This was blamed by the French government partly on the tax privileges enjoyed by the US multinationals and partly on the failure of the European Commission to address the problem. Long before the outbreak of Covid-19, indeed since 2013, the French government had been campaigning to win the agreement of the other EU member states to tax the big tech companies in the countries where they made their profits rather than in those where they were headquartered. However, since European tax policies require unanimity, the French were unsuccessful. When Apple and the government of the Republic of Ireland won their appeal against the Commission's demand for a repayment of tax, and with the US opposed to any change in the way that the firms were taxed, the European Commission was unwilling to risk starting a trade war with the US by pressing the case, preferring to leave the issue to the OECD to negotiate. In any case, it was on weak ground given the large trade surplus that the EU, and France, had with the US and also due to its own unwillingness to address the problem of European (including French) multinational firms and wealthy individuals choosing to be based in Luxembourg to avoid paying tax. Another way in which the French government sought to attack the hegemony of the US tech companies was by pressing for more EU integration on the financing of start-ups, a digital single market to promote innovation in privacy and technological development, and European cloud and data solutions to reduce European reliance on US firms.

In an effort to stop the spread of coronavirus the French government, along with many others, shut down parts of the economy, leading Bruno Le Maire, the economy minister, to promise to nationalize those sectors listed on the CAC 40 that were worst affected if it proved necessary to protect them from hostile takeovers.[4] This led one notable economic historian, Philippe Mioche, to recommend that France should return to the economic planning that had been so successful in regenerating the economy after the end of the Second World War, doing it on a national and then a European level.[5] But, if the pandemic offers an opportunity for the French government to shape or reshape the economy as it recovers, as it found when it sought to recapitalize Air France, in return for agreeing to a temporary relaxation of the rules governing state aid the EU demands that member states should open up those companies receiving such aid to greater competition within the EU. What this means in practice is that Air France should cede extra slots at Paris Orly airport to other European airlines, as German airlines have been obliged to do in several airports. Thus, if the pandemic offers an opportunity to national governments to intervene in their economies, it also offers the European Commission a chance to inject some new dynamism into the stalled liberalization of trade within the single market.

While there are obvious differences in the challenges facing France in the recovery from the pandemic compared with those it faced after the Second World War, not least in the scale of the problems faced in 1945, there are nonetheless some parallels. Now, as then, years of austerity and protection have led to a failure to invest in those sectors of the economy in which world demand is expanding, leaving many people either unemployed or working in sectors where their productivity is low. We have seen that in 1945 one third of the French labour force was still employed in agriculture. While the UK, the United States and Germany had invested in capital goods industries and were producing the sort of goods for which world demand was expanding (cars, aeroplanes, electrical consumer durable goods such as refrigerators and washing machines as well as office equipment), large numbers of French people were continuing to produce food and agricultural products, textiles and clothing and selling them on the protected domestic and colonial markets.

What turned the French economy around after 1945 was, first, the new national consensus in favour of state intervention in the economy that emerged from both the resistance to Nazi occupation and the way in which the occupation was managed by the Vichy government. This consensus in favour of state intervention produced a form of planning that was very different from the Soviet command economy, in which all production and trade was controlled by the state. Apart from the limited number of firms that had been nationalized in 1936 and in the immediate aftermath of the Second World War, most of the French economy remained in private hands. It was the instruments available to the state, particularly its control over credit for investment, that distinguished French planning from the dominant Soviet version. The controls of both a quantitative and qualitative nature over credit ensured that the funding of investment, much of it public, would not lead to inflation, thereby undermining consumption and living standards. Investment was not to be at the expense of consumption. Reforms to the tax system were similarly designed to deliver the objectives of the plan, particularly the introduction of an extra tax on the self-employed that was to end the protection small businesses enjoyed by failing to declare the full extent of their earnings, while the replacement of the cumulative tax on production with a tax on value added, from which investment was exempt, was to increase investment and exports.

Second, it was the ability of the planners to win agreement on a set of priorities for investment across the economy in the private sector as well as the public sector, in agriculture as well as industry and services that contributed to its success. The objective was to change the structure of the French economy so that it ressembled that of other developed countries. While investment in the steel industry, particularly in new wide strip mills, was critical to the transformation of much of the manufacturing sector, leading to an expansion of output and increased demand for labour, so too was investment in agriculture. This enabled labour to be released into higher productivity jobs in industry and services while also increasing the productivity of those who remained working in agriculture.

Third, it was the changes in the nature and scale of trade with other European countries, in particular with West Germany, that, although quite unplanned, contributed to changing the structure of the French economy. It was not only the increased exports from West Germany of the products of mechanical engineering, electrical engineering and transport equipment that sustained investment in France but also West Germany's increasing demand for imports of those products from France, rather than for food and agricultural products as in the 1930s. At the same time, labour was drawn not only from agriculture but also from the textile and clothing sector due to demand in France and in the protected markets of the colonies rising much less rapidly for their products. This led to a new structure of trade in western Europe that, after the formation of the EEC, was increasingly liberalized.

This was an ambitious long-term programme, which was only partially completed before it was changed under the Fifth Republic. In 1958 de Gaulle, influenced by Jacques Rueff, his financial adviser, considered that France had been living beyond its means and set out to cut demand, particularly consumption. At the same time the controls over credit were relaxed, allowing rates of investment and growth of GDP to soar. Investment in industry was increasingly freed from official constraints, and executive orders replaced consensus-building. Between 1961 and 1971 the proportion of total funding provided by the Treasury fell considerably. Apart from a number of technologically advanced but commercially unsuccessful projects in aircraft, space research and computers, which were publicly funded, the choice of most investment was left in the hands of banks, which were now increasingly freed from state controls, or family firms to fund from their own resources. Although de Gaulle retained the organizational structure of planning, it became more like an industrial policy in which the state actively promoted mergers and rationalizations in order to create national champions able to compete with American firms. With the loss of the protected markets in the colonies and exposure to competition in the EEC, the traditional industries of textiles and footwear began to struggle. Only agriculture was offered continued protection under a common policy in the new European Economic Community. As a result of the guaranteed prices and markets offered by the CAP, France, which had the largest area of cultivable land in the EEC, was the largest beneficiary. But equally, because of the CAP, after 1964 there was a much faster increase in the output and exports of French cereals than of the animal farming sector.

What brought the Gaullist model to an end were not only the protests of 1968 and the sporadic outbursts of violence in the poorest parts of

France but the collapse of the international monetary system of Bretton Woods following the sustained pressure put on the dollar by the French government. In the aftermath of the devaluation of the dollar and the quadrupling of the dollar price of oil in 1973, the French economy joined the rest of the developed world in a major recession, the first since 1945. It was the first experience of mass unemployment in France in modern times. With an economy more heavily dependent on imported oil than other developed countries, the incoming French president, Giscard d'Estaing, immediately embarked on a major public investment programme to construct nuclear reactors, with the aim of substituting nuclear energy for oil imports and thereby safeguard the French balance of payments from similar shocks in the future (by 1994 almost 78 per cent of French electricity came from nuclear power). The government also commissioned large infrastructure projects such as high-speed trains and the extension of the Paris metro to the suburbs. But the public investment failed to stimulate private investment at a time when West Germany, Japan and the United States were adjusting to the changes in the international economy and increasing their investment in areas where global demand was rising. These included electronics, information technology, data processing and medical imaging equipment. With 700,000 people, of whom many were women, entering the French labour market for the first time in the 1970s it was the one million new jobs in services that prevented the unemployment figures from rising to nearly two million. However, of the new jobs in services, 797,000 were in services to individuals, particularly in health care, and many were part-time, while 297,000 were in services to firms.

The incoming Socialist government under President Mitterrand hoped to reduce unemployment by expanding both investment and consumption. By nationalizing large numbers of firms in industry and banking, it intended to make up for the lack of private investment in the 1970s while at the same time increasing social spending. But in the absence of a national plan and a set of priorities for investment, and with reduced capacity in manufacturing industry the expansion in demand led to the worst foreign exchange crisis of the postwar era. Rather than reduce and

control investment by agreeing on a set of national priorities, the government cut social spending and consumption. At the same time it reduced
controls over capital movements to encourage foreign investment in the
French economy, while agreeing to the proposal to eliminate all non-tariff
barriers to trade in the European single market.

The objective was to combine trade liberalization with increased social
spending not only in France but across the EC. However, while trade in
some services was liberalized, enabling many French multinational companies to expand into both the European and international markets, most
of the rest of the service sector remained protected not only in France
but across the EU, with domestic barriers to trade in services persisting.
The hope that along with the single market and the single currency there
would be a fund to redistribute income to those who did not benefit was
not realized. Nonetheless, the French government increased the level of
taxation in order to compensate those who were disadvantaged by the
further removal of controls over the economy at a time when mainstream
economists in Britain and the United States were arguing that a reduction in taxes was essential to promote economic growth. In most years
since the early 1980s, taxes, as a proportion of GDP, were higher in France
than anywhere else in the developed world. Yet, despite the high taxes
and redistribution, unemployment, particularly among the young and
unskilled, remained very high. Part of the problem was due to the structure of taxation. In an effort to reduce unemployment successive governments offered inducements to firms to take on extra labour by exempting
them from paying the high rates of employers' contributions to social
security, with the resulting shortfall in receipts made up by introducing
a new tax, the CSG. Levied on a flat-rate basis, it was to raise more than
income tax thereby contributing to the regressivity of the fiscal system.

Despite the high taxes, by the late 2010s France had proved to be the
most attractive country for foreign investment in Europe, as firms that
had previously been nationalized were opened to private ownership.
However, the structure of manufacturing production was slow to evolve
and France continued to specialize in exporting transport equipment,

including aeronautical, nuclear power technology and armaments. In the newer expanding fields of computers and information technologies French firms were unable to challenge the dominant position of the large American and Japanese multinational firms in the international market. In the sectors where it had finally established a trade surplus (food and agricultural products), demand was growing much more slowly.

One major concern of the government throughout the privatization process was to retain control of the companies while selling their share capital, or, at the very least, to prevent the privatized companies from falling into foreign hands and ultimately lead to asset stripping. The government of Dominique de Villepin, having previously tried to reinvigorate French economic competitiveness and boost innovation by offering research funds and tax incentives to a number of sectors including neurosciences, nanotechnology, health and secure communications systems as well as aeronautics, now simply outlawed some foreign mergers or acquisitions. After the 2008 financial crisis, President Nicolas Sarkozy went further and set up a strategic investment fund to protect French firms considered critical to the economy. The method chosen by the Socialist government to stimulate investment was to create a public investment bank offering both loans and the opportunity to issue shares to the state-owned bank.

As a result of the measures put in place since the 1980s, the French growth model has come to rely more on domestic demand than on exports. While high taxation and spending has contributed to sustaining demand, the protection offered to the many small businesses in the service sector has reduced investment. The French model contrasts with the German one, based on a more flexible labour market, higher income inequality and poverty across individuals and age groups and a greater exposure to the international economy. While Germany benefited from the strong recovery and high growth rates of emerging economies after the global financial crisis of 2008–09, with a structure of exports meeting demand, it is now more exposed to sharp swings in global trade.[6] The French economy has grown more slowly, and while its dependence on a small range of exports of goods and services, in particular on sales of aircraft and luxury goods, creates specific vulnerabilities, it benefits from a high level of human capital and no unemployment for high skilled workers. With a higher birth rate than Germany, the share of the working-age population is expected to fall by less in the medium term.

However, one problem facing France that the 2020 pandemic highlighted is that, while it is the second largest market in Europe and the fifth biggest in the world for e-commerce, its digital performance is relatively low. In 2014 the European Commission began to compile an annual index to compare the progress made by each member state in adopting digital technology. In 2019 France was in 15th place, far below the leaders Finland, Sweden, Denmark and the Netherlands and below Malta, Ireland and Estonia.

Table 7.1 Comparative digital performance (Digital Economy and Society Index 2020)

	France		Germany		UK		EU-28
	Rank	Score	Rank	Score	Rank	Score	Score
Overall	15	52.2	12	56.1	8	60.4	52.6
Connectivity	18	49.8	8	59.4	20	48.8	50.1
Human capital	17	47.4	10	56.4	5	63	49.3
Use of internet services	21	53.1	9	61.6	5	73.3	58
Integration of digital technology	11	42	18	39.5	8	54.2	41.4
Digital public services	12	76.7	21	66.4	16	70.8	72

Source: European Commission, *Shaping Europe's Digital Future*.

In 2019, only 17 per cent of French households subscribed to a fixed broadband of at least 100 megabits per second or above, well below the EU average of 26 per cent, although with broadband prices higher than the EU average (the price index in France was 80 against 64 for the EU) this was perhaps understandable. France was also below the EU in the proportion of individuals with digital skills above a basic level (31 per cent in France, 33 per cent in the EU). At the same time, the share of Internet users, at 87 per cent, was higher than the average for the EU, with most people using it for online banking, shopping and selling rather than for social networking or streaming. On the other hand, the number of companies using e-commerce in France was below the EU average and varied considerably with the size of company: only 15 per cent of small and medium-sized companies used it compared with almost 45 per cent of large companies. Where France clearly ranked above average was in the digital provision of public services (see Table 7.1).

Although French governments have drawn up various investment programmes in recent years to improve the country's digital performance, including the provision of life-long learning, the protection afforded to many small businesses, particularly in services, has limited demand. This suggests that if France is to close the digital divide, reduce inequalities and prepare for a carbon-neutral future, greater action will be needed. But whether that action should be at the national level or the European level divides opinion. History suggests that it will be through the government achieving a consensus on the priorities for investment, choosing sectors where demand is expanding globally and reducing protection, that progress will be made. Thus, if the pandemic offers an opportunity to the French government to intervene in the economy to improve living standards and prepare for a carbon-free future in the digital age, it also offers the European Commission a chance to inject some new dynamism into the stalled liberalization of trade within the single market to help it to face that future.

Appendix

Table A.1 Heads of the Provisional Government

Name	Term of office	Political party
Charles de Gaulle	20 Aug 1944–26 Jan 1946	Independent
Félix Gouin	26 Jan–24 Jun 1946	SFIO
Georges Bidault	24 Jun–28 Nov 1946	MRP
Vincent Auriol	28 Nov–16 Dec 1946	SFIO
Léon Blum	16 Dec 1946–22 Jan 1947	SFIO

Table A.2 Presidents of the Council of Ministers of the Fourth Republic

Name	Term of office	Political party
Paul Ramadier	22 Jan–24 Nov 1947	SFIO
Robert Schuman	24 Nov 1947–24 Jul 1948	MRP
André Marie	24 Jul–2 Sep 1948	Radical
Robert Schuman	2–11 Sep 1948	MRP
Henri Queuille	11 Sep 1948–28 Oct 1949	Radical
Georges Bidault	28 Oct 1949–2 Jul 1950	MRP
Henri Queuille	2–12 Jul 1950	Radical
René Pleven	12 Jul 1950–10 Mar 1951	Resistance
Henri Queuille	10 Mar–11 Aug 1951	Radical
René Pleven	11 Aug 1951–20 Jan 1952	Resistance
Edgar Faure	20 Jan–8 Mar 1952	Radical
Antoine Pinay	8 Mar 1952–8 Jan 1953	Independents & Peasants
René Mayer	8 Jan–28 Jun 1953	Radical
Joseph Laniel	28 Jun 1953–19 Jun 1954	Independents & Peasants
Pierre Mendès France	19 Jun 1954–17 Feb 1955	Radical
Christian Pineau	17–23 Feb 1955	SFIO
Edgar Faure	23 Feb 1955–1 Feb 1956	Radical
Guy Mollet	1 Feb 1956–13 Jun 1957	SFIO
Maurice Bourgès-Maunoury	13 Jun–6 Nov 1957	Radical
Félix Gaillard	6 Nov 1957–14 May 1958	Radical
Pierre Pflimlin	14 May–1 Jun 1958	MRP
Charles de Gaulle	1 Jun 1958–8 Jan 1959	UNR

Table A.3 Prime ministers of the Fifth Republic

Name	Term of office	Political party
Michel Debré	8 Jan 1959–14 Apr 1962	UNR
Georges Pompidou	14 Apr 1962–10 Jul 1968	UNR
Maurice Couve de Murville	10 Jul 1968–20 Jun 1969	UDR
Jacques Chaban-Delmas	20 Jun 1969–6 Jul 1972	UDR
Pierre Messmer	6 Jul 1972–27 May 1974	UDR
Jacques Chirac	27 May 1974–26 Aug 1976	UDR
Raymond Barre	26 Aug 1976–31 Mar 1978	Independent
Raymond Barre	31 Mar 1978–21 May 1981	UDF
Pierre Mauroy	21 May 1981–17 Jul 1984	PS
Laurent Fabius	17 Jul 1984–20 Mar 1986	PS
Jacques Chirac	20 Mar 1986–10 May 1988	RPR
Michel Rocard	10 May 1988–15 May 1991	PS
Edith Cresson	15 May 1991–2 Apr 1992	PS
Pierre Bérégovoy	2 Apr 1992–29 Mar 1993	PS
Édouard Balladur	29 Mar 1993–17 May 1995	RPR
Alain Juppé	18 May 1995–3 Jun 1997	RPR
Lionel Jospin	3 Jun 1997–6 May 2002	PS
Jean-Pierre Raffarin	7 May 2002–31 May 2005	UMP
Dominique de Villepin	31 May 2005–15 May 2007	UMP
François Fillon	17 May 2007–10 May 2012	UMP
Jean-Marc Ayrault	15 May 2012–31 Mar 2014	PS
Manuel Vals	31 Mar 2014–6 Dec 2016	PS
Bernard Cazeneuve	6 Dec 2016–15 May 2017	PS
Édouard Philippe	15 May 2017–3 Jul 2020	UMP then LR
Jean Castex	3 Jul 2020–	LR

Table A.4 Presidents

Name	Term of office	Political party
Vincent Auriol	1947–53	SFIO
René Coty	1954–58	Independent
Charles de Gaulle	1959–69	UNR
Georges Pompidou	1969–74	UNR
Valéry Giscard d'Estaing	1974–81	Independent Republicans
François Mitterrand	1981–95	PS
Jacques Chirac	1995–2007	UMP
Nicolas Sarkozy	2007–12	UMP
François Hollande	2012–17	PS
Emmanuel Macron	2017–	LREM

Notes

PREFACE

1. Bootle, *The Trouble with Europe*, 114.
2. Dormois, *The French Economy in the Twentieth Century*.
3. Although Sarkozy made no mention of this in his book *Testimony: France, Europe, and the World in the Twenty-first Century*.
4. See OECD, *Beyond GDP: Measuring What Counts for Economic and Social Performance*; Stiglitz, *Globalization and Its Discontents*.
5. Fitoussi & Saraceno, "European economic governance: the Berlin–Washington consensus".
6. This was known as the High-Level Group on Measurement of Economic Performance and Social Progress (see OECD, *Beyond GDP*).
7. Fourastié, *Les trente glorieuses ou la révolution invisible de 1946 à 1975*.

1. INTRODUCING THE FRENCH ECONOMY

1. The first official measurements date from 1833, when a general statistics office was created within the ministry of trade.
2. Fourastié, *Les trente glorieuses*.
3. Milward & Saul, *The Development of the Economies of Continental Europe 1850–1914*.
4. Wieviorka (ed.), *La France en Chiffres de 1870 à nos jours*, 103.
5. McMillan, *Twentieth-Century France: Politics and Society, 1898–1991*, 47.
6. Magraw, "Not backward but different? The debate on French 'economic retardation'" in Alexander (ed.), *French History since Napoleon*.
7. Milward & Saul, *Economic Development of Continental Europe 1780–1870*.

8. Cummins, "Why did fertility decline? An analysis of the individual level economic correlates of the nineteenth century fertility transition in England and France?"

9. Armengaud, "Du Malthusianisme démographique au Malthusianisme économique" in Braudel & Labrousse (eds), *Histoire Économique et Sociale de la France*, 22.

10. O'Brien & Keyder, *Economic Growth in Britain and France, 1780–1914: Two Paths to the Twentieth Century*, 137.

11. Magraw, "Not backward but different?"

12. Lévy-Leboyer & Bourguignon, *The French Economy in the Nineteenth Century: An Essay in Econometric Analysis*.

13. Pinkney, *Napoleon III and the Rebuilding of Paris*.

14. Lane, *Industry and Society in Europe: Stability and Change in Britain, Germany and France*, 36 (figure refers to the 1920s).

15. Lévy-Leboyer & Bourguignon, *French Economy*, 8.

16. Dormois, *L'Économie française face à la concurrence britannique à la veille de 1914*.

17. Wieviorka, *La France en Chiffres*.

18. Dormois, "France: the idiosyncrasies of volontarisme" in Foreman-Peck & Federico (eds), *European Industrial Policy: The Twentieth-Century Experience*, 58–97.

19. Dormois, *L'Économie française face à la concurrence britannique à la veille de 1914*, 87.

20. Wieviorka, *La France en Chiffres*.

21. Millward, *The State and Business in the Major Powers: An Economic History 1815–1939*, 18.

22. Chadeau, "State-owned industry in France" in Tonelli (ed.), *The Rise and Fall of State-Owned Enterprise in the Western World*.

23. Millward, *State and Business*, 65.

24. Pinchemel, *France: A Geographical Survey*, 222.

25. Schremmer, "Taxation and public finance: Britain, France and Germany" in Mathias & Pollard (eds), *The Cambridge Economic History of Europe, Volume VIII*, 398.

26. Lynch, "The Haig-Shoup mission to France in the 1920s" in Brownlee, Ide & Fukagai (eds), *The Political Economy of Transnational Tax Reform*.

27. Wieviorka, *La France en Chiffres*, 103.

28. See Shennan, *Rethinking France: Plans for Renewal 1940–1946*, 99.

29. Chadeau, "State-owned industry in France".

2. THE CHANGING FRENCH ECONOMIC MODEL

1. McMillan, *Twentieth-Century France*, 153–7.

2. Although the left-wing populist movement La France Insoumise is calling for the formation of a constituent assembly to write the constitution of a Sixth Republic to replace what they consider to be the presidential monarchy of the Fifth Republic.

3. Baumier, *Les paysans de l'an 2000*, 29.

4. Milward, *The New Order and the French Economy*, 277.

5. Kuisel, *Capitalism and the State in Modern France: Renovation and Economic Management in the Twentieth Century*, 142.

6. Baum, *The French Economy and the State*, 9–10.

7. Rousso, "L'economie: pénurie et modernisation" in Azéma & Bédarida (eds), *La France des années noires*, 455.

8. Kuisel, *Capitalism and the State*, 86–7.

9. Shennan, *Rethinking France*, 232; Kuisel, *Capitalism and the State*, 147.

10. Shennan, *Rethinking France*, 46–9.

11. Patat & Lutfalla, *A Monetary History of France in the Twentieth Century*.

12. Faugère, *Les politiques salariales en France*.

13. Chadeau, "State-owned industry in France".

14. *Ibid.*

15. Chapman, *France's Long Reconstruction: In Search of the Modern Republic*, 166–7.

16. Monnet, *Controlling Credit, Central Banking and the Planned Economy in Postwar France, 1948–1973*, 13.

17. Quennouëlle-Corre, "The state, banks and financing of investments in France from World War II to the 1970s".

18. Lynch, "Resolving the paradox of the Monnet Plan: national and international planning in French reconstruction".

19. Margairaz, *L'État, les finances et l'économie. Histoire d'une conversion 1932–1952*.

20. Jabbari, *Pierre Laroque and the Welfare State in Postwar France*, 132–55.

21. Piketty, *Les hauts revenus en France au XXe siècle. Inégalités et redistributions 1901–1998*, 284.

22. Membership of trade unions is much lower in France than in neighbouring countries.

23. Chemla, "The French social security system", in ILO, *The Right to Social Security in the Constitutions of the World: Broadening the Moral and Legal Space for Social Justice.*

24. Lynch, "A tax for Europe: the introduction of value added tax in France".

25. Chadeau, "State-owned industry in France", 206.

26. Milward, *The European Rescue of the Nation-State*, 137.

27. Lynch, *France and the International Economy.*

28. Chapman, *France's Long Reconstruction*, 192.

29. Lynch, "The powerlessness of employees in France: the spread of income taxation, 1945–1980" in Huerlimann *et al.* (eds), *Worlds of Taxation.*

30. Monnet, *Controlling Credit: Central Banking and the Planned Economy in Postwar France, 1948–1973.*

31. Margairaz & Tartakowsky, *L'État détricoté. De la Résistance à la République en marche*, 75.

32. *Ibid.*, 64.

33. Szarka, *Business in France: An Introduction to the Economic and Social Context*, 57.

34. McArthur & Scott, *Industrial Planning in France*, 490.

35. Cohen, *Modern Capitalist Planning: The French Model*, 248.

36. Liggins, *National Economic Planning in France*, xviii.

37. *Ibid.*, 165.

38. Lauber, *The Political Economy of France: From Pompidou to Mitterrand*, 10.

39. *Ibid.*

40. Szarka, *Business in France*, 58; Millward, *State and Business.*

41. Bordo *et al.*, "France and the Bretton Woods International Monetary System 1960 to 1968" in Reis (ed.), *International Monetary Systems in Historical Perspective.*

42. Van der Wee, *Prosperity and Upheaval: The World Economy 1945–1980*, 488.

43. Millward, *State and Business*, 226.

44. Monnet, *Controlling Credit.*

45. *Ibid.*

46. Szarka, *Business in France*, 51.

47. Chadeau, "State-owned industry in France", 197.

48. *Ibid.*, 245.

49. *Ibid.*

50. Berne & Pogorel, "Privatization experiences in France" in Köthenbürger, Sinn & Whalley (eds), *Privatization Experiences in the European Union*.

51. Cohen, "Lessons from the nationalization nation: state-owned enterprise in France"; Margairaz & Tartakowsky, *L'État détricoté*, 89.

52. A. Tonnelier, "Le FSI se cherche toujours une identité", *Le Monde*, 30 April 2012.

53. OFCE, *L'économie française, 2019*, 66–7.

54. P. Roger, "Le succès de la BPI n'est pas exempt de critiques", *Le Monde*, 16 November 2016.

55. OFCE, *L'économie française, 2019*, 13.

56. France Stratégie, "La planification: idée d'hier ou piste pour demain?", 17 June 2020.

3. GROWTH AND STRUCTURAL CHANGE IN THE FRENCH ECONOMY, 1945–2018

1. Maddison, *Dynamic Forces in Capitalist Development*, 6–7, 50; Crafts & Toniolo, "European economic growth, 1950–2005: an overview".

2. In 2018 the trade balance of commercial services of France was $291 billion, behind the United States with a balance of $808 billion, the UK with $373 billion and Germany with $326 billion.

3. In 2018 the trade balance of goods of France was $582 billion, behind China with $2,487 billion; the US with $1,664 billion; Germany with $1,561 billion; Japan with $738 billion; the Netherlands with $727 billion; and the Republic of Korea with $605 billion. The UK was tenth with $486 billion.

4. Stromberg, *Fathers, Families, and the State in France, 1914–1945*, 186.

5. UN Department of Economic and Social Affairs, Population Division, *World Population Prospects 2019*. The average age in Germany is 46, in the UK it is 41, and in the Republic of Ireland it is 38.

6. INSEE, *France, portrait social, Édition 2019*.

7. Mouré, "The French economy since 1930" in Alexander, *French History since Napoleon*, 374.

8. Baum, *The French Economy and the State*, 36.

9. Lynch, *France and the International Economy*, 99.

10. Mouré, "The French economy since 1930".

11. Carré *et al.*, *French Economic Growth*, 117.

12. *Ibid.*, 21.

13. Tapinos, *L'Immigration étrangère en France*, 31.

14. *Ibid.*

15. Fourastié & Fourastié, *Jean Fourastié entre deux mondes.*

16. Tapinos, *L'Immigration étrangère*, 16.

17. Baumier, *Les paysans de l'an 2000.*

18. Milward, *The European Rescue*, 244.

19. A term attributed to Raymond Aron.

20. Carré *et al.*, *French Economic Growth*, 550–51.

21. Baumier, *Les paysans de l'an 2000*, 86–95.

22. Barral, *Les Agrariens Français de Méline à Pisani*, 293–9.

23. Godelier, "Usinor: the first French wide strip mill" in Aylen & Ranieri (eds), *Ribbon of Fire: How Europe Adopted and Developed US Strip Mill Technology (1920–2000).*

24. Ranieri & Aylen, "The importance of the wide strip mill and its impact" in Aylen & Ranieri, *Ribbons of Fire.*

25. In 2018 hydroelectricity was about 13 per cent of French electricity production.

26. Chick, *Electricity and Energy Policy in Britain, France and the United States since 1945*, 88.

27. Broder, *Histoire économique de la France au XXe 1914–1997*, 274.

28. Hecht, "L'empire nucléaire. Les silences des 'trente glorieuses'" in Pessis *et al.* (eds), *Une autre histoire des 'trente glorieuses'.*

29. De Carmoy, "French energy policy and the impact of the European Community energy policy" in Dreyfus, Morizet & Peyrard (eds), *France and EC Membership Evaluated.*

30. Broder, *Histoire économique de la France*, 276.

31. Pincemel, *France: A Geographical Survey*, 223.

32. Ardagh, *The New France: A Society in Transition 1945–73*, 154–5.

33. See Spire "The spread of tax resistance: the antitax movement in France in the 1970s", and *Résistances à l'impôt, attachement à l'Etat. Enquête sur les contribuables français.*

34. Hollifield, "Immigration and modernization" in Hollifield & Ross (eds), *Searching for the New France*, 122.

35. Delorme, *De Rivoli à Bercy. Souvenirs d'un inspecteur des finances 1952–1998*, 137–8.

36. *Ibid.*

37. Among the *pieds noirs* were Louis Althusser, Jacques Attali, Albert Camus, Jacques Derrida and Yves Saint Laurent.

38. Johnman & Lynch, "The road to Concorde: Franco-British relations and the supersonic project"; Johnman & Lynch, "A treaty too far? Britain, France and Concorde, 1961–1964"; Johnman & Lynch, "Technological non-cooperation: Britain and Airbus, 1965–1969".

39. Berend, *An Economic History of Twentieth-Century Europe*, 266.

40. INSEE, *Fresque historique du système productif.*

41. INSEE, *Le mouvement économique en France, 1949–1979*, 79.

42. Millward, *State and Business*, 216–17.

43. Hau, "Les grands naufrages industriels français" in Lamard & Stoskopf (eds), *1974–1984: Une Décennie de désindustrialisation?*

44. Broder, *Histoire économique de la France*, 277.

45. De Carmoy, "French energy policy and the impact of the European Community energy policy", in Dreyfus *et al.* (eds), *France and EC Membership Evaluated*, 41.

46. *Ibid.*, 41–2.

47. INSEE, *Tableaux de l'économie française 1984*, 136.

48. Lane, *Industry and Society in Europe*, 93.

49. INSEE, *Tableaux de l'économie français 1986.*

50. Lane, *Industry and Society*, 93.

51. Mouré, "The French economy since 1930", 385.

52. Howarth, "The legacy of state-led finance in France and the rise of Gallic market-based banking".

53. INSEE, *Tableaux de l'économie française 1988*, 142.

54. Coppolaro, "Globalizing GATT: The EC/EU and the trade regime in the 1980s–1990s".

55. Heyer & Timbeau, "L'économie française depuis un demi-siècle" in OFCE, *L'économie française, 2019.*

56. Berne & Pogorel, "Privatization experience in France".

57. However, between 2006 and 2009 as many as 60 employees committed suicide, leading to a public inquiry into working practices. See P. Robert-Diard, "Procès France Télécom: 'Ces suicides ont eu valeur d'alerte'", *Le Monde*, 11 May 2019.

58. Eurostat, *50 Years of Figures on Europe. Data 1952–2001.* Available at https://ec.europa.eu.

59. Dormois, *The French Economy in the Twentieth Century*, 126.

60. *Ibid.*

61. Demmou, "Le recul de l'emploi industriel en France entre 1980 et 2007. Ampleur et principaux déterminants: un état des lieux".

62. Wieviorka, *La France en Chiffres*, 131–2.

63. Frigant, Jullien & Lung, "L'industrie automobile: une vigueure renouvelée" in Colletis & Lung (eds), *La France industrielle en question: analyses sectorielles*; Wieviorka, *La France en Chiffres*.

64. Guéry, "L'État partout et nulle part".

65. INSEE, *Tableaux de l'économie française, 2018*.

66. See survey conducted by EY Consulting, reported by J.-M. Bezat "Les industriels étrangers croient toujours dans les atouts de la France", *Le Monde*, 13 January 2020.

67. Howarth, "Legacy of state-led finance".

68. J.-M. Normand, "Le secteur des services menacé de déclin en France", *Le Monde*, 16 June 2011.

69. Guillou & Nesta, "La compétitivité de l'appareil productif français: état des lieux et perspectives" in OFCE, *L'économie française 2018*.

70. For the first time ever, the Socialist party held a nationwide open contest to select the presidential candidate.

71. L. Benchabane, "Les doutes et les fragilités du secteur nucléaire français", *Le Monde*, 8 December 2019.

4. REGIONAL INEQUALITY

1. Gravier, *Paris et le désert français*.

2. Bonnet *et al.*, "Les inégalités de revenu entre les départements français depuis cent ans".

3. *Ibid.*

4. Lamard & Stoskopf, *1974–1984*, 17.

5. Robb, *The Discovery of France*, 13.

6. Aldrich & Connell, *France's Overseas Frontier: Départements et Territoires D'Outre-Mer*.

7. In 2003 the population of the northern French part of Saint Martin (the southern part is Dutch) voted to secede from Guadeloupe to form a separate overseas collectivity of France. It remains part of the European Union.

8. French overseas territories and departments have an EEZ of 3,791,998 square miles, which accounts for 96.7 per cent of France's EEZ. The total area of the French Republic's EEZ is 4,514,000 square miles, which is about

8 per cent of the world's exclusive economic zones, while the country's land area represents only 0.45 per cent of the world's land area. France also claims part of the Canadian EEZ for their Saint Pierre and Miquelon territory.

9. Candau & Rey, "International trade in outermost Europe: a comparative analysis of Mayotte Island and French Overseas Departments", 123–46.

10. *Ibid.*

11. On 8 July 2019 the French government signed convergence contracts with the overseas territories following the shocking victory of the RN in the 2019 elections to the European Parliament. P. Roger "L'exécutif tente de reconquérir les outre-mer avec la signature des premiers contrats de convergence", *Le Monde*, 8 July 2019.

12. Jamet, "Meeting the challenges of decentralisation in France" in OECD, *Economic Survey of France*.

13. Forrest, "Paris versus the provinces; regionalism and decentralism since 1789" in Alexander, *French History since Napoleon*.

14. Kayser & Kayser, *95 régions*, 62.

15. These were the Association pour le développement et l'industrialisation de la région Alsace (ADIRA) and the Comité de Liaison des Intérêts bretons (CELIB).

16. Bodiguel & Buller, "Environmental policy and the regions in France" in Loughlin & Mazey (eds), *The End of the French Unitary State*, 93.

17. Denton *et al.*, *Economic Planning and Policies in Britain, France and Germany*, 314–17.

18. Bauchet, *Economic Planning: The French Experience*, 196.

19. Denton *et al.*, *Economic Planning*, 314.

20. Douence, "The evolution of the 1982 regional reforms: an overview" in Loughlin & Mazey (eds), *End of the French Unitary State*.

21. Liggins, *National Economic Planning in France*, 233. In 1970 this was increased to 22 when Corsica was separated from Provence Côte d'Azur for planning purposes.

22. Kayser & Kayser, *95 régions*, 5.

23. Although, by 2018 it was estimated that as many as 40 per cent of French people could no longer afford to go away for a summer holiday.

24. Bouneau, "Les tensions de la politique d'aménagement touristique du littoral français de 1962 à 1974. L'avènement d'un tourisme de masse?" in Griset (ed.), *Georges Pompidou et la modernité. Les tensions de l'innovation 1962–1974*.

25. Denton *et al.*, *Economic Planning*, 326

26. Wolff, "Decazeville: expansion et déclin d'un pôle de croissance".

27. Kayser & Kayser, *95 régions*.

28. Douence, "Evolution of the 1982 regional reforms", 10.

29. *Ibid.*

30. Le Galès, "Regional economic policies: an alternative to French economic dirigisme?" in Loughlin & Mazey, *End of the French Unitary State*, 79.

31. Jamet, "Meeting the challenges of decentralisation".

32. *Ibid.*

33. The regional prefect was the prefect of the department in which the regional capital was located.

34. See OECD (2007), "Regions at a Glance". France was the seventh lowest after Sweden, Japan, Greece, Finland, ranking just behind Australia, the Netherlands, and Finland.

35. Davezies, *La crise qui vient. La nouvelle fracture territoriale*.

36. In 2020 the Commissariat général à l'égalité des territoires became the Agence nationale de la cohésion des territoires.

37. B. Jérôme, "Nouvelles régions: 'Raboter les identités, c'est prendre le risque de replis négatifs'", interview with Jacques Lévy, *Le Monde*, 16 November 2014.

38. *Ibid.*

39. Davezies, "Politiques publiques: le social et le spatial".

40. C. Mayer, "Comment Bordeaux est devenu un bastion des 'gilets jaunes'", *Le Monde*, 20 February 2019.

41. Rodríguez-Pose, "The revenge of the places that don't matter (and what to do about it)".

42. Sagot, *Gentrification et paupérisation au cœur de l'Île de France*

43. S. Mehl and L. Soullier, "De Perpignan à Orange: sur a route de l'extrême droite", *Le Monde*, 20 February 2020.

44. C. Ducourtieux, "Covid-19: le cri d'alarme d'un médecin britannique face à un hôpital public au bord de la saturation", *Le Monde*, 11 January 2021.

5. INTERPERSONAL INEQUALITY

1. These figures do not capture the full scale of the problem, since they ignore those who were forced to work part-time and those who gave up looking for work. There were over 1.5 million people who wanted to work but were unable or unwilling to look for a job and were thus excluded from the official statistics. See INSEE, *France, Portrait social, Édition* 2019.

2. Nizet, *Fiscalité, économie et politique. L'impôt en France, 1945–1990*, 394.

3. Prasad, *The Politics of Free Markets: The Rise of Neoliberal Economic Policies in Britain, France, Germany and the United States.*

4. OECD, "Revenue Statistics", 2019, and European Commission, Taxation and Customs Union. Data on Taxation, ec.europa.eu.

5. *Ibid.*

6. IMF Investment and capital stock statistics, database.

7. E. Barthet & M. Charrel, "Inégalités: les faiblesses du modèle français", *Le Monde*, 28 September 2018.

8. See Smith, *France in Crisis*, 3.

9. Greiner, "France" in Van Vugt & Peet (eds), *Social Security and Solidarity in the European Union.*

10. Vlandas, "Labour market developments and policy responses during and after the crisis in France".

11. Garbinti, Goupille-Lebret & Piketty, "Accounting for wealth inequality dynamics: methods, estimates and simulations for France".

12. All figures are taken from Barthet & Charrel, "Inégalités".

13. Sauvy, *Histoire économique de la France entre les deux guerres (1931–1939),* 378.

14. Dutton, *Origins of the French Welfare State: The Struggle for Social Reform in France, 1914–1947,* 212.

15. Athari *et al.*, "Quarante ans d'évolution de la démographie française: le vieillissement de la population s'accélère avec l'avancée en âge des *baby-boomers*". In INSEE, *France, portrait social*, Édition 2019.

16. Gauchon, *Le modèle économique français*, 100.

17. De Castro Fernandez *et al.*, "The economic effects of a tax shift from direct to indirect taxation in France".

18. OECD, *Economic Survey of France 2015*, 2.

19. Spohr, "Germany's labour market policies: how the sick man of Europe performed a second economic miracle" in Compton & 't Hart (eds), *Great Policy Successes.*

20. Vlandas, "Labour market developments".

21. Carré *et al.*, *French Economic Growth*, 53–4.

22. Margairaz & Tartakowsky, *L'État détricoté*, 37.

23. Wieviorka, *La France en Chiffres*, 170.

24. *Ibid.*

25. *Ibid.*

26. OECD, *Economic Survey of France 2018*.

27. *Ibid.*

28. OECD, *Economic Survey of France 2019*.

29. INSEE, *France, portrait social, Édition 2019*.

30. *Ibid.*

31. Eurostat, *Sustainable Development in the European Union. Monitoring report on progress towards the SDGs in an EU context*, 2019 edition.

32. Le Secours Catholique-Caritas France, *État de la pauvreté en France 2018*.

33. V. Morin, "Enquête PISA 2018: L'école française toujours aussi inégalitaire", *Le Monde*, 4 December 2019.

34. Prost, *Petite histoire de la France au XXe siècle*, 87–8.

35. Bourdieu & Passeron, *Les Héritiers. Les étudiants et la culture*.

36. Falcon & Bataille, "Equalization or reproduction? Long-term trends in the intergenerational transmission of advantages in higher education".

37. L. Gérard, "L'employabilité, enjeu majeur de la réforme Pénicaud", *Le Monde*, 19 April 2018.

38. Brinbaum *et al.*, "Situation sur le marché du travail: status d'activité, accès à l'emploi et discrimination" in Beauchemin, Hamel & Simon (eds), *Trajectoires et origines*.

39. INSEE, *Tableaux de l'économie française*, 2019.

40. INSEE, *Enquête emploi en continu 2013-2017*; Meurs, L'hommeau & Okba, "Emplois, salaires et mobilité intergénérationnelle" in Beauchemin *et al.*, *Trajectoires et origines. Enquête sur la diversité des populations en France*.

41. See Brinbaum, "Incorporation of immigrants and second generations into the French labour market".

42. Förster & Thévenot, "Inégalite des revenus et protection sociale: les enseignements de l'analyse internationale de l'ocde" in Palier & Roussel (eds), *Stratégies de croissance, emploi et protection social*.

43. Goujard & Guérin, "Boosting growth in France and making reforms beneficial to all".

6. THE FRENCH ECONOMY AND EUROPEAN INTEGRATION

1. In an interview broadcast on the BBC's *Andrew Marr Show* in January 2018, President Macron admitted that French people would probably have voted to leave the EU if presented with a similar choice to the Brexit referendum.

2. Boltho & Eichengreen, "The economic impact of European integration".

3. The French government devoted considerable effort and money towards mixing different grades of coal to try to produce more of their own coking coal in this period; see Milward, *The European Rescue*, 57.

4. Lynch, *France and the International Economy*, 63–4.

5. Gillingham, *Coal, Steel, and the Rebirth of Europe, 1945–1955*.

6. De Carmoy, "French energy policy".

7. Milward, *The European Rescue*, 200.

8. *Ibid.*, 173–4.

9. Lynch, *France and the International Economy*, 169–73.

10. CHEF (Comité pour l'histoire économique et financière de la France) (ed.), *Le commerce extérieur français de Méline à nos jours*.

11. Lynch, *France and the International Economy*, 178–80.

12. *Ibid.*, 180–82.

13. Balassa, *Trade Liberalization among Industrial Countries*, 45.

14. Milward, *Politics and Economics in the History of the European Union*, 80.

15. Milward, *The European Rescue*, 314–15.

16. INSEE, *Fresque historique du système productif*.

17. Cyncynatus & Floch, "L'agriculture dans la CEE. Les échanges extérieurs de produits agro-alimentaires".

18. Dinan, *Ever Closer Union*, 343.

19. Wieviorka, *La France en Chiffres*, 112.

20. In 2018 it had fallen to 34 million tonnes. INSEE, *Tableaux de l'économie française 2020*.

21. Anderson, "Ever closer union?".

22. Buzelay, "The impact of the Single Market on the French economy: strengths and weaknesses" in Dreyfus *et al.* (eds), *France and EC Membership Evaluated*, 12.

23. Cecchini *et al.*, *The European Challenge 1992: The Benefits of a Single Market*.

24. Gulvin, "The French economy and the end of the Cold War" in Chafer & Jenkins (eds), *France From the Cold War to the New World Order*, 123.

25. *Ibid.*, 115–25.

26. Ilzkovitz *et al.*, "Steps towards a deeper economic integration: the internal market in the 21st century. A contribution to the Single Market Review".

27. At the time Monti was president of Bocconi University in Milan. He went on to serve as prime minister of Italy from 2011 to 2013. He had been a European Commissioner from 1995 to 2004; see Monti, "A new strategy for the Single Market: at the service of Europe's economy and society".

28. Mion & Ponattu, "Estimating economic benefits of the Single Market for European countries and regions".

29. The political accident was the collapse of East Germany.

30. A protocol provided that the UK would not be obliged to enter the third stage of EMU without a separate decision to do so by its government and parliament.

31. These criteria were that a state's budget deficit could not exceed 3 per cent of GDP, its national debt could not exceed 60 per cent of GDP, the inflation rate could not be higher than 1.5 percentage points above the rate of the three best-performing member states and its exchange rate had to be stable within the European Exchange Rate Mechanism (ERM) for at least two years.

32. There is considerable debate about how agreement was actually reached. See, for example, Dyson & Featherstone, *The Road to Maastricht: Negotiating Economic and Monetary Union*. Disagreements may not be resolved until the official archives for the period have been opened.

33. Bilger, "The European monetary system and French monetary policy" in Dreyfus, Morizet & Peyrard (eds), *France and EC Membership Evaluated*, 101.

34. Lynch, *France and the International Economy*, 13.

35. See Mourlon-Droul, *A Europe Made of Money: The Emergence of the European Monetary System*.

36. Blanchard & Muet, "Competitiveness through disinflation: an assessment of the French macroeconomic strategy".

37. Margairaz & Tartakowsky, *L'État détricoté. De la Résistance à la République en marche*, 121–7.

38. Vail, "Europe's middle child: France's statist liberalism and the conflicted politics of the euro".

39. INSEE, *Tableaux de l'économie française, 2018*.

40. See the survey by EY cited by J.-M. Bezat "Les industriels étrangers croient toujours dans les atouts de la France", *Le Monde*, 13 January 2020.

41. See Fitoussi & Saraceno, "European economic governance", 479–96.

42. Howarth & Schild, "France and European mcroeconomic policy coordination: from the Treaty of Rome to the euro area sovereign debt crisis" in *Modern and Contemporary France*, 171–90.

43. Although Mayotte, which forms part of the Comoros islands, rejected independence.

44. This was after many thousands of Algerians were killed by the French in 1945 for calling for independence.

45. For greater detail, see Lynch, *France and the International Economy*, 186–209.

46. Lebanon left the Franc Zone in 1948; the states of former Indochina were given their own currency under the terms of the French withdrawal agreement in December 1954; Moroccco, Algeria and Tunisia left between 1956 and 1962; and Guinea-Conakry left in 1958. Madagascar left in 1973.

47. Members of the BCEOA were Côte d'Ivoire, Dahomey (known from 1975 as Bénin), Upper Volta (which became Burkina Faso in 1983), Mauritania, Niger and Senegal.

48. Members of the BCEAEC were Cameroon, Central African Republic, Chad, Congo and Gabon.

49. In addition to the five original members (without Mauritania, which withdrew) it now included Guinea-Bissau, Mali and Togo.

50. Masson & Pattillo, "Monetary Union in West Africa (ECOWAS). Is it desirable and how could it be achieved?".

51. European Council decision of 23 November 1998.

52. Masson & Pattillo, "Monetary Union in West Africa (ECOWAS)".

53. Lavallée & Lochard, "The empire strikes back: French-African trade after independence", 390–412.

54. D. Pilling & N. Munshi, "Macron signals rethink on French-backed Africa currency", *Financial Times*, 16 December 2019.

55. C. Bensimon & M. de Vergès, "Malgré la mort annoncée du franc CFA, l'éco n'est pas encore né", *Le Monde*, 12 July 2020.

56. Whether the reserves are used as collateral to enable the French Treasury to borrow on more favourable terms is unclear.

57. Germany remains the most important trading partner, supplying 18 per cent of French imports and taking 14 per cent of its exports in 2018.

58. See *Ouest-France*, 28 January 2021.

7. CONCLUSION

1. However, the left-wing populist movement La France Insoumise made continued membership of the EU conditional on a reform of its monetary policy, common agricultural policy and environmental policy.

2. Marine Le Pen, the youngest daughter of Jean-Marie Le Pen the founder of the Front National, became the leader of the FN in 2011.

3. Skype, a company launched by Swedish, Danish and Estonian entrepreneurs, was bought by Microsoft in 2011.

4.   See I. Chaperon, "Coronavirus: Bruno Le Maire n'exclut pas des nationalisations", *Le Monde*, 18 March 2020.

5.   See Ph. Mioche, "Après le coronavirus: 'Pourquoi ne pas penser aussi à la planification à la française?'", *Le Monde*, 17 April 2020. Also *Le Plan Monnet. Genèse et Élaboration 1941–1947*.

6.   European Commission, *Cruising at Different Speeds*.

Bibliography

Aldrich, R. & J. Connell 1992. *France's Overseas Frontier: Départements et Terri-toires D'Outre-Mer*. Cambridge: Cambridge University Press.

Alexander, M. (ed.) 1999. *French History since Napoleon*. London: Arnold.

Anderson, P. 2021. "Ever closer union?", *London Review of Books* 43(1), 7 January.

Ardagh, J. 1973. *The New France: A Society in Transition 1945–1973*. London: Penguin.

Armengaud, A. 1979. "Du Malthusianisme démographique au Malthusianisme économique" in F. Braudel & E. Labrousse, *Histoire Économique et Sociale de la France, 1880–1914*. Paris: PUF.

Athari, E., S. Papon & I. Robert-Bobée 2019. "Quarante ans d'évolution de la démographie française: le vieillissement de la population s'accélère avec l'avancée en âge des *baby-boomers*" in INSEE, *France, portrait social, Édition 2019*. Paris: INSEE.

Aylen, J. & R. Ranieri (eds) 2012. *Ribbon of Fire: How Europe Adopted and Devel-oped US Strip Mill Technology (1920–2000)*. Perugia: Pendragon.

Azéma, J.-P. & F. Bédarida (eds) 1993. *La France des années noires*. Paris: Seuil.

Balassa, B. 1967. *Trade Liberalization among Industrial Countries*. New York: McGraw Hill.

Barral, P. 1968. *Les Agrariens Français de Méline à Pisani*. Paris: Armand Colin.

Bauchet, P. 1964. *Economic Planning: The French Experience*. London: Heinemann.

Baum, W. 1958. *The French Economy and the State*. Princeton, NJ: Princeton University Press.

Baumier, J. 1979. *Les paysans de l'an 2000*. Paris: Plon.

Beauchemin, C., C. Hamel & P. Simon (eds) 2015. *Trajectoires et origines. Enquête sur la diversité des populations en France*. Paris: INED.

Berend, I. 2006. *An Economic History of Twentieth-Century Europe*. Cambridge: Cambridge University Press.

Berne, M. & G. Pogorel 2006. "Privatisation experiences in France" in M. Köthen-bürger, H.-W. Sinn & J. Whalley (eds), *Privatization Experiences in the Euro-pean Union*, CESifo Seminar Series.

Bilger, F. 1993. "The European monetary system and French monetary policy" in F.-G. Dreyfus, J. Morizet & M. Peyrard (eds), *France and EC Membership Evaluated*. London: Pinter.

Blanchard, O. & P. Muet 1993. "Competitiveness through disinflation: an assessment of the French macroeconomic strategy". *Economic Policy* 16: 11–56.

Bodiguel, M. & H. Buller 1995. "Environmental policy and the regions in France" in J. Loughlin & S. Mazey (eds), *The End of the French Unitary State*. London: Frank Cass.

Boltho, A. & B. Eichengreen 2008. "The economic impact of European integration". Centre for Economic Policy Research, Discussion Paper 6820, May.

Bonnet, F., H. d'Albis & A. Sotura 2020. "Les inégalités de revenu entre les départements français depuis cent ans". Available at: https://halshs.archives-ouvertes.fr/halshs-02536856.

Bootle, R. 2014. *The Trouble with €urope*. London: Nicholas Brealey.

Bordo, M. D., D. Simard & E. N. White 1995. "France and the Bretton Woods International Monetary System 1960 to 1968" in J. Reis (ed.), *International Monetary Systems in Historical Perspective*. London: Palgrave Macmillan.

Bouneau, C. 2006. "Les tensions de la politique d'aménagement touristique du littoral français de 1962 à 1974. L'avènement d'un tourisme de masse?" In P. Griset (ed.), *Georges Pompidou et la modernité. Les tensions de l'innovation 1962–1974*, 107–21. Brussels: Peter Lang.

Bourdieu, P. & J.-C. Passeron 1964. *Les Héritiers. Les étudiants et la culture*. Paris: Les Éditions de Minuet.

Braudel, F. & E. Labrousse 1979. *Histoire Économique et Sociale de la France, 1880–1914*. Paris: PUF.

Brinbaum, Y. 2018. "Incorporation of immigrants and second generations into the French labour market: changes between generations and the role of human capital and origins". *Social Inclusion* 6(3): 104–18.

Brinbaum, Y., D. Meurs & J.-L. Primon 2015. "Situation sur le marché du travail: status d'activité, accès à l'emploi et discrimination" in C. Beauchemin, C. Hamel & P. Simon (eds), *Trajectoires et origines. Enquête sur la diversité des populations en France*. Paris: INED.

Broder, A. 1998. *Histoire économique de la France au Xxe: 1914–1997*. Paris: Ophyrs.

Brownlee, W., E. Ide & Y. Fukagai (eds) 2013. *The Political Economy of Transnational Tax Reform*. Cambridge: Cambridge University Press.

Buzelay, A. 1993. "The impact of the Single Market on the French economy: strengths and weaknesses" in F.-G. Dreyfus, J. Morizet & M. Peyrard (eds), *France and EC Membership Evaluated*. London: Pinter.

Candau, F. & S. Rey 2014. "International trade in outermost Europe: a comparative analysis of Mayotte Island and French Overseas Departments". *European Journal of Comparative Economics* 11(1): 123–46.

Carré, J-J., P. Dubois & E. Malinvaud 1976. *French Economic Growth* (translated from the French by John P. Hatfield). Stanford, CA: Stanford University Press.

Cecchini, P., M. Catinat & A. Jacquemin 1988. *The European Challenge 1992: The Benefits of a Single Market*. Aldershot: Wildwood House.

Chadeau, E. 2000. "State-owned industry in France" in P. Tonelli (ed.), *The Rise and Fall of State-Owned Enterprise in the Western World*. Cambridge: Cambridge University Press.

Chafer, T. & B. Jenkins (eds) 1996. *France From the Cold War to the New World Order*. London: Macmillan.

Chapman, H. 2018. *France's Long Reconstruction: In Search of the Modern Republic*. Cambridge, MA: Harvard University Press.

CHEF (Comité pour l'histoire économique et financière de la France) (ed.) 1993. *Le commerce extérieur français de Méline à nos jours*. Paris: Imprimerie Nationale.

Chemla, E. 2016. "The French social security system" in ILO, *The Right to Social Security in the Constitutions of the World: Broadening the Moral and Legal Space for Social Justice*, Global Study, Volume 1, Europe.

Chick, M. 2007. *Electricity and Energy Policy in Britain, France and the United States Since 1945*. Cheltenham: Elgar.

Cohen, P. 2010. "Lessons from the nationalization nation: state-owned enterprise in France". *Dissent* 57(1): 15–20.

Cohen, S. 1969. *Modern Capitalist Planning: The French Model*. London: Weidenfeld & Nicholson.

Colletis, G. & Y. Lung (eds) 2006. *La France industrielle en question: analyses sectorielles*. Paris: La Documentation française.

Commissariat général au plan 1953. *Rapport sur la réalisation du plan de modernisation et d'équipement de l'Union française, année 1952*. Paris.

Compton, M. & P. 't Hart (eds) 2019. *Great Policy Successes*. Oxford: Oxford University Press.

Coppolaro, L. 2018. "Globalizing GATT: The EC/EU and the trade regime in the 1980s–1990s". *Journal of European Integration History* 24(2): 335–52.

Crafts, N. & G. Toniolo 2008. "European economic growth, 1950–2005: an overview". CEPR Discussion Paper No. 6863.

Cummins, N. 2009. "Why did fertility decline? An analysis of the individual level economic correlates of the nineteenth century fertility transition in England and France". PhD thesis, London School of Economics.

Cyncynatus, M. & J.-M. Floch 1992. "L'agriculture dans la CEE. Les échanges extérieurs de produits agro-alimentaires". INSEE Résultats. Système productif (1989–2001), No. 187, May.

Davezies, L. 2009. "Politiques publiques: le social et le spatial". *Revue Projet* 310(3): 22–31.

Davezies, L. 2012. *La crise qui vient. La nouvelle fracture territoriale.* Paris: Seuil.

De Carmoy, G. 1993. "French energy policy and the impact of the European Community energy policy" in F.-G. Dreyfus, J. Morizet & M. Peyrard (eds), *France and EC Membership Evaluated.* London: Pinter.

De Castro Fernandez, F., M. Perelle & R. Priftis 2018. "The economic effects of a tax shift from direct to indirect taxation in France". Brussels: European Commission, DG Economic and Financial Affairs.

Delorme, G. 2000. *De Rivoli à Bercy. Souvenirs d'un inspecteur des finances 1952–1998.* Paris: CHEFF.

Demmou, L. 2010. "Le recul de l'emploi industriel en France entre 1980 et 2007. Ampleur et principaux déterminants: un état des lieux". *Economique et Statistique* 438–440: 273–96.

Denton, G., M. Forsyth & M. MacLennan 1968. *Economic Planning and Policies in Britain, France and Germany.* London: Allen & Unwin.

Dinan, D. 1999. *Ever Closer Union.* London: Macmillan.

Dormois, J.-P. 1997. *L'Économie française face à la concurrence britannique à la veille de 1914.* Paris: L'Harmattan.

Dormois, J.-P. 1999. "France: the idiosyncrasies of volontarisme" in J. Foreman-Peck & G. Federico (eds), *European Industrial Policy: The Twentieth-Century Experience,* 58–97. Oxford: Oxford University Press.

Dormois, J.-P. 2004. *The French Economy in the Twentieth Century.* Cambridge: Cambridge University Press.

Douence, J.-C. 1995. "The evolution of the 1982 regional reforms: an overview" in J. Loughlin & S. Mazey (eds), *The End of the French Unitary State,* 10–25. London: Frank Cass.

Dreyfus, F.-G., J. Morizet & M. Peyrard (eds) 1993. *France and EC Membership Evaluated.* London: Pinter.

Dutton, P. 2002. *Origins of the French Welfare State: The Struggle for Social Reform in France, 1914–1947.* Cambridge: Cambridge University Press.

Dyson, K. & K. Featherstone 1999. *The Road to Maastricht: Negotiating Economic and Monetary Union.* Oxford: Oxford University Press.

Eck, J.-F. 1988. *Histoire de l'économie française depuis 1945.* Paris: Armand Colin.

European Commission 2019. "Cruising at different speeds: similarities and divergences between the German and French economies". Economic and Financial Affairs Discussion Paper 103, July.

European Commission 2020. *Shaping Europe's Digital Future*, February. Available at: https://ec.europa.eu/.

European Commission, Taxation and Customs Union. Data on Taxation. Available at: https:// ec.europa.eu/.

Eurostat 2003. *50 years of Figures on Europe. Data 1952–2001.* Available at: https:// ec.europa.eu/.

Eurostat 2019. *Sustainable Development in the European Union: Monitoring Report on Progress Towards the SDGs in an EU context – 2019 edition.*

Falcon, J. & P. Bataille 2018. "Equalization or reproduction? Long-term trends in the intergenerational transmission of advantages in higher education". *European Sociological Review* 34(4): 335–47.

Faugère, J.-P. 1988. *Les politiques salariales en France.* Paris: La Documentation française.

Fitoussi, J.-P & F. Saraceno 2013. "European economic governance: the Berlin–Washington Consensus". *Cambridge Journal of Economics* 37(3): 479–96.

Foreman-Peck, J. & G. Federico (eds) 1999. *European Industrial Policy: The Twentieth-Century Experience.* Oxford: Oxford University Press.

Forrest, A. 1999. "Paris versus the provinces; regionalism and decentralism since 1789" in M. Alexander (ed.), *French History since Napoleon,* 106–126. London: Arnold.

Förster, M. & C. Thévenot 2016. "Inégalite des revenus et protection sociale: les enseignements de l'analyse internationale de l'ocde" in B. Palier & R. Roussel (eds), *Stratégies de croissance, emploi et protection social,* 65–91. Paris: La Documentation française.

Fourastié, J. 1979. *Les trente glorieuses ou la révolution invisible de 1946 à 1975.* Paris: Fayard.

Fourastié J. & J. Fourastié 1994. *Jean Fourastié entre deux mondes. Mémoires en forme de dialogues avec sa fille Jacqueline.* Paris: Beauchesne.

Frigant, V., B. Jullien & Y. Lung 2006. "L'industrie automobile: une vigueure renouvelée" in G. Colletis & Y. Lung (eds), *La France industrielle en question: analyses sectorielles.* Paris: La Documentation française.

Garbinti, B., J. Goupille-Lebret & T. Piketty 2019. "Accounting for wealth inequality dynamics: methods, estimates and simulations for France", Working paper GATE 2019-35. Available at: https://halshs.archives-ouvertes.fr/hal shs-02401488.

Gauchon, P. 2015. *Le modèle économique français.* Fifth edition. Paris: PUF.

Gillingham, J. 1991. *Coal, Steel, and the Rebirth of Europe, 1945–1955.* Cambridge: Cambridge University Press.

Glaeser, E. 2011. *Triumph of the City: How Our Greatest Invention Makes Us Richer, Smarter, Greener, Healthier and Happier.* London: Macmillan.

Godelier, E. 2012. "Usinor: the first French wide strip mill" in J. Aylen & R. Ranieri (eds), *Ribbon of Fire: How Europe Adopted and Developed US Strip Mill Technology (1920–2000)*, 193–203. Perugia: Pendragon.

Goujard, A. & P. Guérin 2019. *Boosting Growth in France and Making Reforms Beneficial to All*. Paris: OECD.

Gravier, J.-F. 1947. *Paris et le désert français*. Paris: Flammarion.

Greiner, D. 2000. "France" in J. Van Vugt & J. Peet (eds), *Social Security and Solidarity in the European Union*, 50–64. New York: Physica Verlag.

Griset, P. (ed.) 2006. *Georges Pompidou et la modernité. Les tensions de l'innovation 1962–1974*. Brussels: Peter Lang.

Guéry, A. 2019. "L'État partout et nulle part". *Le Débat* 206(4): 177–92.

Guillou, S. & L. Nesta 2017. "La compétitivité de l'appareil productif français: état des lieux et perspectives" in OFCE, *L'économie française 2018*. Paris: La Découverte.

Gulvin, C. 1996. "The French economy and the end of the Cold War" in T. Chafer & B. Jenkins (eds), *France: From the Cold War to the New World Order*. London: Macmillan.

Hau, M. 2009. "Les grands naufrages industriels français" in P. Lamard & N. Stoskopf (eds), *1974–1984: Une Décennie de désindustrialisation?*, 15–35. Paris: Picard.

Hecht, G. 2013. "L'empire nucléaire. Les silences des 'trente glorieuses'" in C. Pessis *et al.* (eds), *Une autre histoire des "trente glorieuses"*. Paris: la Découverte.

Heyer, É & X. Timbeau 2018. "L'économie française depuis un demi-siècle" in OFCE, *L'économie française 2019*. Paris: La Découverte.

Hollifield, J. 1991. "Immigration and modernization" in J. Hollifield & G. Ross (eds), *Searching for the New France*. London: Routledge.

Howarth, D. 2013. "France and the international financial crisis: the legacy of state-led finance", *Governance* 26(3): 369–95.

Howarth, D. & J. Schild 2017. "France and European mcroeconomic policy coordination: from the Treaty of Rome to the euro area sovereign debt crisis", *Modern and Contemporary France*, 25(2): 171–90.

Ilzkovitz, F., A. Dierx, V. Kovacs & N. Sousa 2007. "Steps towards a deeper economic integration: the internal market in the 21st century. A contribution to the Single Market Review". European Commission, Economic Papers, No. 271, January.

INSEE 1974. *Fresque historique du système productif*. Paris.

INSEE 1981. *La crise du système productif*. Paris.

INSEE 1981. *Le mouvement économique en France, 1949–1979*. Paris.

INSEE 1984. *Tableaux de l'économie française 1984*.

INSEE 1986. *Tableaux de l'économie française 1986.*

INSEE 1988. *Tableaux de l'économie française 1988.*

INSEE 2014. *Les comptes nationaux annuels, base 2014.* Available at: https://www. insee.fr/fr/metadonnees/source/serie/s1030.

INSEE 2015. *Marché du Travail. Séries longues.*

INSEE 2018. *Enquête emploi en continu 2013–2017.*

INSEE 2018. *Tableaux de l'économie française 2018.*

INSEE 2019. *Évolution de la population. Bilan démographique en 2019.*

INSEE 2019. *France, portrait social, Édition 2019.*

INSEE 2019. *Tableaux de l'économie française 2019.*

INSEE 2020. *Tableaux de l'économie française 2020.*

Jabbari, E. 2012. *Pierre Laroque and the Welfare State in Postwar France.* Oxford: Oxford University Press.

Jamet, S. 2007. "Meeting the challenges of decentralisation in France" in OECD, *Economic Survey of France.* Paris: OECD.

Johnman, L. & F. Lynch 2002. "The road to Concorde: Franco-British relations and the supersonic project". *Contemporary European History* 11(2): 229–52.

Johnman, L. & F. Lynch 2002. "A treaty too far? Britain, France and Concorde, 1961–1964". *Twentieth Century British History* 13(3): 253–76.

Johnman, L. & F. Lynch 2006. "Technological non-cooperation: Britain and Airbus, 1965–1969". *Journal of European Integration History* 12(1): 125–40.

Kayser, B. & J.-L. Kayser 1971. *95 régions.* Paris: Seuil.

Köthenbürger, M., H.-W. Sinn & J. Whalley (eds) 2006. *Privatization Experiences in the European Union.* Cambridge, MA: MIT Press.

Kuisel, R. 1981. *Capitalism and the State in Modern France: Renovation and Economic Management in the Twentieth Century.* Cambridge: Cambridge University Press.

Lamard, P. & N. Stoskopf (eds) 2009. *1974–1984: Une Décennie de désindustrialisation?* Paris: Picard.

Lane, C. 1995. *Industry and Society in Europe: Stability and Change in Britain, Germany and France.* Aldershot: Elgar.

Lauber, V. 1983. *The Political Economy of France: From Pompidou to Mitterrand.* New York: Praeger.

Lavallée, E. & J. Lochard 2019. "The empire strikes back: French-African trade after independence". *Revue internationale économique* 27 (1): 390–412.

Le Galès, P. 1995. "Regional economic policies: an alternative to French economic dirigisme?" in J. Loughlin & S. Mazey (eds), *The End of the French Unitary State.* London: Frank Cass.

Lévy-Leboyer, M. & F. Bourguignon 1990. *The French Economy in the Nineteenth Century: An Essay in Econometric Analysis*. Cambridge: Cambridge University Press.

Liggins, D. 1975. *National Economic Planning in France*. Farnborough: Saxon House.

Loughlin, J. & S. Mazey (eds) 1995. *The End of the French Unitary State*. London: Frank Cass.

Lynch, F. 1984. "Resolving the paradox of the Monnet Plan: national and international planning in French reconstruction". *Economic History Review* 37(2): 229–43.

Lynch, F. 1997. *France and the International Economy from Vichy to the Treaty of Rome*. London: Routledge.

Lynch, F. 1998. "A tax for Europe: the introduction of value added tax in France". *Journal of European Integration History* 4(2): 67–87.

Lynch, F. 2013. "The Haig–Shoup mission to France in the 1920s" in W. Brownlee, E. Ide & Y. Fukagai (eds), *The Political Economy of Transnational Tax Reform*. Cambridge: Cambridge University Press.

Lynch, F. 2018. "The powerlessness of employees in France: the spread of income taxation, 1945–1980" in G. Huerlimann, W. Brownlee & E. Ide (eds), *Worlds of Taxation: The Political Economy of Taxing, Spending, and Redistribution since 1945*. London: Palgrave Macmillan.

Maddison, A. 1991. *Dynamic Forces in Capitalist Development*. Oxford: Oxford University Press.

Margairaz, M. 1991. *L'État, les finances et l'économie. Histoire d'une conversion 1932–1952*. Paris: Imprimerie Nationale.

Margairaz, M. & D. Tartakowsky 2018. *L'État détricoté. De la Résistance à la République en marche*. Paris: Éditions du Détour.

Masson, P. & C. Pattillo 2001. "Monetary Union in West Africa (ECOWAS). Is it desirable and how could it be achieved?" Occasional Paper 204, IMF, 14 February.

Matas, J. 2017. *Panorama du commerce extérieur*. Paris: La Documentation française.

Mathias, P. & S. Pollard (eds) 1989. *The Cambridge Economic History of Europe, Volume VIII*. Cambridge: Cambridge University Press.

McArthur, J. & B. Scott 1969. *Industrial Planning in France*. Cambridge, MA: Harvard University Press.

McMillan, J. 1992. *Twentieth-Century France: Politics and Society, 1898–1991*. London: Arnold.

Meurs, D., B. L'hommeau & M. Okba 2015. "Emplois, salaires et mobilité intergénérationnelle" in C. Beauchemin, C. Hamel & P. Simon (eds), *Trajectoires et origines. Enquête sur la diversité des populations en France*. Paris: INED.

Millward, R. 2013. *The State and Business in the Major Powers: An Economic History 1815–1939*. London: Routledge.

Milward, A. 1970. *The New Order and the French Economy*. Oxford: Clarendon Press.

Milward, A. 1992. *The European Rescue of the Nation-State*. London: Routledge.

Milward, A. 2005. *Politics and Economics in the History of the European Union*. Abingdon: Routledge.

Milward, A. & B. Saul 1973. *The Economic Development of Continental Europe 1780–1870*. London: Allen & Unwin.

Milward, A. & B. Saul 1977. *The Development of the Economies of Continental Europe 1850–1914*. London: Allen & Unwin.

Mioche, Ph. 1987. *Le Plan Monnet. Genèse et Élaboration 1941–1947*. Paris: Publications de la Sorbonne.

Mion, G. & D. Ponattu 2019. "Estimating economic benefits of the Single Market for European countries and regions". Bertelsmann Stiftung, Policy Paper.

Monnet, E. 2018. *Controlling Credit: Central Banking and the Planned Economy in Postwar France, 1948–1973*. Cambridge: Cambridge University Press.

Monti, M. 2010. "A new strategy for the Single Market: at the service of Europe's economy and society", Report to the President of the European Commission, May.

Mouré, K. 1999. "The French economy since 1930" in M. Alexander (ed.), *French History since Napoleon*. London: Arnold.

Mourlon-Droul, E. 2012. *A Europe Made of Money: The Emergence of the European Monetary System*. Ithaca, NY: Cornell University Press.

Nizet, J.-V. 1991. *Fiscalité, économie et politique. L'impôt en France, 1945–1990*. Paris: LGDJ.

O'Brien, P. & C. Keyder 1978. *Economic Growth in Britain and France, 1780–1914: Two Paths to the Twentieth Century*. London: Allen & Unwin.

OECD 2007. *Economic Survey of France*. Paris: OECD.

OECD 2018. *Economic Survey of France*. Paris: OECD.

OECD 2019. *Economic Survey of France*. Paris: OECD.

OECD 2019. "Revenue Statistics". Paris: OECD.

OECD 2020. "Income Inequality". Paris: OECD.

OFCE 2018. *L'économie française 2019*. Paris: La Découverte.

Palier, B. & R. Roussel (eds) 2016. *Stratégies de croissance, emploi et protection sociale*. Paris: La Documentation française.

Patat, J.-P. & M. Lutfalla 1990. *A Monetary History of France in the Twentieth Century*. London: Macmillan.

Pessis, C., S. Topçu & C. Bonneuil 2013. *Une autre histoire des "Trente Glorieuses". Modernisation, contestations et pollutions dans la France d'après-guerre*. Paris: La Découverte.

Piketty, T. 2001. *Les hauts revenus en France au XXe siècle. Inégalités et redistributions 1901–1998*. Paris: Grasset.

Piketty, T. 2003. "Income inequality in France, 1901–1998". *Journal of Political Economy* 111(5): 1004–42.

Pinchemel, P. 1969. *France: A Geographical Survey*. London: Bell & Sons.

Pinkney, D. 1958. *Napoleon III and the Rebuilding of Paris*. Princeton, NJ: Princeton University Press.

Prasad, M. 2006. *The Politics of Free Markets: The Rise of Neoliberal Economic Policies in Britain, France, Germany and the United States*. Chigago, IL: University of Chigago Press.

Prost, A. 1992. *Petite histoire de la France au XXe siècle*. Paris: Armand Colin.

Quennouëlle-Corre, L. 2005. "The state, banks and financing of investments in France from World War II to the 1970s". *Financial History Review* 12(1): 63–86.

Ranieri, R. & J. Aylen 2012. "The importance of the wide strip mill and its impact" in J. Aylen & R. Ranieri (eds), *Ribbon of Fire: How Europe Adopted and Developed US Strip Mill Technology (1920–2000)*, 13–75. Perugia: Pendragon.

Reis, J. (ed.) 1995. *International Monetary Systems in Historical Perspective*. London: Macmillan.

Robb, G. 2016. *The Discovery of France*. London: Picador.

Rodríguez-Pose, A. 2018. "The revenge of the places that don't matter (and what to do about it)", *Cambridge Journal of Regions, Economy and Society* 11(1): 189–209.

Sagot, M. 2019. *Gentrification et paupérisation au cœur de l'Île de France. Évolutions 2001–2015*. Paris: IAU.

Sarkozy, N. 2007. *Testimony: France, Europe, and the World in the Twenty-first Century*. New York: HarperCollins.

Sauvy, A. 1967. *Histoire économique de la France entre les deux guerres (1931–1939)*. Paris: Fayard.

Schremmer, D. E. 1989. "Taxation and public finance: Britain, France and Germany" in P. Mathias & S. Pollard (eds), *The Cambridge Economic History of Europe, Volume VIII*, 315–494. Cambridge: Cambridge University Press.

Secours Catholique-Caritas France 2018. État de la pauvreté en France 2018.

Shennan, A. 1989. *Rethinking France: Plans for Renewal 1940–1946*. Oxford: Clarendon Press.

Smith, T. 2004. *France in Crisis: Welfare, Inequality and Globalization since 1980*. Cambridge: Cambridge University Press.

Spire, A. 2013. "The spread of tax resistance: the antitax movement in France in the 1970s", *Journal of Policy History* 25(3): 444–60.

Spire, A. 2018. *Résistances à l'impôt, attachement à l'Etat. Enquête sur les contribuables français*. Paris: Seuil.

Spohr, F. 2019. "Germany's labour market policies: how the sick man of Europe performed a second economic miracle" in M. Compton & P. 't Hart (eds), *Great Policy Successes*. Oxford: Oxford University Press.

Stiglitz, J. 2002. *Globalization and Its Discontents*. London: Penguin.

Stromberg, C. 2003. *Fathers, Families, and the State in France, 1914–1945*. Ithaca, NY: Cornell University Press.

Szarka, J. 1992. *Business in France: An Introduction to the Economic and Social Context*. London: Pitman.

Tapinos, G. 1975. *L'Immigration étrangère en France*. Paris: Presses Universitaires de France.

Vail, M. 2015. "Europe's middle child: France's statist liberalism and the conflicted politics of the euro" in M. Matthijs & M. Blyth (eds), *The Future of the Euro*. Oxford: Oxford University Press.

Van der Wee, H. 1986. *Prosperity and Upheaval: The World Economy 1945–1980*. London: Viking.

Van Vugt, J. & J. Peet (eds) 2000. *Social Security and Solidarity in the European Union*. New York: Physica Verlag.

Vlandas, T. 2016. "Labour market developments and policy responses during and after the crisis in France". *French Politics* 15(1) : 75–105.

Wieviorka, O. (ed.) 2015. *La France en Chiffres de 1870 à nos jours*. Paris: Perrin.

Wolff, J. 1972. "Decazeville: expansion et déclin d'un pôle de croissance". *Revue économique* 23(5): 753–85.

Index